The Film and Media Creators' Guide to Music

Music plays an integral role in the experience of film, television, video games, and other media—yet for many directors, producers, and media creators, working with music can be a baffling and intimidating process. *The Film and Media Creators' Guide to Music* bridges the gap between musical professionals and the creators of film and other media projects, establishing a shared language while demystifying this collaborative journey. Organized with a modular chapter structure, the book covers fundamental topics including:

- Why (and when) to use music in a project
- How to talk about music
- Licensing existing music
- Commissioning original music
- Working with a composer

Geared toward emerging and established creators alike, this book takes a practical approach to the process of finding the best music for all forms of moving image. *The Film and Media Creators' Guide to Music* offers hands-on advice for media creators, providing readers with the confidence to approach the planning, commissioning, creation, and placement of music in their projects with the awareness, understanding, and vocabulary that will enable them to be better collaborators and empowered storytellers. For students and professionals working across film and media, this book is the essential guide to using music creatively and effectively.

Vasco Hexel is a composer, author, and educator. He leads the Masters Programme in Composition for Screen at the Royal College of Music, London, UK.

The Film and Media Creators' Guide to Music

VASCO HEXEL
ROYAL COLLEGE OF MUSIC, LONDON

NEW YORK AND LONDON

First published 2019

by Routledge
711 Third Avenue, New York, NY 10017

and by Routledge
2 Park Square, Milton Park, Abingdon, Oxon, OX14 4RN

Routledge is an imprint of the Taylor & Francis Group, an informa business

© 2019 Taylor & Francis

The right of Vasco Hexel to be identified as author of this work has been asserted by him in accordance with sections 77 and 78 of the Copyright, Designs and Patents Act 1988.

All rights reserved. No part of this book may be reprinted or reproduced or utilised in any form or by any electronic, mechanical, or other means, now known or hereafter invented, including photocopying and recording, or in any information storage or retrieval system, without permission in writing from the publishers.

Trademark notice: Product or corporate names may be trademarks or registered trademarks, and are used only for identification and explanation without intent to infringe.

Library of Congress Cataloging-in-Publication Data
Names: Hexel, Vasco, 1980- author.
Title: The film and media creators' guide to music / Vasco Hexel.
Description: New York, NY: Routledge, 2018.
Identifiers: LCCN 2018018301 (print) | LCCN 2018023054 (ebook) |
ISBN 9781315165752 (ebook) | ISBN 9781138055728 (hardback) |
ISBN 9781138055735 (pbk.)
Subjects: LCSH: Motion picture music–Production and direction.
Classification: LCC ML2075 (ebook) | LCC ML2075 .H48 2018 (print) |
DDC 781.5/4–dc23
LC record available at https://lccn.loc.gov/2018018301

ISBN: 978-1-138-05572-8 (hbk)
ISBN: 978-1-138-05573-5 (pbk)
ISBN: 978-1-315-16575-2 (ebk)

Typeset in Avenir and Dante
by Deanta Global Publishing Services, Chennai, India

Contents

Foreword by John Ottman	*viii*
Acknowledgments	*xii*

Introduction	**1**
Rationale behind This Book	1
Who Is This Book For?	2
How to Read This Book	3
Ten Guiding Principles for Media Music	6

1	**Why Use Music at All?**	**10**
	1.1 Getting Started	10
	1.2 Rules and Principles	13
	1.3 Film Music as Language	15
	1.4 How Overt or Subtle Should Music Be?	17
	1.5 Conventional Roles and Functions of Narrative Music	19
	Notes	40

2	**Different Types of Narrative Media Music**	**41**
	2.1 Introduction	41
	2.2 Diegetic Music	41
	2.3 Non-Diegetic Music	42
	2.4 Special Cases and Creative Possibilities	43
	2.5 Immersive and Interactive Music	49
	Note	51

vi Contents

3 How to Think and Talk about Music   **52**

3.1 Introduction   52
3.2 How to Listen to Music   56
3.3 Existing Music as a Reference   59
3.4 Categorizing Music: Styles, Genre, Form   60
3.5 Building Blocks of Music: Melody and Harmony   62
3.6 Building Blocks of Music: Instrumentation   68
3.7 Musical Attributes: Tempo and Rhythm   77
3.8 Musical Attributes: Volume and Dynamics   79
3.9 Musical Attributes: Timbre   81
Notes   84

4 When to Think and Talk about Music   **85**

4.1 Introduction   85
4.2 Season to Taste: Adding Music at the End   95
4.3 The Mixed Blessing of Temp Tracks   96
4.4 You Cannot "Temp" Originality   103
4.5 Reversing the Workflow: Music-First   106
Notes   110

5 Licensing Existing Music   **112**

5.1 Introduction   112
5.2 Obtaining a Synchronization License for
     a Piece of Music   115
5.3 Getting Your Head around Music Royalties   122
5.4 Using Licensed Music   124
5.5 Using Production Music   145
Notes   148

6 Commissioning Original Music   **149**

6.1 Introduction   149
6.2 Introducing Musical Themes   152
6.3 Original Songs   161
6.4 Musicals   164
6.5 Costs and Budgets   170
6.6 The Commissioning Contract   183
Notes   188

Contents **vii**

7	**Collaborating with a Composer**	**189**

	7.1 Introduction	189
	7.2 Finding and Choosing a Composer	190
	7.3 Onboarding the Composer	197
	7.4 The Media Composer's Workflow	202
	7.5 Different Modes of Collaboration	216
	7.6 Change the Music, Not the Composer	224
	7.7 Lasting Partnerships	226
	Notes	228

8	**Finalizing Your Project**	**230**

	8.1 Introduction	230
	8.2 Digital Film Technology and Its Impact on Music	231
	8.3 Digital Soundtrack Creation and Its Impact on Music	240
	8.4 The Dubbing Session	248
	8.5 The Importance of Cue Sheets	253
	8.6 Takeaways	254
	8.7 Looking Ahead	255
	Notes	256

Further Listening	*259*
Further Reading: Film Composer Biographies	*261*
About the Author	*262*
Glossary	*264*
Index	*275*

Foreword

It's been said that music soothes the soul. Well, music in media may not always soothe, but it is, in fact, the very heart of a project. Whether for a profound moment between two lovers or an attack by malevolent aliens, a composer gives life to the scene. You could say a media composer can play God. But, as this invaluable and comprehensive book will illustrate, composing is not about having a God complex; instead, it's about being a musical collaborator, surgeon, therapist, architect, diplomat, and benevolent slave to the project—all in one.

Media music is a strange animal. And a media composer needs to be one. If you're classically trained in music theory, you must endeavor to *unlearn* many of the things you have learned. ("Use the Force, Luke.") And if your musical knowledge is scant, you must immerse yourself in watching and listening to the works of the masters. (You have to know how to use that light saber first.) The most ingenious solution for creating a profound moment in a scene, for instance, may not even be "musical" at all. This is where the traditionally trained composer may struggle. Conversely, a project may require well-thought-out themes with a beginning, middle, and end (shouldn't most?). Or, there may be a long sequence that requires a musical journey to be designed like a fine tapestry. This is where a young composer (or media creator, for that matter) whose only exposure has been to modern "repeat bar" ostinato or drone scores will struggle. Additionally, it may not dawn on either composer or filmmaker to implement music that's completely against the grain for profound effect, such as operatic music over a murder; this is where the filmmaking sensibility comes into play for both composer and media creator.

In high school, I played clarinet; but I learned my scoring sensibilities by watching and making movies. Actually, another big influence for me was watching the original *Star Trek* TV series and its strong use of themes and motifs. I was a busy filmmaker, making Super 8 movies and "scoring them" with music by luminary film composers of whom I was a fan. After graduating from USC film school, I taught myself how to use a simple MIDI studio I assembled. Soon I was re-scoring my friends' student films, learning as I went along. I also began listening to symphonies from twentieth-century symphonic composers such as Dvorak, Holst, and Vaughan Williams because their symphonies sounded like thematic film scores. I also wrote pieces of music, even short symphonies. So, you could say, back then, I was that self-taught newbie who loved listening to and making music for films. Also, being a filmmaker, or storyteller, helps me see things from a different angle and influences how I approach writing film scores.

So, if the classically trained and the newbie composer walked into the chamber from *The Fly* together, the "strange animal" that emerged would be a perfect media composer. You've heard it before, and will read in this book again, that media composers must, above all, be storytellers and collaborators. And there's good reason for this mantra. You may write cool music, but if you can't tell a story with it on the media canvas before you, your compositions will be hopelessly alien to that canvas. And if you're a media producer or director and aren't mindful of this notion, great opportunities could be lost in how you conceive a scene or collaborate with or instruct the composer. Just as an architect with a flair for modern design must first consider the basic needs of the occupants and the building's foundation, a composer must understand the project from the media maker's perspective. What is the goal of the character? What is the problem the character faces? What is the scene *about*? What are the shortcomings of the scene and how can you *clarify* things? One of the biggest codes to crack is how to translate a media creator's needs into music. The more you put yourself into his/her head—or are able to communicate your perspective in *their* language—the more effective and enjoyable your craft will be. The icing on the cake is the identity and cleverness you bring to it.

Very early in my career, I was initially terrified to veer from the temp score. But as I wrote more and more, I recognized my own isms and personality emerging. At first, I wasn't sure of them. But when I realized my instincts and style worked, there was a point where I let go and just let me be me. Once you become more comfortable in your own skin, you may actually end up with a style. For instance, no matter how prolific and varied their scores were, you always know you're listening to works of Goldsmith, Williams,

x Foreword

Barry, Horner, and others. These composers had their own unique voice, and this made them sought after. Even James Horner relied heavily on the temp in his very early scores, versus his later works where he came into his own. But style is not necessarily defined by how the compositions sound. A style, most importantly, is the very instincts and *sensibilities* of how a composer or filmmaker *uses* music.

There are so many profoundly composed scenes in the lexicon of film to cite as examples to study. But before I leave you to embark into the pages of this indispensable book, I implore you to take the time to study three scenes, no matter if you compose for games or live action or wish to produce or direct them. Perhaps these scenes are from a bygone era, but there's little chance you will not be enlightened or inspired by them. They're timeless.

"The Enterprise" from *Star Trek: The Motion Picture* (1979, score by Jerry Goldsmith)

I think of this scene for many reasons. First, it's an example of a dying art form—the long developing composition—and of the long developing scene. I often wonder how a composer with knowledge of only modern, thematically limited scores would ever be able to sustain such a sequence. Often described as the "Enterprise striptease," the sequence is a slow reveal of this beautiful and loyal ship, a symbol of a hopeful future. Similarly, the scene is a striptease of Goldsmith's wondrous theme. If he hadn't put himself through the agony of writing a full-fledged main theme (A-B-A structure), the resplendent musical journey of this scene would be impossible; and, most certainly, aimless. Notice the intelligent evolution of the piece, its taste and majestic grandeur, hitting all the right points masterfully. (In fact, the whole score is a superb example of motifs and themes intertwining to tell a story.)

"The Truck Chase" from *Raiders of the Lost Ark* (1981, score by John Williams)

To be sure, Williams weaves in his Indiana Jones theme, but he also creates a masculine seven-note repeating truck chase motif. This not only sharpens the scene's focus but gives it a personality all its own. His reprisal of the motif near the end of the scene when the tables turn for Indiana is greatly responsible for the elation, humor, and absolute satisfaction of it all. *Raiders* is a masterpiece of thought-out themes, motifs, and their intelligent implementation, not to mention the deftness and approach of the music in between these themes. *A story is being told.*

As a side note, action scenes today often lack clarity and clearly set goals. This puts even more onus on the composer to help the audience understand the stakes (or at least make us feel like there are some) and clarify the action. Even within a modern music template, there's room for motifs to help clarify action. This is what separates run-of-the-mill and expert music ... and productions.

"Descending the Staircase" from *Poltergeist* (1982, score by Jerry Goldsmith)

For ghosts coming down a staircase into someone's home, the first inclination would be to write evil horror music. But, actually, that's a less scary approach! The chills instead come from Goldsmith's mournful elegy. As the ghosts activate a camera in the living room, the music is ethereally longing. This inspired idea makes the scene oddly believable ... and therefore far more unsettling than an obvious approach. In his heyday (1960s through the late 1970s), Goldsmith strived to go beneath the surface—for instance, using electronics to echo trumpets in *Patton* to reflect Patton's belief of his own reincarnation. *Poltergeist*, like so many of his films, was transformed and *elevated* by Goldsmith's filmmaking instincts. He gave them an indelible soul. Not generic, not interchangeable.

These scenes are all musically expository in nature. But there's also the very important area of delicate and psychological *dialog underscoring*, which this book will also explore. *The Film and Media Creators' Guide to Music* is the bible for anyone dipping his/her toe into the media music waters, or those who are already knee-deep in it. It spans the universe of music media from the creative to the nuts-and-bolts business side. It will be your trusty companion from which you will never part.

Make it your primary goal to elevate whatever it is you're creating. Don't settle for music that can be easily swapped out for any other kind. Music is the very spirit of a project. Make it uniquely yours.

I wish you the best of luck in your quest to deepen our experience and inspire us in whatever media you score or create.

You're the God of your craft.

John Ottman
film composer and editor

Acknowledgments

I thank my students on the Masters Programme in Composition for Screen at the Royal College of Music, London, for making my work worthwhile.

I am grateful to my editor Genevieve Aoki at Routledge for supporting this book and seeing it through to completion.

This book would not have been possible without the first-hand insights and wisdom shared by numerous media composers and orchestrators when they visited the Royal College of Music: Jeff Atmajian, Michael Giacchino, George Fenton, Rolfe Kent, Rachel Portman, Howard Shore. Mel Wesson, Gabriel Yared, and Hans Zimmer.

My interviews with Joe Kraemer, John Ottman, Rachel Portman, and Hauschka at SoundTrack_Cologne over the years have informed my writing. I also had the pleasure to hear games composer Jason Graves and film composer Marco Beltrami speak at SoundTrack_Cologne and the Krakow Film Music Festival respectively.

My colleague and friend Gary Yershon has inspired me with his unparalleled enthusiasm and energy.

I thank my ever-supportive colleague Matthias Hornschuh for his spirit and energy, even in difficult times.

I thank my good friend Andrew Simmons for countless hours of insightful film music discussions, trivia, and banter, as well as for his impeccable proofreading skills!

I thank my family in Germany, in the UK, and in the US for their unwavering encouragement.

Most of all, I thank my husband Zomo Fisher for his guidance and support.

The completion of this book was supported by a grant from The Film Music Foundation (FMF).

Introduction

Rationale behind This Book

This book is the product of my ten-plus years working with aspiring media composers and student filmmakers. I have had the pleasure and privilege of meeting some of the most talented and inspired emerging professionals, whose passion for their craft made teaching and advising them a joy. Since the professional field they hope to enter is all about networking and collaboration, I have always promoted collaborative links between student composers and filmmakers, coaching them during their collaborative journey. Early on, I discovered that many young filmmakers had a keen and articulate vision for their projects. Many of them also loved music. But they often did not know how to make effective use of music in their projects, nor how to communicate their ideas and requirements in ways a musician might understand: The filmmakers and composers did not have a shared language to have a constructive dialogue. Speaking more generally, media creators, whether they are aspiring, emerging, or established, even if they love music, may never have been encouraged to think about the narrative and aesthetic potential of music in ways that can unlock a reasoned and reflected approach to media music. Some media creators even have an irrational fear of music.

With this book, I hope to alleviate that fear, and to show readers how they may think and talk about music in ways that are conducive to a constructive collaborative creative process. I hope to equip media creators with the awareness, understanding, and language that will enable them to be better collaborators and empowered storytellers. No one expects media creators to be music specialists: All they need to do is to open their ears and creative minds to the

2 Introduction

wonderful expressive potential that music can offer them—and then to invite music specialist to join them in a fruitful collaboration on their next project.

Who Is This Book For?

This book is for aspiring, emerging, and established directors, producers, and creators of audiovisual multimedia, including films, television content, video games, virtual reality (VR) experiences, and interactive installations. Whether you are a hobbyist, a student, a young professional, or an experienced pro, anyone hoping to gain better understanding of the use of music in audiovisual multimedia, and to acquire a more grounded conceptual grasp and suitable vocabulary, will benefit from reading this book. This guide may also be helpful to screenwriters, editors, sound designers, music supervisors, dubbing engineers, and, of course, composers (who may or may not be musically trained).

This book offers hands-on practical advice to media creators and thus should be relevant to any student of filmmaking, media production, and video game design. As a textbook, this book may be used at undergraduate or postgraduate levels. The material requires no prior knowledge about media music and can serve as a useful companion during an introductory course to media music, be it theoretical or practical. Taking into account the large number of examples given in the following chapters for further viewing and listening, the material may sustain a whole semester. The material can subsequently serve as a reference guide. Select passages may inform focused group discussions. Ample reference to films, TV shows, and video games may provide useful starting points for practical exercises and/or further research. This book can also be a practical companion during a collaborative project. Where media students collaborate with musicians, both parties will benefit from consulting this book.

This guide may offer inspiration to professional directors and producers of audiovisual multimedia who wish to gain better understanding of the use and creation of music for their projects. With a practical focus, this book explores key concepts that apply equally to all forms of moving image, including features films, narrative television programs, documentary formats, short-form web content, video games, multimedia installations, and VR.

This book does *not* champion composers or pursue any other music agenda. No one will force you to use music or to use music of a particular style. Not to use any music in a project can sometimes the best choice. However, this should be a reasoned choice, weighing up different options, not just the route of least resistance. If any music is to be used, multimedia creators may choose to use existing or newly composed music. This book addresses the sourcing, planning, and implementation of all types of music, including licensed tracks and newly commissioned scores, addressing key considerations and concerns that can arise with both options. This book has ten key objectives:

Ten Objectives

1. To nourish a general appreciation of media music, its narrative potential, and aesthetic value.
2. To help media creators fill knowledge gaps about (media) music.
3. To guide media creators towards a better grasp of music concepts and to show how these can align with the creative and dramatic aims of their project.
4. To introduce media creators to the language required for a dialogue about music creation.
5. To provide examples of effective uses of media music.
6. To make independent and stylistically non-prescriptive suggestions with the project's creative success at heart.
7. To give advice on planning, licensing, and commissioning of existing and newly composed music.
8. To encourage media creators to make bold choices, to look beyond contemporary trends, not to copy or conform, and to be innovative.
9. To inform best practice through enhanced mutual understanding between key creative stakeholders.
10. To help reduce frustration and wasteful creative processes.

How to Read This Book

Scope

The advice offered in this book is applicable to all **linear media**: Narrative film, television, screen documentary, and the tools and techniques they commonly share, whether they are indie, art house, or mainstream, low- or big-budget. The advice offered here is also relevant for creators of interactive, **non-linear media**, such as video games. Creators of video games may already be aware of the expressive and narrative similarities between their medium and linear visual ancestors. When it comes to the roles and functions of narrative music, these, broadly speaking, apply in similar ways in video games as they do in linear media. There are a few special cases where video games and VR place special demands on music creation and implementation and these are raised where relevant. Wherever possible, this book draws on recent examples from films, TV, and video games that are widely available and/or will already be familiar to many readers. There are some exceptions where reference is made to older

4 Introduction

films and TV programs, because they may illustrate an important point. The reader will find that this book does not advocate any particular style or genre of music; it is stylistically non-prescriptive and comprehensive in terms of different types and usages or music. Furthermore, this book gives equal weighting to a discussion of existing and newly commissioned music to be used in a project.

Structure

This book is written in a **modular structure**. Each chapter is self-contained and does not require the reader to have read the preceding chapters. However, readers who choose to read the chapters in order will find that they loosely trace the successive creative processes of media production. If this book is assigned as a course text, the course leader may choose to recommend selected chapters or sections for reading to fit in with their teaching plan. Each chapter is broken down into numbered sections and related sub-sections. **Section headers flag** what the next session is about and readers may choose to skip sub-sections. To help guide the reader, important terms and key considerations are highlighted in **bold**. Key **Takeaways** are summarized at the end of each section.

Terminology

Key terminology is explained in the text wherever it is first mentioned and also in the Glossary. There are a few terms that readers will see throughout:

- **"Onboarding"** is the process of integrating a new employee into an organization. It is used here to refer to the holistic process of hiring and briefing a music supervisor and/or composer.
- **"Creative stakeholders"** are all the creative personnel involved in the project, including the director, producer, sound designer, composer, editor, set designer, etc. They have a vested interest in the creative success of the project.
- **"Project owners"** is used here to refer to those creative stakeholders who are in charge of a project, usually the director, producers, and studio executives, commissioning editors (in broadcasting), and audio directors (in video games). The term refers to creative ownership and responsibility but also reflects the fact that project owners have authority over other creative stakeholders and their work.

- **"Filmmakers"** is used as an umbrella term for directors and producers. In the realm of filmmaking, they are project owners.
- **"Media creator"** is a broader term that includes project owners in film, television, audiovisual media installations, media web content, and video games.

No Need to Rush

This book should not be read quickly. For readers wishing to gain a better understanding of the expressive potential of music in audiovisual multimedia, there is a lot to take in. This book tackles some big issues and there is a lot to discover. Readers should allow themselves to take notes, take breaks, listen to the **music examples**, watch some of the films and TV shows, and play some of the games discussed in these pages. If this book is assigned as a course text, it can sensibly accompany a whole semester, and then serve as a companion for the students' future projects. There are hundreds of **references** to films and TV shows and video games in this book. For disambiguation, the year of initial release is stated—for example, *"Gladiator* (2000)." Further information about all the references, including names of key personnel, is readily available online. All examples cited in this book were available on DVD, Blu-ray, paid download, or various streaming providers at the time of writing.

The **Further Reading** sections at the end of each chapter provide pointers for readers wishing to explore a chosen subject in more detail. There is also a **Further Listening** section at the end of this book, which recommends ten films, TV shows, and video games to consider for their respective use of music. Finally, there is a list of **Film Composer Biographies**.

Legal Matters

There are some sections on music licensing, music commissioning, and other legal considerations. It is important that media creators gain a basic grasp of these issues, as they are an essential part of the creative process. Mistakes with contracts and payments can have costly repercussions, or delay or prevent a project from being cleared for release. However, this book only gives some introductory pointers and guidelines, to help uncover knowledge gaps. Advice given here does *not* replace specialist legal advice, which should be sought if and whenever media creators are unclear about any aspect of music licensing and commissioning. Legal council is readily available for these highly

6 Introduction

specialized matters. Contract and cue sheet templates and further guidance are also available online.

Listening Companion

Accompanying this book are Apple Music and Spotify streaming **Playlists** containing nearly 300 tracks, over 18 hours of music, for your consideration. Throughout this book, if a song or cue title is underlined, it can be found in the streaming playlists—for example, Prokofiev's Peter and the Wolf. The Apple Music playlist contains all underlined tracks at the time of writing. The Spotify playlist is largely identical, except for small variations due to respective availability of tracks on the two services.

- **Apple Music** companion playlist (Apple Music subscription required, student discount available): https://tinyurl.com/yb2c3yax
- **Spotify** companion playlist (Spotify Premium recommended, student discount available): https://tinyurl.com/y7bmfae8

Only a few pieces mentioned in this book were not available for streaming at the time of writing. Virtually all music mentioned in this book was still available on CD, however, including some older or less-well-known film scores. Order from the vendor of your choice.

Ten Guiding Principles for Media Music

Before we get started, there are ten guiding principles that you may choose to follow to set you on course towards best practice conducive of an effective and rewarding creative dialogue with composers and music supervisors:

1. Don't Be Afraid.
2. There Are No Rules.
3. Music Needs a Vision.
4. You Are Not Alone.
5. Collaborate.
6. Communicate.
7. Delegate.
8. Value Music.
9. Be Bold.
10. Own Your Project.

1. Don't Be Afraid

There is no need to fear what music might do to a project. Such fear is usually borne out of lack of experience and practice and will lessen with each positive creative experience. Of course, music can have a powerful impact on the viewing or gaming experience. But this impact can be channeled and controlled. The expressive and emotive powers of music in audiovisual multimedia are nothing to be afraid of.

2. There Are No Rules

There are tried and tested conventions and principles that media music has commonly adhered to. These can be readily observed. There are also roles and functions that media music commonly serves. However, these are not fixed rules that everyone must obey. Some of the most fascinating and rewarding music uses have broken with convention to good effect. Media creators should always feel free to experiment and try new ways of incorporating music in their projects.

3. Music Needs a Vision

Media creators should have a vision for music in their project: What purpose should music serve? What roles should it play? How important is music to the project? What kind of music might best serve the project? This vision may be inspired by other projects—past practice—and refer to and borrow from what has come before. The media creator's vision will, in turn, inform creative discussions held with key collaborators. If a vision for the project at hand is not forthcoming, remember Principle 4:

4. You Are Not Alone

Media creators should seek the input of key creative specialists, at every stage in the project's gestation. Whether early conversations in the conceptual phase help develop ideas (including for music uses), or a creative dialogue during production supports the music supervisor's and/or composer's work: You need not be alone on your creative journey and you will likely feel the benefit of a fruitful joint venture.

5. Collaborate

Close collaboration between media creators and a music supervisor will go a long way towards sourcing the best, most suitable existing music for a project. Collaborating closely with a composer will greatly increase the chances of arriving at an original score that fulfills the project requirements *and* is created in a collaborative setting that supports rewarding creative working conditions

6. Communicate

Frequent, honest, and articulate communication is vital to ensure all creative stakeholders are aligned on aims and objectives. No party should exclude the other from creative conversations. Any and all concerns should be voiced as soon as they arise. A lack or breakdown of communication is almost always the root cause of frustrating working conditions and of wasteful work processes.

7. Delegate

Project owners should trust their collaborators, including music supervisors and composers, to do their respective jobs. These creative stakeholders are highly trained specialists who will make their best effort for the project at hand. Project owners who struggle to let the music team get on with their work may end up getting in the way, hampering progress towards the best music solutions. The music team needs time and space to come up with ideas. Although frequent and open communication is important, micro-management will not inspire a composer to do their best work.

8. Value Music

Music, whether it is licensed or newly commissioned for a project, is a valuable tool that can transform any project for the better. Composers, songwriters, and music producers spend years refining their skills and craft, and they require expensive equipment to do their work. High-quality music is not free and no media creator who values their project should ever expect to be given music free of charge. This is a matter of respecting a fellow creative's craft and to compensate them for their contribution to the project, no matter what the budget and scope of the project may be.

9. Be Bold

Project owners may find inspiration in past projects and in the work of their peers and contemporaries, but emerging trends are too often picked up across media markets by emulators and copycats. This includes imitative music choices, scoring styles, and focusing on a few celebrity composers. The music industry eagerly feeds and reaffirms these fads, however passing they may be. Bold and brave media creators will seek out new modes of expression rather than serving the flavor of the day. Exploring novel ways to implement music in a project, looking at musical styles and sources left and right of the center ground, and/or inviting the contribution of new voices and less than established musicians, may lead to surprising and refreshing results.

10. Own Your Project

In order for the music team to be able to do the best job, sourcing creating the best music for the project, the project owners must be reliable and consistent with their input. If a creative stakeholder (for example, a film producer) starts commenting on music and their opinion contradicts the creative conversations previously held between the director and the composer, then the director should stand up for the composer and shield them from potentially confusing and perhaps harmful criticism or conflicting creative demands. Of course, creative stakeholders may change their mind on any aspect of the project, including music. But changes, opinions, and evolving feelings about the music should always be communicated clearly and openly. Crucially, project ownership should be clearly assigned from the start so that the music team knows whom they are actually working for and answerable to.

Why Use Music at All?   **1**

1.1 Getting Started

> I think music is one of the most effective ways of preparing an audience and reinforcing points that you wish to impose on it. The correct use of music, and this includes the non-use of music, is one of the great weapons that the filmmaker has at his disposal.[1]
>
> *Stanley Kubrick, director*

Understanding the Needs of the Project

During the conceptual stages of any media project an understanding should evolve as to what the project as a whole should achieve—creatively, narratively, and perhaps commercially. A grasp of the scale and scope of the project will firm up as the concept takes shape. These considerations will determine the needs of the project in terms of budget, logistics, and production timelines. Furthermore, initial thoughts on genre, style, tone, and underlying (post-)production aesthetic may form. It is never too early to think about any and all component parts of the project. Some scripts will cite a specific location, such as Times Square. Whether or not that actual location is feasible depends on the production budget, scheduling, shooting permits, etc. Circumstances may dictate that an alternative location be dressed to look like Times Square, to reduce production costs or to benefit from tax incentives in a different filming location. Perhaps the script ends up developing in such a way that a generic town square will do. Sometimes a project banks on famous

Why Use Music at All? **11**

talent and much effort may go into securing that person. Early planning may stipulate a particular kind of setting for the project, such as a landscape, a season, or time period. Ideas for visual flair and other attributes may arise (sets, costumes, special effects), some soon to be dismissed along the way, others to be developed further.

Thought can and should be given to sound and music as well. There are many ways in which sound and music can transform your project. Asking some questions including "what will we *hear* of what we *see*?" or "what will we *see* of what we *hear*?" may stir some fruitful creative thoughts. Although sound and music may not actually be created and/or fixed until production and post-production, early planning can catalyze useful reflection on the nature, role, and functions of sound and music in the context of the project as a whole.

Considering the Role and Function of Music in the Project

Can music play a role in the project at hand? Should it? Will it? Why use music at all? There are many compelling examples of films that use no music at all, or very little. As Kubrick says in the opening quotation to this chapter, the non-use of music can be perfectly reasonable and highly effective. Alfred Hitchcock's psychological thriller *Rope* (1948) uses no composed underscore after an initial opening title. Set in an apartment on a single evening, the film relies only on source music, when Phillip (Farley Granger) plays Poulenc on the piano. The confined setting of the film, like a stage play, reasonably precludes the use of music that might feel intrusive. Sidney Lumet's *Network* (1976) uses no composed music. The film's contemporary setting and *vérité* style arguably require an immediacy from which musical underscore might detract. Although they are of a horror genre, where music can play a highly effective role, *The Blair Witch Project* (1999) and *Cloverfield* (2008) also operate without music. In both films, the narrative logic of a handheld camcorder point-of-view renders music superfluous. Austrian director Michael Haneke consistently uses only source music, i.e., music the characters can hear. German director Maren Ade pursues the same strategy in *Toni Erdmann* (2016). In the most compelling and creatively rewarding projects where no or very little music is used, this non-use has been carefully considered and planned. In each instance, the absence of music arguably required as much creative deliberation as the presence of music. It is for these reasons that Hitchcock's *The Birds* (1963) and Darren Aronofsky's *Mother!* (2017) credit

12 Why Use Music at All?

composers as music consultants (Bernard Herrmann and Jóhann Jóhannsson respectively), even though no original music is used.

On the other hand, there are countless examples of audiovisual multimedia that do use music to powerful ends. Media music can be a valuable asset for immersive storytelling. Music may come in many forms and guises (see later in the chapter). It may be newly composed for a project or compiled from existing sources. Media music may be of any musical style, form, and instrumentation. Considering whether to use any music at all may lead to broader considerations: How heavily will the project rely on music? How much music should there be? These are questions that can be asked early on, even if they may not be answered until further down the line.

Music is exceedingly effective as a structuring and framing device. Well-judged placement of music can completely transform the viewing or gaming experience. The highly dramatic crop duster sequence in Hitchcock's *North by Northwest* (1956, score by Bernard Herrmann) is left un-scored until the plane crashes into the truck (and the main character escapes unharmed). Just by looking at the final film, it is of course impossible to know what creative considerations and discussions went into this scene. But it seems likely that Hitchcock, who was certainly aware of the power of music, planned this selective non-use early on. In other suspenseful scenes, *North by Northwest* features music prominently—for example, during the climactic chase on Mount Rushmore. Sergio Leone chose to leave the opening reel of *Once Upon a Time in the West* (1968, score by Ennio Morricone) un-scored, instead placing heightened emphasis on sound effects and, in conjunction with a slow visual and editing pace, effectively highlighting a sense of discomforting heat and inactivity in the scene. Numerous films make effective use of the sparse placement of music, selectively delineating the structure of the film with music entries and, in turn, giving added importance, a voice, to music when it is used. The judiciously sparse use of music can be highly effective.

Takeaways

- Project planning in the early stages should consider sound and music.
- The absence of (original) music deserves as much creative deliberation as the presence of (original) music.
- Media music is an asset at the media creator's disposal for immersive storytelling.

1.2 Rules and Principles

There are **no fixed rules** for the use of music in audiovisual multimedia. Although music has always accompanied moving images from long before the advent of synchronized sound, no hard and fast rules have emerged that dictate how media music should sound or what it should do. If ten experienced media composers were asked to score the same scene, working to the same brief, and with the same resources at their disposal, they would nevertheless all come up with different music solutions. Whilst on the one hand this introduces a certain level of uncertainty to every new project, it also opens up a multitude of exciting possibilities. Historically, we can of course observe prevalent modes of practice in a chosen canon—for example, how a certain set of filmmakers preferred to use music or how a group of composers happened to score films in similar ways. For example, in her 1987 book, "Unheard Melodies: Narrative Film Music," the scholar Claudia Gorbman chose to focus on so-called Classical Hollywood films, a period in Hollywood filmmaking that formed a unified body of works, with underlying scoring principles that could, in hindsight, be observed and summarized.[2] Gorbman highlighted that music in classical Hollywood films tended to be orchestral scores in the so-called new-Romantic style. She also showed that "**narrative film music**" followed certain principles in the ways it related to the other "**narrative vehicles**" (dialogue and sound design): Music would be devised in such a way that it would remain "inaudible," subordinated to the other narrative vehicles and not drawing conscious attention to itself. Gorbman tied this in with Classical Hollywood films' general aim to mask the technical artifact that is "film," i.e., hiding cameras and microphones, building convincing sets, employing certain editing techniques, etc., basically anything that might distract the viewer from fully immersing themselves in the narrative. Whilst Gorbman's analysis was fascinating, the scoring principles she observed are not universally applicable to films outside the Classical Hollywood canon. And scoring principles are not rules anyway, just a collected view on what was commonly done because it had proven effective and what would, therefore, likely work again.

In the ever-evolving field of audiovisual multimedia, no one is interested in insisting on rules. Of course, there are some conventions that are fairly fixed. For example, where dialogue and sound design are present in a film or TV show or game, music will often stay out of the way, sonically, so as not to obstruct those elements. Then again, there are many examples where music overpowers the dialogue, for dramatic or other expressive reasons. Media music continually evolves as a storytelling tool among other elements. Style and genre conventions will inform creative ideas, as will current trends

14 Why Use Music at All?

and prevalent industry standards. When considering music as an expressive asset, you need not worry about how things *should* be done but, instead, how you might best achieve the desired effect. Observing past practice can bring inspiring insights and help avoid costly mistakes, redundant workflows, and inefficient planning. You may come across examples you particularly like or dislike. Whenever this happens, it is worth exploring what can be learned about the creative process that led to a particular result. It is worth asking, "How did they do that?" especially if the result seems worth emulating. But there should always be scope for subversion, to challenge what has come before, to hack processes, and to do whatever feels right in order to pursue the most effective and creatively rewarding product possible.

Incidentally, in the right context, *any* **music can be media music**, regardless of style, instrumentation, no matter when it was written or by whom. There are endless possibilities when it comes to finding the "right" music for a project. The task is to clarify the dramatic, emotional, narrative needs of the project and to determine what role music should play. There may never be one quick answer to this and it is worth allowing time and creative thinking space to work towards solutions. It is never too early to invite collaborative partners to join the creative process. A composer and/or music supervisor can interface with ideas even at treatment stage and may help energize and inspire the development of the project. Even though at the earliest stages there may not yet be a budget for development, let alone production, a creative team may speculatively come together, their collaborative effort in turn improving chances for getting the project off the ground. Throughout the collaborative process, you might ask what the obvious solution to any given creative challenge would be. You might also ask what the opposite of the obvious, perhaps an unconventional, even shocking, solution would be. Veering to the left or right of the proverbial middle of the road can produce fascinating results. Remaining mindful of and articulating your own set of references and bearing in mind that your collaborators will have their set of references as well, ultimately there is always the intended target audience to consider, and they, too, will have a set of references and will receive the product from that perspective.

Takeaways

- There are no fixed rules for the use of music in audiovisual multimedia.
- There are some conventions that have proven helpful. For example, music will often stay out of the way of dialogue, sonically.
- Any music can be media music, in the right context.

1.3 Film Music as Language

Pictures can universally signify an object: Show someone a picture…

…and they will think, "tree." Spoken or written language can convey meaning by prior agreement and convention: Person reads, "tree" and pictures…

…a tree. The word "tree" is of course an arbitrary convention in just one language. Other languages use different words to signify the same thing: "Baum," arbre," "árbol." Although, in the right context, media music can serve as an effective storytelling tool, it does not hold inherent meaning on its own. There is, arguably, no such thing as "sad" or "happy" or "scary" music because **music is not indicative**. As an abstract art form, music will make listeners think or feel different things, their response to varying degrees determined by prior conditioning, current situational experience, and state of mind. Unlike written and spoken words, music certainly cannot communicate specifics such as "the beautiful princess lived in a lovely castle and enjoyed cake for breakfast." Susanne Langer refers to music as an "unconsummated symbol" that in the

16 Why Use Music at All?

Figure 1.1 Notation Example.

context of audiovisual media is "consummated," or channeled into meaning by the medium it accompanies.[3] Music can be thought of as a language (it contains signifiers that seem to be saying something) that cannot be reliably and predictably decoded by the listener (unclear signified). A musical phrase may *seem* to be communicating *something*, but one cannot fix that meaning. Play someone this... (Figure 1.1)

...and it may not say anything to them or make them think of anything in particular. Of course, some listeners may have prior associations with a particular piece of music or a style of music. So, when they hear that piece or music of that style, they may be reminded of prior associations. When drawing on **music as a storytelling tool**, as narrative music, it is helpful to reflect on these cultural and contextual ("semantic") associations because they will shape the audience's perception of music in the context of the final project. One person's love song is another person's break-up anthem. What sounds foreign to a local audience may sound perfectly "at home" in a foreign market.

Although there are some musical compositions that tell specific stories (so-called program music such as Prokofiev's "Peter and the Wolf"), these stories are prescribed in and framed by the works' respective titles, program notes, or spoken narrative. The fact that music alone is a **signifier without a definitive signified** actually makes it a *more* powerful and flexible storytelling tool in an audiovisual **context**: In order to guide the audience towards the intended meaning and narrative result, whatever that may be, music is **mediated** by and must be **channeled** by the other component parts of the audiovisual experience.

Takeaways

- Music is a signifier without a definitive signified.
- Music is not indicative.
- Music comes with the baggage of audiences' prior associations.
- Media music must be channeled by the other component parts of the multimedia experience.
- Narrative music exists among other storytelling tools.

1.4 How Overt or Subtle Should Music Be?

How noticeable or prominent should music be? A project may feature music overtly or in subtle ways. Many media creators in recent decades have opted for a "subtle" approach to music, especially film and TV directors. "I need very little here"; "I want nothing too big"; "I want to have something quite sparse and quiet," are fairly typical instructions to the music team. Opting for an understated or simple or quiet musical solution may be the perfect choice for a scene, a character, and a project as a whole. But such musical restraint should be carefully considered. It must not be borne out of a fear of expressive music. Demanding restraint of a composer is absolutely fine, so long as they are allowed to understand the reasoning behind the request. Subtlety should not mask a lack of vision, sense, or aims and dramatic purpose for music on the part of the project owners. Too many films and television programs over the years have fallen for the minimalist trap, opting for cowardly musical underscores that are barely audible, subdued, and non-expressive. These kinds of scores are really dull for a composer to write and rarely the best creative solution. There absolutely is a time and place for restraint. Some of the most compelling film scores know when to let the film breathe, when to rest, where to remove all but the bare minimum of musical expressivity. A measured and understated approach to scoring can be the appealing opposite of something garish or pompous or melodramatic. A competent composer will be the first to request that certain moments in a project remain un-scored or be given only a very sparse musical treatment. Some great examples of subtle scoring solutions include:

- *The Dark Knight* (2008)—Mel Wesson's contribution as "ambient music designer" facilitated the seamless fusion of sonically conceived music and musically conceived sound design. The technologically enabled creative process made it possible for the film to have a staggering 130 minutes of "music," which at times operates at extremely low relative volume levels (compared to dialogue and sound design).
- *Moonlight* (2016)—Nicholas Britell's beautiful score is sparsely placed throughout the film and judiciously allows extended passages without music.
- *Birdman or (The Unexpected Virtue of Ignorance)* (2014)—The placement of music toys with the ambiguity of source (on-screen or off-scree). Antonio Sanchez's solo drumming subverts the notion what constitutes a "score."

18 Why Use Music at All?

- *No Country for Old Men* (2007)—Although some subtle synthesizer tones allegedly survive in the final film, composer Carter Burrell, who worked closely with the Coen Brothers on this project, eventually talked himself out of a job: The team jointly agreed that music could and would not add anything of use to this film. Crucially, this was a mutual decision that organically emerged from the creative process.
- *Mother!* (2017)—Darren Aronofksy worked with composer Jóhann Jóhannsson for several months, going as far as screening versions of the film with music, before then deciding the film worked better without composed underscore. Jóhannsson was eventually credited as "Music and Sound Consultant," not dissimilar to Bernard Herrmann's consulting on Hitchcock's *The Birds* (1963).

There absolutely is also a time and place for bold and in-your-face scoring solutions. For example, TV and online commercials commonly rely on prominent music placements, because it is well understood that music is an effective ally in quickly setting the tone in a format where everything is compressed into just a few seconds. The need for immediacy is served well with poignant music placements. Numerous feature films and video games contain segments in which music is given prominence, if only temporarily. Where music is pushed to the foreground of the soundtrack, the audience is more likely consciously to notice it. Some examples of effective bold music uses include:

- *Psycho* (1960)—Even though Hitchcock originally wanted the groundbreaking shower scene without music, Herrmann presented him with a score for the scene. The director finally conceded that the scene worked better with music. There is nothing subtle about music in this scene, the shrieking string stabs brutally mirroring the knife stabs.
- *Ex Machina* (2014)—The result of the close collaboration between the director Alex Garland and the composers Geoff Barrow and Ben Salisbury, music in this psychological thriller is prominently placed in the soundtrack. The score drives the increasing tension forward and is strikingly effective. It may also be one of the few instances in the history of film music where (spoiler alert!) music "lies" to the audience, early on siding with Ava (Alicia Vikander) and suggesting that Nathan (Oscar Isaac) is the one to be feared.
- *Requiem for a Dream* (2000)—Clint Mansell's unforgiving <u>Lux Aeterna</u>, which has been used many times in commercials and film trailers since the release of this film, is just one of several cues that are allowed to make

Why Use Music at All? **19**

a strong statement and help heighten the sense of terror and dread in this drama.

- *Love Actually* (2003)—Yes, it's probably cheesy, and, yes, it's a rom-com, but when, near the end of the film, young Sam (Thomas Sangster) runs after his would-be love interest, a rousing music cue amplifies our collective sense of joy.
- *Star Trek* (2009)—Michael Giacchino's majestic theme for the starship Enterprise is given prominent placement in J.J. Abrams's entries to the franchise, surely to the delight of invested fans.
- *Blade Runner 2049* (2017)—Paying sonic homage to the score for the original *Blade Runner* (1982), Hans Zimmer and Benjamin Wallfisch's synthesizer score is foregrounded several times in Denis Villeneuve's visually stunning sequel.

On every project, opportunities for musical prominence should be discussed, carefully weighing up dramatic and aesthetic implications. In paying close attention to the expressive and creative possibilities that arise from using music in a project; in exposing oneself to a range of musical ideas and influence; and by inviting a capable composer and/or music supervisor along during a project's early planning stages, all creative stakeholders will be in a better position to make reasoned suggestions regarding music, and all scoring choices can emergence organically from the collaborative process.

> **Takeaways**
> - There is a time and place for restraint, but subtle music uses should not mask a lack of vision, sense of aims and dramatic purpose for music on the part of the director.
> - There is a time and place for bold and in-your-face scoring solutions.

1.5 Conventional Roles and Functions of Narrative Music

The following overview of the roles and functions narrative media music has conventionally played is fairly comprehensive, but it should not be considered prescriptive or dogmatic. Always feel free to explore new possibilities and push boundaries on your next project. Media music never acts in isolation but contributes to the cumulative effect of all storytelling tools. When analyzing multimedia, it may become apparent that wherever media music occurs, it tends to serve several purposes at once. (See Table 1.1.)

20 Why Use Music at All?

Table 1.1 Overview: Conventional Roles and Functions of Media Music

Added Value	Music raises the aesthetic quality and effect.
Creating Atmosphere and Setting the Tone	Music sets up the prevalent experiential atmosphere or tone of the project.
Delineating Structure	Music acts as a structuring device in film and other audiovisual media.
Direct Attention	Music provides focus and point-of-view perspective in narrative situations that might otherwise be ambiguous.
Establish Characters	Music identifies individual characters or characterizes a protagonist in a certain way.
Comedy	Music creates a sense of, supports, or amplifies comedy.
Provide Continuity	Music provides sonic continuity between shots.
Supporting Dialogue	Music accompanies dialogue to a narrative and dramatic end (e.g., pacing, development, emotional charge).
Geographic Location	Music establishes a geographic location by using instruments and musical styles typical of a place or country.
Further Meaning and Narrative	Music tells the audience/player something that is not already implied or apparent in the visuals or from context.
Establish Time Period	Music indicates a time period by using period instruments and musical styles.
Dramatic/Narrative Pace	Music provides a sense of higher speed and urgency.
Indicating Mood and Stirring Emotions	Music evokes an emotional response from the audience or indicates the mood of a scene, character, etc.

Added Value

Media music will, in synergy with other audiovisual elements, raise the overall aesthetic quality and effect for the audience or player. The scholar Michel Chion has called this contribution "added value."[4] It is up to the creative stakeholders to channel the intended cumulative aesthetic to the desired effect, whatever that may be. Intention and outcome will differ greatly depending on the project at hand and aesthetic considerations may not always be easy to articulate. Where active discussions do take place (certainly in advertising!), aesthetic aims can be served by music, among other elements.

- In *TRON: Legacy* (2010), for example, Daft Punk's sleek and calculated synthesizer score elegantly serves the glossy visual style of the film, envisioned by director Joseph Kosinki, who had previously only worked on commercials.
- In *Thor: Ragnarok* (2017), Mark Mothersbaugh's score is predominantly orchestral and dignified during scenes that are set in Asgard and on Earth. By contrast, scenes set on the zany planet Sakaar are accompanied by playful vintage synthesizers reminiscent of 1980s arcade games.

Creating Atmosphere and Setting the Tone

Music can be highly effective in setting up the prevalent experiential atmosphere or tone of the project. The use of a particular melody, a chord progression, a choice of instrument or instrumental colors, a musical style, and general mood or attitude in the music can all work towards establishing an intended tone. Using music to create atmosphere is of course also commonplace in everyday life, where atmospheric background music is omnipresent in restaurants, supermarkets, shopping malls, theme parks, hotel lobbies, and even elevators. Visitors and customers subliminally are being primed for their experience, be it luxurious, relaxing, fun, or exciting.

Main Titles and Opening Cues

Opening title themes (or "**main titles**") or overtures used to be a common device to engage the audience and set the tone for the film or TV show (see also Chapter 6). Perhaps by coincidence, some of these opening titles proved so powerful that they served as effective branding tools as well, staying with the audience long after the film or episode had finished. Some of the best-loved film and TV scores are arguably best remembered for their respective main title. Without exception, main titles will aim to set the tone and atmosphere in line with the film or show they introduce, including *Star Wars*, *Superman*, *Braveheart*, *Mission: Impossible*, *Star Trek: The Next Generation*, *Game of Thrones*, or *Westworld*. Even in the absence

22 Why Use Music at All?

of an opening title or overture, music in multimedia can serve as a **tone-setter** or **primer**.

- *American Beauty* (1999)—The cue <u>Dead Already</u> accompanies Lester Burnhams's (Kevin Spacey) opening monologue. The sparse nature of the music leaves space for the monologue, while also setting a jocular tone that prevents this segment from feeling overly serious or sentimental. The tone of this opening is broadly indicative of the ensuing film.
- Music in the opening passage of the Coen Brothers' <u>*Fargo*</u> (1996) establishes a grounded and perhaps somewhat bleak tone for this crime drama set in wintery Minnesota.
- The first composed cue in *The Social Network* (2010), <u>Hand Covers Bruise</u>, can be heard as Mark Zuckerberg walks across the Harvard campus back to his dorm after his girlfriend has just broken up with him in a bar. The cue comprises an undulating synthesizer buzz, a short piano motif, and sparsely placed deep bass pulses, creating an atmosphere of foreboding, a sense of something important being about to happen (the invention of Facebook).

"Cool" Music

The concept of "**cool**" is an elusive and shifting attribute: What was "cool" yesterday is "lame" today. Music can contribute to the notion of "cool" if desired but this effect must be gauged in a contemporary context (i.e., what is "cool" right now?) and with the intended target market in mind. The use of a pop music idiom and electronic instruments certainly made *Beverly Hills Cop* (1984, the cue <u>Axel F</u>) feel modern and hip at the time of its release. The music for *Top Gun* (1986, the cue <u>Top Gun Anthem</u>) and *Days of Thunder* (1990) followed the same trend, albeit with a different musical style. John Powell's music for the *Bourne* franchise (for example, the cue <u>Treadstone Assassins</u> from *The Bourne Identity*, 2002) relies on electric guitars, edgy strings, and rhythmic loops, providing a contemporary edge. Ramin Djawadi's score for *Iron Man* (2008, <u>Mark II</u>) is similar in this respect. The opening title for HBO's *The Sopranos* (1999–2007) is the song <u>Woke up This Morning</u> by the band Alabama 3, which greatly contributed to setting the show's cool tone. The exciting blend of synthesizers and large orchestra helped create the sleek and glossy style of Kosinski's *TRON: Legacy* (2010, <u>Son of Flynn</u>) reminiscent of fashion or make-up commercials the director had previously focused on.

Romance

Music is an excellent aid when it comes to indicating **romance and sensuality**. Love themes, suggestive of a love interest within the narrative, are among the most common stock devices for musical underscoring.

- *Blade Runner* (1982)—For his Love Theme, composer Vangelis uses saxophone, a scoring cliché that probably no longer has currency, but was exceedingly effective at the time.
- *Avatar* (2009)—In The Bioluminescence of the Night, ethereal glass mallets, gentle synths, and strings for the cautious romantic outing of the two protagonists.
- *Star Wars—Return of the Jedi* (1983)—Luke and Leia Theme starts off quietly with a solo horn and then gradually builds, suggestive of the tentative and unsure bond the two characters feel between each other.

Music need not flag a specific love interest but can also serve to set a romantic, sensual, or outright sexual tone more generally:

- *Basic Instinct* (1997)—Jerry Goldsmith's full orchestral score adds sensuous depth to this twisted thriller—for example, with the cue Pillow Talk.
- *Fifty Shades of Grey* (2015)—In the cue Did That Hurt? Danny Elfman works with visceral sonic texture and different timbres, ranging from warm to cold, gentle to abrasive.
- *The English Patient* (1997—Gabriel Yared's nuanced and fragile score elegantly supports the unfolding romance, for example, in the cue As Far as Florence / Rupert Bear.

Crime and Sleaze

Jazz and other popular music idioms are commonly used to accompany criminals and **crime thrillers** such as *The Talented Mr. Ripley* (1999), among many others. There is perhaps an unsavory quality about criminal characters and their illegal activities that is not best served by more traditional scoring styles. A notable exception is Michael Kamen's score for *Die Hard* (1988), where the composer adapts "Ode to Joy" from Beethoven's Symphony No. 9 in D Minor, Op. 125—"Choral:" IVb Presto—"O Freunde, nicht diese Töne!" to accompany the main villain Hans Gruber, giving him an air of sophistication and

German-ness. John Paesano's music for Marvel's *Daredevil* (2015–) reserves a recognizable theme for the main character (<u>Main Title</u>), underscoring the rest of the show with driving rhythms underneath a blend of strings, guitars, and throbbing synthesizers. **Film noir** in particular draws on jazz to complement its distinctive visual style—for example, in *Chinatown* (1974) and *Taxi Driver* (1976, the music from <u>Main Title</u> recurs frequently throughout the film). There are scoring staples including saxophone, jazz combo (piano, upright bass, drums), big bands, and seductive strings that immediately help set a *noir* atmosphere. Tom Ford's neo-noir *Nocturnal Animals* (2016, <u>Wayward Sisters</u>) selectively opts for a beautiful strings theme that is reminiscent of Bernard Herrmann's work for Hitchcock.

Delineating Structure

Structural Relationship between Music and Image

Music can act as a structuring device in film and other audiovisual media. Filmmakers as far back as Sergei Eisenstein have explored and theorized the structural implications of using music in conjunction with the moving image. When music and visuals are combined, they enter into a structural relationship, among others. This may be noticeable at the macro-level (e.g., a film's act structure, a TV episode, a video game level), or the incidental micro-level (e.g., how much relates to visual cuts or movement within the image). Where a composer provides original music for a project, they can act as structurer, actively shaping the cumulative structure of "music + moving image" as experienced by the audience or player.

Narrative Structure

Narrative structure can be delineated by the presence and absence of music. Music may serve as a structural **marker** and provide **punctuation marks**, by providing audiovisual coincidence (an event in the music occurring at the same time as a visual event or cut), or by use of judiciously placed music start and end points. Music can also help **separate** sections in the visual medium— for example, a studio logo from the beginning of a film (see also Chapter 6). Another time, music may **bind** together separate sections—for example, leading from one scene to another. Music may be used to hold together **montage** sequences (see also Chapter 5), which are commonly used in film and television to indicate passage of time, travelling a distance, making progress. Music may also help set the **pace** of a scene or segment, with musical attributes such as pitch, rhythm, and tempo interacting with the audiovisual flow in such a way that the resulting effect is one of increased or decreased speed (see also Chapter 8). For example, fast and highly rhythmic music will often accompany chase and fight scenes, whereas contemplative or romantic settings are accompanied congruently by slow and calm music.

"Form" in Music

The respective form and structure of music and moving images may not immediately be compatible. When describing a piece of music, the term "**form**" refers to the structure of the musical composition as a whole. Traditionally, there have been shorter forms, such as a song or a prelude, and relatively longer forms, including symphonies and operas. Concepts of forms govern the way a composer organizes musical material over the course of a composition. Some of these concepts are fairly strict, such as a Bach-style fugue (hear, for example, the fugue from Toccata and Fugue in D Minor, BWV 586, II. Fugue) or a so-called sonata-allegro form (for example, Piano Sonata in D Major, K.381: I. Allegro, by Wolfgang Amadeus Mozart). These traditional forms stipulate exactly how melodies and harmonic structure may be organized. Other forms are more flexible, such as the symphony, which can take on a wide range of inner structures, including the number of movements and overall length. Since most media music compositions comprise relatively short pieces, called "cues," the overarching form is not often discussed. A composer may consider using thematic material across a number of cues within a longer film or video game (see also Chapter 6). But they will not normally plan thematic layouts in the way they would when writing a string quartet in the style of Beethoven.

Contrarily, with the composition of interactive video game music, there are structural implications that must be considered, and music produced in such a way so that different score elements can be flexibly recombined to accompany real-time gameplay. Music may need to loop as long as it takes a player to get to a certain point in the game. Music may also need to shift gears suddenly—for example, if the player chooses to attack an opponent. The composer will liaise with the programmers and audio director to plan and implement music with the game engine.

26 Why Use Music at All?

Structure in Music

It should be kept in mind that musical compositions <u>do</u> have structure. This structure can be devised flexibly to suit the needs of the project, but nevertheless there is a sense of structural coherence and integrity that a composer will hope to achieve and maintain. You will not normally need to discuss the structure of a cue, let along the detailed measure-by-measure development of a composition. But thinking of structure in music can helpfully intersect with structural concerns in the narrative and visual editing. There are overlaps and synergies that can be explored, and the composer should welcome a dialogue with the team to address these structural concerns. Composer Marco Beltrami (*World War Z* (2012), *Logan* (2017)) feels that "people today are so afraid of giving music or themes space to breathe and play out. Compare Hitchcock or Leone: There is so much space (for music)."[5] Orchestrator and conductor Jeff Atmajian agrees: "If you think of somebody like Hitchcock or Sergio Leone, the way they would shoot long scenes […] where they knew music would be the only thing that would make that really work. They left that space for it."[6] Academy Award-winning composer Gabriel Yared (*The English Patient* (1997), *The Talented Mr. Ripley* (1999)) conceives of film and music as conversation: "In a spoken conversation, if one person speaks, the other is silent. Give music space and room. Invite music to elevate film."[7] Considering the structure of the narrative alongside structural aspects of music, you may choose to allow extra space for music in some places.

- The <u>Main Title</u> from *To Kill a Mockingbird* (1962) is a good example of an opening title theme, where music is given the time and space to develop.
- In a memorably lyrical moment, Luke Skywalker faces the binary sunset in *Star Wars: Episode IV—A New Hope* (1977), and a rousing complete statement or the Luke Skywalker/Force Theme is provided by full symphony orchestra.
- There is a lovely scene in John Favreau's live action adaption of *The Jungle Book* (2016) after Mowgli has helped the elephants recue their baby from a sinkhole: Composer John Debney is given time to quote an extended passage of the main melody from the song "The Bare Necessities," in a heart-warming rendition with full orchestra (<u>Mowgli and the Pit</u> from 2:24)

Direct Attention

Music can provide focus and point-of-view perspective in narrative situations that might otherwise be ambiguous.

- *Altered States* (1980)—John Corigliano's unsettling score mirrors the main character's drug-induced mental journey.
- *Vertigo* (1958)—Bernard Herrmann's score features a number of themes that differentiate Scotty's love interest Madeleine from her alter ego, Carlotta (for example, in the cue <u>Scotty Trails Madeleine</u>), also highlighting Scotty's infatuation with her/them.
- In video games, music is a valuable asset to guide players towards a goal and steer them in a particular direction. Working in conjunction with other sound and visual elements, music can motivate players in the gameplay progress or dissuade players from veering too far off course.

Establish Characters

Music can help identify individual characters, effectively labeling or branding them early on in a narrative. The most obvious way music can help establish character is by use of **character-specific themes or motifs**. These may be melodies, chord progressions, or, in the case of the *Terminator* franchise, simply a recognizable drum pattern (e.g., in <u>Main Title Terminator 2 Theme</u>.) A character's theme is first established by accompanying the character with their musical theme. Later on, the character may then be referred to by music alone, in their absence. When a musical theme is assigned to the character, it will usually be indicative of their character traits and intentions. The theme not only identifies the characters, it also *characterizes* them. A story's hero, villain, love interest, interloper, benevolent elder will receive very different musical treatments. Some scores use only one, or very few, recurring themes (e.g., *Jaws* (1975)) whereas other films have dozens (the *Star Wars* franchise and *the Lord of the Rings* trilogy each have more than 40 recurring themes.) Musical themes need not be attached to a specific character but can serve a film as a whole. Alan Silvestri's theme <u>I'm Forrest ... Forrest Gump</u> for *Forrest Gump* (1994) or Henry Mancini's <u>Moon River</u> for *Breakfast at Tiffany's* (1961) are distinctive themes that are not necessarily attached to their respective main character but rather the narrative as a whole. In both examples, however, the thematic material helps set the main characters in a certain sympathetic light.

Music can serve more generally to **characterize a protagonist** in a certain way. For example, it is a bit of a cliché that villains love classical music, presumably pairing an evil streak with intellectual highbrow taste. Hannibal Lecter enjoys Bach's Goldberg variations (<u>Goldberg Variations, BWV 988: Aria</u>) in *The Silence of the Lambs* (1991). Alexandra listens to a private performance Brahms's String Quartet in C Minor in *Marvel's Defenders* (2017).

28 Why Use Music at All?

By contrast, the emotional or psychological fragility of characters can be suggested by use of empathetic music, as is the case in:

- *To Kill a Mockingbird* (1962)—Elmer Bernstein's gentle theme for Boo Radley (the cue <u>Boo Who?</u>).
- *Brokeback Mountain* (2005)—Gustavo Santaolalla's understated theme for Ennis Del Mar and Jack Twist (e.g., the cue <u>Brokeback Mountain 1</u>).
- *Moonlight* (2016)—Nicholas Britell's soothing theme for Little (<u>Little's Theme</u>).

Music can also **distance the audience from a character**, or characters from each other, instilling a sense of alienation or otherness in:

- *Planet of the Apes* (1968)—Jerry Goldsmith's largely atonal score for a film that depicts a cash of culture between humans and highly evolved apes (e.g., <u>Main Title</u>).
- *Snow Falling on Cedars* (1999)—James Newton Howard's haunting score accompanies the clash of Japanese and Caucasian communities in post-WWII 1950s US
- *Lawrence of Arabia* (1962)—Music helps render a sense of "foreignness" in this British-American epic, an historical drama film based on the life of T.E. Lawrence (e.g., <u>Overture</u>).

Comedy

Music is invariably called upon to help create a sense of, to support, or amplify comedy. There is a long tradition in music history for musical comedy—for example, *opera buffa* and *operettas* are lighthearted and comedic in terms of music but also in terms of subject matter and situational comedy. In a film or TV show, if a scene is not funny, music is unlikely to succeed in making it so. Music in comedy can come in different guises and serve different purposes, but timing is often key: the way music is fitted to a scene and where music starts and stops can make a big difference to whether or not a scene is funny. There is **slapstick** comedy in which musical gestures often are closely synchronized to the on-screen action, essentially mimicking sound effects. Taken to an extreme, such close matching of musical gestures and on-screen actions is called "mickey-mousing," pioneered by composer Carl W. Stalling, who worked for Walt Disney on the groundbreaking animation *Steamboat Willie* and the *Silly Symphonies* series and later for Warner Bros. on *Looney Tunes* and *Merrie Melodies*.

Having established that the quirky nature of some jazz music can be drawn upon for comedic effect, notably with Henry Mancini's <u>The Pink Panther Theme</u>, countless straightforward **comedies**, films, and TV shows draw on a similar musical palette. In recent years, the prime-time soap *Desperate Housewives* and comedy shows *Ugly Betty* (2006–2010), *Unbreakable Kimmy Schmidt* (2015–), and *The Good Place* (2016–) all draw on lighthearted musical underscoring for comedic effect. It could be said that in these examples lighthearted music is in agreement with the comical setting of the respective show.

Music can conjure a sense of low-stakes mischief in **crime-comedies**, providing the requisite tongue-in-cheek tone predominantly with composed underscore (in, for example, Soderbergh's *Ocean's 11* (2001, e.g., <u>Boobytrappin</u>) or Spielberg's *Catch Me If You Can* (2002)) or with a combination of composed and compiled music (e.g., *The Nice Guys* (2016), <u>Theme from "The Nice Guys"</u>). Jazz, funk, and other pop music idioms often are the go-to here.

Romantic comedies commonly rely on music to maintain a light and humorous tone even when at times a character may be struggling with heartache etc. Whilst much of the comedy is, once again, situational (not relying solely on music), score and song choices can go a long way towards helping the audience remember that the program they are watching is less than serious. By contrast, Elmer Bernstein's serious and highly dramatic orchestral score for the spoof comedy *Airplane!* (1980) proved that comedy music need not be funny at all. In fact, the juxtaposition of ultra-serious music with a farcical setting can bring hilarious results. Since then, the same effect has been used in many films and TV shows, including:

- *Zoolander* (2001)—David Arnold underscores this spoof (fashion) crime thriller with *faux* spy/action music.
- *Austin Powers: International Man of Mystery* (1997)—George Clinton's serious quasi-Bond score provides a dramatic musical backdrop to the comedy.
- *Robin Hood—Men in Tights* (1993)—Hummie Mann's tuneful and bold orchestral score for this Mel Brooks spoof of Kevin Reynolds's star-studded film is every bit as ambitious as Michael Kamen's original.

Provide Continuity

In audiovisual multimedia, a range of filming and editing techniques help the audience suspend their disbelief and critical distance. Music is an additional asset that can provide continuity across multiple shots, sonically "gluing" together what is visually separate. Especially with increasing editing speeds, continuous music can fulfill a binding and unifying function, be it in busy action sequences or during a visual montage. Countless video games since the earliest days have drawn on music for an added sense of continuity, including runner games, shooter games, strategy, and puzzle games. Music can help bridge temporal and spatial jumps or gaps in the narrative. These include transitions to a flashback or visions of a distant future that suddenly appear to a character. A connection can be made between different characters across time periods, as, for example, in *The Hours* (2002), by use of continuous music. When characters travel a long distance in the space of seconds, music can help bridge the distance. In *The Muppets* (2011), the characters point out the "traveling by map" trick to humorous effect.

Supporting Dialogue

The idea that music can support the spoken word to a narrative end, be it sonically, emotionally, and/or dramatically, perhaps dates back all the way to *recitative* in sixteenth-century opera and oratorio. In audiovisual multimedia, music can help with the pacing of the delivery of lines (akin to punctuation), underline and emphasize key points, and develop along dialogue to gradually build tension, or mystery, aggression, benevolence, etc. If music and dialogue are not only to coexist but also work effectively in conjunction, joint planning of these elements is required. There are countless inspired examples for music supporting dialogue. To name just a few:

- When the Joker, brutally beaten by Batman in the interrogation room sequence in *The Dark Knight* (2008), finally agrees to name the location of Harvey Dent, subtle meandering gongs underpin his evil scheming (he soon reveals that he has also abducted Rachel).
- When *Amélie* (2001) whisks a blind man down a busy street and describes for him all the sights and impressions he cannot see, the accompanying music grows increasingly energized, paralleling the blind man's experience of joy.
- When Riggan experiences yet another moment of crisis in *Birdman or (The Unexpected Virtue of Ignorance)* (2014), he has a fight with his imagined super hero alter ego. Frantic drumming highlights Riggan's (Michael Keaton) chaotic inner turmoil and punctuates the dialogue to visceral effect, further amplified by the noise caused by Riggan trashing his dressing room.

Geographic Location

Where are we? Music is highly effective in establishing a geographic location. Using specific instruments and musical idiosyncrasies of a country or region, music can serve as subliminal shorthand:

- shakuhachi flute = Japan
- didgeridoo = Australia
- throat singing = Tibet
- samba rhythms = Brazil
- gamelan = Indonesia
- balalaikas = Russia
- bagpipes = Scotland.

These are just some of many musical clichés that reliably flag entire cultures. Despite the term's negative connotation, clichés are of course just signs that signal well. If media music is effectively and quickly to signpost a geographic setting to an audience, then these wholesale appropriations of musical cultures can be perfectly suitable. For some projects a purist approach may be required that reflects musical cultures more truthfully—for example, by working with musicians from that culture. Other times it can be acceptable for stylistic adaptations to be quite superficial. Composer Alf Clausen once said that whenever he had to write "ethnic" music for *The Simpsons* (1989–) he would spend no more than twenty minutes on researching the respective culture before composing his cue.[8] By contrast, a composer might spend months researching musical customs if an accurate rendition is desired.

- *A River Runs through It* (1992)—Copland-esque strings, harp, solo violin and a sustained simplicity of tonal language serve this film set in early twentieth-century Montana (<u>A River Runs through It</u>).
- *Brokeback Mountain* (2005)—Breaking away from Wild West clichés, strings and acoustic guitar nevertheless help establish a rural Western setting (<u>Brokeback Mountain 1</u>).
- *Brave* (2012)—Patrick Doyle provides vivacious tunes on bagpipes and fiddles for a fairytale set in the Scottish Highlands (<u>The Games</u>).
- *The Hunt for Red October* (1990)—Basil Poledouris's score skillfully helps tell apart the Russian and American sailors, including inspired use of Russian hymns sung by the Red Army Choir (<u>Main Title</u>).
- *The Lion King* (1994)—South African singer Lebo M opens <u>Circle of Life</u> and immediately transports the audience to Africa. Tribal percussion and choirs supplement the orchestral score throughout.

32 Why Use Music at All?

- *Prometheus* (2012)—The unusual and strained sound of high French horn in the opening cue <u>Life,</u> paired with ethereal choral hums are suggestive of an alien world.
- *Ratatouille* (2007)—Michael Giacchino's score evokes the French setting by use of acoustic guitar, piano, accordion, and by quoting the French national anthem in the <u>Main Theme</u> and in <u>Welcome to Gusteau's</u>.
- *Syriana* (2005)—Syrian/Lebanese percussion and strings in a distinctive tonal language help transport the audience to the Levant (<u>Beirut Taxi</u>).

Sometimes the nature of a musical score appears to disagree with the geographic setting of the film. In *The Last of the Mohicans* (1992), three trappers protect a British colonel's daughter during the conflict between the French and Native American tribes. Trevor Jones and Randy Edelman's orchestral score is distinctly biased towards a white Western cultural realm, possibly to make the film palatable for the presumed target audience (<u>Main Title</u>). Maurice Jarre's synthesizer score for *Witness* (1985) blatantly contradicts the rural setting in an Amish community (<u>Building the Barn</u>). This was a conscious choice made by the composer: director Peter Weir wanted a score that was cold and had emotional distance. As a result, the tone and style of the music does not support the geographic setting of the film.

Dream State

Rather than an actual geographic location, music may also **suggest a dream state** and it may also help differentiate between characters' real-life experience versus a dream reality.

- John Corigliano's ambitious aleatoric score for *Altered States* (1980) accompanies the main protagonist's drug-induced hallucinations.
- Hans Zimmer's score for *Inception* (2010) amplifies the mesmerizing visual experience and highlights the life-threatening stakes in the dream world the characters enter (<u>Dream Is Collapsing</u> and <u>Time</u>).
- Newman's score for *American Beauty* (1999) does not clearly distinguish in tone between Lester Burnham's dream-states and waking hours but the music provides sympathetic beautiful padding in the dream scene in which Angela appears to Lester, bedded on rose petals on the ceiling (<u>Arose</u>).
- Karen O and the Kids devise a child-like and largely comforting score for *Where the Wild Things Are* (2009), possibly suggesting young Max is dreaming his encounter with the large wild beasts (<u>Igloo</u>).

Further Meaning and Narrative

There are many different situations in which music can tell the audience something that is not already implied by context, or apparent in the visuals, or expressed in spoken words by the protagonists. There are many different ways in which this can be achieved. For example, a character may seem at ease and look friendly, but music suggests that something sinister is afoot. Perhaps the character has ill intentions towards someone, or they are struggling with an inner conflict or obsession. Jonny Greenwood's score for *There Will Be Blood* (2007, <u>There Will Be Blood</u>) may at first seem incongruous with the story of a gold digger who lives the American Dream to become a wealthy oil tycoon. Considered in the broader context of the story, however, it becomes apparent that the music primarily focuses on the corrupting effects of greed and wealth on the individual. In a similar fashion, albeit by different musical means, Greenwood focuses on the troubled inner world of Freddie Quell (Joaquin Phoenix) in *The Master* (2012).

Music can also foreshadow a narrative development. In *Star Wars—Episode I: The Phantom Menace* (1999), music suggests that young Anakin will one day turn into Darth Vader, whose theme can be heard on a subtle oboe when young Anakin puts on his backpack outside his hut. Invested fans have speculated that Supreme Leader Snoke, first seen in *Star Wars—Episode VII: The Force Awakens* (2015), is the fabled Darth Plagueis: The latter was mentioned to adolescent Anakin by Senator Palpatine in *Star Wars: Episode III—Revenge of the Sith* (2005) and speculation over the two characters being one and the same arose because the musical theme (low male voices singing) used to accompany both is very similar (<u>Snoke</u>).

Establish Time Period

When are we? Music can help indicate a time period by using period instruments and musical styles. Individual approaches can range from purist to liberal. With a purist approach, music will strive for an accurate emulation of the music of the particular time period that is being depicted in the narrative.

The Past

This may require direction quotation from past repertoire, which incidentally can serve as excellent shorthand to indicate a time period. A more liberal approach

34 Why Use Music at All?

will borrow or emulate aspects of period music but adapt and embellish that music to serve other needs in the project. Depending on the project, composed or compiled music may best serve the purpose of establishing a time period.

- *American Graffiti* (1973)—George Lukas's breakthrough film uses a large number of licensed pop songs for this film set in 1962.
- *Glow* (2017–)—Set in 1980s Los Angeles, this show aptly draws on licensed songs in conjunction with period props and outfits.
- *Dangerous Liaisons* (1988)—For this film, set in eighteenth-century France, composer George Fenton adapts George Frederick Handel [1685–1759] in his composed underscore. The film also uses existing pieces of the time period, including Vivaldi, Gluck, and Bach.

The Future

Where a narrative is set in the future, composers and music supervisors may explore different types of music:

- *Blade Runner* (1982)—Vangelis opts for synthesizers for the film's futuristic setting but also a saxophone for the love theme, a popular sound when this film was made (<u>Main Titles</u>).
- *Minority Report* (2002)—John Williams's score for this film is fully orchestral and largely shuns synthesizers or drum grooves that one might have expected from this futuristic action-thriller (<u>Minority Report</u>).
- *2001: A Space Odyssey* (1968)—Kubrick famously opted for a compilation score comprising existing pieces by Ligeti (<u>Lux Aeterna</u>), Khachaturian, Richard Strauss, and Johann Strauss II.

Outliers

There are many outliers in which music does not reflect the time period in which the narrative is set. There can be any number of reasons why one may choose to opt for other musical solutions. Pure or adapted period music may feel ill-suited to serve the project, or it may fail to engage and appeal to the intended target audience.

- *Mr. Turner* (2014)—Mike Leigh expressly did not want a period score but instead agreed with composer Gary Yershon that they would focus on the increasingly abstract nature of Turner's paintings (<u>Mr. Turner</u>).

Why Use Music at All? **35**

- *Gladiator* (2000)—This film, whose targeted mainstream audience would hardly recognize what authentic ancient Roman/Germanic music sounded like, has a large-scale orchestral score in a popular music idiom, featuring Australian singer Lisa Gerrard (<u>Now We Are Free</u>).
- *1492: Conquest of Paradise* (1992)—This fully synthesized score was a commercial hit in its own right but, stylistically, has nothing to do with the film's fifteenth-century setting.

Dramatic/Narrative Pace

Music can help provide a sense of higher speed and urgency in a scene or segment, pushing the action forward by use of rhythmic patterns, agitated musical lines, and energetic gestures. Any chase sequence, escape, countdown, or deadline in the narrative will benefit from music.

- *Unstoppable* (2010)—Harry Gregson-Williams's loop-based score provides relentless drive, amplifying the effect of Tony Scott's high-octane visual style.
- *The Italian Job* (2003)—John Powell's score for this re-make of the 1969 original is fast-paced and highly energetic, effectively distracting from the fact that some of the action is actually rather slow-moving: For example, in the <u>Tunnel Run</u> segment, the Mini Coopers are driving quite slowly.
- *Dunkirk* (2017)—Zimmer's score helps deliver a breathless experience by use of incessant ticking and clicking (<u>Supermarine</u>.)

Indicating Mood and Stirring Emotions

Music may not be intrinsically emotional, but media music can effectively evoke an emotional response from the audience. In the right context, music can move an audience to tears, make them cheer for the hero, or jump with fright. Finding the emotional truth of each moment in the narrative is one of the great challenges for all media creators and composers. Music can be an ally to help amplify the emotional charge of a scene or segment.

Action and Adventure

In epic **adventures** (*Ben Hur* (1959), *Star Wars* franchise, *Gladiator* (2000), *Indiana Jones* franchise, and *Game of Thrones* (2011–), to name a few), music can whisk the audience along and enfranchise them to a collective struggle and an emotional journey. The use of large-scale instrumental forces and grand musical gestures (brass fanfares, heavy percussion, bright strings) helps underline a sense of greatness of the characters portrayed and the importance of their actions. The individual audience member is enticed to empathetically join in with a collective struggle. **Hymns and anthems** are part of cultures worldwide, sung to uphold a sense of unity, belonging, and collective (national) pride. In multimedia, anthem-like music can be drawn upon to conjure the same effect. For example, the aptly named <u>Top Gun Anthem</u> in *Top Gun* (1986) uplifts the victory celebrations after aerial combat.

The plight of one becomes the plight of many (including that of the audience):

- when a **struggle is overcome** (for example, in the cue <u>Run Forrest Run</u> in *Forrest Gump* (1994), when young Forrest escapes the kids that are taunting him).
- when a narrow **escape** succeeds (as, for example, in the L.A. getaway sequence in Emmerich's *2012* (2009)).
- when a sports **trophy is won** (see countless sports movies).

War epics and **military conflict** are frequently accompanied by large-scale scores. The style of music in such projects can vary, depending on budgets, time period depicted, target audience, etc. For example, three films depicting submarine warfare receive very different musical treatments:

- *Crimson Tide* (1995, <u>Main Theme</u>)
- *Hunt for Red October* (1990, <u>Hymn to Red October (Main Title)</u>)
- *Das Boot* (1981, <u>Titel</u>)

Even where the same conflict is depicted, music can be very different depending on the director's intentions. One might compare, for example, these two Vietnam films:

- *Apocalypse Now* (1979)—The use of Wagner's pompous <u>Ride of the Valkyries</u> remains controversial.
- *Tigerland* (2000, <u>Tigerland</u>)—Nathan Larson's score for this Joel Schumacher film is surprisingly small-scale, using a solo *k'ni* (a Vietnamese violin-type instrument), drums, and electric guitar.

Triumph

To help evoke a sense of heroic triumph, or generate a sense of ritual or ceremony, distinguishing a great individual (= the hero) from the masses (in the narrative and also the audience). Michael Kamen's theme for *Robin Hood: Prince of Thieves* (1991, Robin Hood Prince of Thieves), Williams's themes for *Superman* (1978, Theme from Superman) and *Raiders of the Lost Ark* (1981, Raiders March), and Elmer Bernstein's theme for *The Magnificent Seven* (1960, Main Title and Calvera) are just a few of the greatest heroic fanfares in film music.

Awe and Wonder

There are many ways in which music can help create wondrous atmosphere or highlight a character's amazed response to a situation. A range of instruments may provide sounds that are unusual or unfamiliar to the audience, or a tonal palette may be devised that sounds dark or mesmerizing.

- The musical dialogue with the aliens near the end of *Close Encounters of the Third Kind* (1977, Wild Signals), where music gradually evolves into a colorful sonic mesh, is a good example.
- Music underlines the stunning visuals and amplifies Casey's sense of awe as she first explores the futuristic city in *Tomorrowland* (2015).
- The cue Ice Dance in *Edward Scissorhands* (1990) beautifully complements the visuals when Edward creates ice sculptures, to Kim's amazement (incidentally, winning her heart).
- Scotty's impeding obsession with Madeleine becomes obvious in the way she is framed in the restaurant in *Vertigo* (1958, cue Scotty Trails Madeleine), both visually and musically.

Depictions of magic reliably rely on music for added sparkle and wonder. One might consider, for example, the transformation sequence, in Disney's animated *Beauty and the Beast* (1991, Transformation), Elliott's first encounter with E.T. in *E.T.: The Extra-Terrestrial* (1982, the cue Meeting E.T.), and the *Harry Potter* franchise, famously Hedwig's Theme.

Horror and Fear

Horror and music are perhaps inseparable, but music is also called upon more broadly every time a sense of fright, fear, or trepidation is to be

38 Why Use Music at All?

indicated (felt by a character) or induced (in the audience). Sometimes the use of music will be overt and in-your-face. Other times, subtle gestures suffice to achieve a desired effect. A wide range of styles of music can be effective in a horror context. There are many films and games where perfectly lovely music may accompany terrifying visuals, the resulting effect being all the more troubling. Reversely, harmless images may be accompanied by a harsh musical noise-scape, together delivering a frightening experience for the audience.

Some films, including Hitchcock's masterpiece *Psycho* (1960, <u>Murder</u>), rely on aggressive gestures to parallel the on-screen action. James Newton Howard, who composed the score for *The Sixth Sense* (1999, <u>Hanging Ghosts</u>), is confident that his music has a profound impact on the film: According to him, it "wasn't scary without music, I guarantee you."[9] Contrarily, music in *Stranger Things* (2016–, <u>Stranger Things</u>) tends to be more broadly atmospheric, largely eschewing sudden or aggressive scoring devices.

Jason Graves's award-winning scores for the *Dead Space* games (2008, <u>Dead Space Theme</u>) is a prime example of extrovert and visceral horror music, setting a new benchmark for truly horrific underscoring. As ever, music does not operate in isolation, but it is the implementation of music among other elements that makes for terrifying game-play. The *Doom*, *Halo*, and *Resident Evil* series, among so many others, also draw on music in ingenious ways, often relying on dark and brooding colors and/or sudden heavy impacts.

Benjamin Wallfisch's score for *It* (2017, <u>Every 27 Years</u>), Komeda's score for *Rosemary's Baby* (1968, <u>Main Theme</u>), and Andrews's score for *Donnie Darko* (2001, the cue <u>Cellar Door</u>) all use lullabies, children's voices, and generally cute and cuddly music, which heighten the resulting sense of horror in the context of the other storytelling elements. The powerful effect resulting from the unlikely juxtaposition of seemingly incongruous "music + narrative context" is similar to very serious music operating in the context of comedies (see earlier examples).

Sadness and Tragedy

Music will reliably be of service in moments of sadness, tragedy, and loss. A careful balance must be struck between the other storytelling elements, and also considering the context in which a sad moment occurs, so as to not tip the emotional balance over the top. Invariably, for the audience to feel sad, characters and situations must be prepared and constructed.

Music alone will not make for a sad scene, but a certain kind of music used in the right context will help bring tears to everyone's eyes. The familiar cliché "cue the violins" is indicative of scoring tools of a bygone era that may no longer be effective. Once again, it should be stressed that there probably is no such thing as "sad music." There is, however, a range of different musical solutions that will help make a scene or scenario feel sad, if used at the right time and after suitable preparation. Investible characters, a plausible and engaging plot, compelling stakes, and a convincing delivery (by the actors) all contribute towards the successful setting up of a sad scene. **Timing is essential**: Cueing music too soon might prevent an audience from engaging with the scene. Cueing it too late might mean missing an opportunity. There are a vast number of films and TV shows that have tackled sadness, tragedy, and loss: Compare the uses of music therein. Some obvious examples include:

- *Beaches* (1988)—There is nothing intrinsically sad about Bette Midler's song Wind beneath My Wings, but when it is heard in the film, it is utterly devastating, its lyrics relating to the story the audience has followed up to this point.
- *Titanic* (1997)—Jack's death is accompanied by a simple flute tune that is related to the main theme (My Heart Will Go on), in its understated manner nevertheless amplifying the emotional charge of the moment.
- *Good Will Hunting* (1997)—Music stays almost completely clear of the "It's not your fault" scene, in which a psychiatrist (played by Robin Williams) has a breakthrough with his patient Will Hunting (Matt Damon), entering only at the very end when Will has already broken down.
- *Dancer in the Dark* (2000)—Music in this challenging quasi-musical provides an aesthetic counterpoint to the bleak place where the main character Selma Jezkova (played by Björk) lives. The execution scene, led up to by the song 107 Steps, sets up perhaps one of the most devastating moments in the film.

Takeaways

- There is a wide range of conventional roles and functions of media music that are tried and tested.
- Always feel free to explore new possibilities and push boundaries on your next project.
- Media music never acts in isolation but contributes to the cumulative effect of all storytelling tools.

40 Why Use Music at All?

> **Further Reading**
>
> Bordwell, D., J. Staiger, and K. Thompson. *The Classical Hollywood Cinema: Film Style and Mode of Production to 1960.* London and New York: Routledge, 1985.
> Chion, M. *Audio-Vision: Sound on Screen.* New York: Columbia University Press, 1994.
> Eisenstein, S. *The Film Sense.* New edition. London: Faber & Faber, 1986.
> Gorbman, C. *Unheard Melodies: Narrative Film Music.* London: BFI Publishing, 1987.
> Kalinak, K.M. *Settling the Score: Music and the Classical Hollywood Film.* Madison, WI: University of Wisconsin Press, 1992.

Notes

1 Robert Emmett Ginna. "Stanley Kubrick Speaks for Himself." EW.com, 9 April 1999. http://ew.com/article/1999/04/09/stanley-kubrick-speaks-himself/, accessed 25 January 2018.
2 C. Gorbman. *Unheard Melodies: Narrative Film Music.* London: BFI Publishing, 1987, p. 73.
3 S.K. Langer. *Philosophy in a New Key: A Study in the Symbolism of Reason, Rite, and Art* (1942) 3rd edition. Cambridge, MA: Harvard University Press, 1978, p. 240.
4 M. Chion. *Audio-Vision: Sound on Screen.* New York: Columbia University Press, 1994, p. 5.
5 Beltrami in a talk at the Transatlantyk International Film Festival, Poznan on 8 August 2013.
6 Atmajian in a personal interview in London on 14 June 2011.
7 Yared during a visit to the Royal College of Music, London on 21 April 2016.
8 Clausen in a talk at the Berklee College of Music, Boston in April 2003.
9 C. Reynolds and M. Brill. "On the Art and Craft of Film Music: A Conversation with James Newton Howard." *Hopkins Review* 3(3) (2010): 320–351, p. 331.

Different Types of Narrative Media Music

2

2.1 Introduction

Broadly speaking, there are two different types of music in narrative media. So-called **diegetic music** (or **source music**) has its source within the narrative and inhabits the same narrative space as dialogue and sound effects. Diegetic music can be heard by the characters in the narrative—for example, in a shopping mall, a restaurant, an elevator, in a club, at a party, etc. **Non-diegetic music** (or **extra-diegetic music**) accompanies the narrative but does not originate from within the narrative. Non-diegetic music is external to the narrative environment and cannot be heard by the characters. Most of the time, it is obvious whether music is diegetic or non-diegetic. This is conveyed by narrative context, the sound quality of the music, etc. Sometimes, it is less than clear whether music has its source inside or outside the narrative, and media creators can toy with conventions to good effect (see later in the chapter).

2.2 Diegetic Music

Diegetic music may be heard in a scene depicting a party, a funeral, a sporting event, etc. Any and all music of any style can be diegetic music, be it purely instrumental or songs. Diegetic music may sometimes have its source pointed out within the narrative—for example, when a band is playing in a venue, a string quartet is playing at a wedding reception, or a DJ is shown spinning records in a club. Maybe an establishing shot shows speakers from which music emanates. Characters may also *perform* music themselves: Holly Golightly sings <u>Moon River</u> in *Breakfast at Tiffany's* (1961). Maverick and

42 Different Types of Narrative Media Music

Goose sing <u>Great Balls of Fire</u> in *Top Gun* (1986). Other times, characters may simply sing along to the radio or a band performing or sing in the shower.

The need for diegetic music should become obvious at scripting stage, and there will be implications for music selection and licensing (more on that in Chapter 5). A character may put a record on the record player, a cassette into the tape deck, or a CD into the CD-player. A character may put a coin in a jukebox and select a song. A character may be shown flicking through an iPod and listening to a piece of music on her headphones. A character may turn on the radio in their car. In *American Psycho* (2000), investment banker and serial killer Patrick Bateman (Christian Bale) talks at length about source music that is playing in his home. In different scenes, he puts CDs in his home stereo before he then talks about the music of Huey Lewis and the News, Phil Collins, and Whitney Houston. In Wes Anderson's *The Life Aquatic with Steve Zissou* (2005), oceanographer Zissou (Bill Murray) plays music during his crew's underwater excursions. He repeatedly refers to this music when he turns it on, and even dances to it in one scene.

2.3 Non-Diegetic Music

Any and all music of any style and form can be non-diegetic music, be it purely instrumental or songs. A newly commissioned underscore (see also Chapter 6) is almost always non-diegetic. Nearly all of the best-loved orchestral film music of the last 100+ years has been non-diegetic, with very few exceptions where filmmakers chose purposely to toy with the audience (see later in the chapter). There are countless examples for non-diegetic music in film, television, and video games (in the last, particularly during filmic introductions and linear transitions). Even though audiences will not always pay conscious attention to non-diegetic music (or to any music in media, for that matter), non-diegetic music can be a powerful storytelling tool.

Takeaways

- Broadly speaking, there are **two different types of narrative media music.**
- **Diegetic music** has its source within the narrative and inhabits the same narrative space as dialogue and sound effects.
- **Non-diegetic,** or **extra-diegetic music,** accompanies the narrative but does not originate from within the narrative.
- Newly commissioned composed underscore is almost always non-diegetic.

2.4 Special Cases and Creative Possibilities

It can be interesting to explore different balances between diegetic and non-diegetic music and to subvert the notion of music being *either* within *or* outside the narrative. This requires careful planning with the aid of a music supervisor, music editor, and/or a composer. Any music placement, be it diegetic, non-diegetic, or something in between, has implications for project preparation and execution. When pursuing unconventional modes of expression, including music usages, you need to communicate ideas clearly, to align on shared goals and work collaboratively towards the intended outcome. The examples given here are by no means exhaustive. These should serve as pointers to give media creators some ideas for less than conventional music usages.

Taking Liberties with Diegetic Music

You can take some liberties when placing source music in a scene. Audiences will accept a source off-screen even when that source is not first introduced on-screen. For example, it is not always necessary to show a character putting on a record for the audience to understand from context that music is playing in a living room. Furthermore, audiences will accept the sound quality of the music to be quite pure—without the clichéd crackling from a record player or hiss from a cassette tape—and still believe that the music is meant to be coming from a diegetic source (radio, tape, record). In George Lucas's *American Graffiti* (1973), disc jockey Wolfman Jack is repeatedly heard from a notional radio source, announcing songs during his late-night radio show. Lucas does not strictly adhere to narrative logic whereby the characters would have to be near a radio (be it in one of the many cars, in a diner, etc.) to hear the radio show. Instead, the continuous audio from the radio show occupies a sonic space shared by the film's characters across different locations. In Damien O'Donnell's *East Is East* (1999), Neenah Khan (Archie Panjabi) dances to the song "Inhi Logon Ne" from the Bollywood film *Pakeezah* (1972), a well-known tragic tale of forbidden love. Neenah breaks into an impromptu dance to the song with the aid of a nearby broom, making for a comedic setting. Her brother is bobbing his head along in time with the music. Although the source of the music is not visible, the audience is led to assume the music is playing from a record player or tape deck off-screen.

44 Different Types of Narrative Media Music

No Extra-Diegetic Music

Some filmmakers prefer to work entirely without non-diegetic music. This can be reasonably justified by a film's style, genre, and subject matter. Social realism films, for example, have tended not to draw on extra-diegetic music in order not to tip towards melodrama or moralistic finger pointing. A range of examples for films and TV shows entirely without extra-diegetic music include:

- The Dogme 95 filmmakers subscribed to the rule that music must not be used unless it occurs where the scene is being shot.
- Alfred Hitchcock opted to have no underscore in *The Birds* (1963), favoring carefully crafted sound design and some diegetic music. His go-to composer Bernard Herrmann was involved as a sound consultant and helped devise synthesized sounds of bird noises.
- Austrian director Michael Haneke works exclusively with diegetic music—for example, in *Funny Games* (1997) and *Caché* (2006).
- The HBO series *The Wire* (2002–2008) used diegetic music almost exclusively, except during some montage segments. The absence of composed underscore heightens a sense of realism and immediacy.
- Maren Ade's *Toni Erdmann* (2016) uses only diegetic music, including in a nightclub scene and when Ines Conradi (Sandra Hüller) suddenly performs Whitney Houston's ballad "The Greatest Love of All."

Very Little Extra-Diegetic Music

Some films use very little non-diegetic music, perhaps because there are many diegetic music entries or because the style of the film stipulates sparse scoring. The sparse use of non-diegetic music should be a reasoned choice:

- Robert Zemeckis's *Cast Away* (2000) contains no music once Chuck Noland (Tom Hanks) has washed up on the desert island, highlighting the protagonist's isolation from society.
- Ken Loach's acclaimed *I, Daniel Blake* (2016) contains very little composed music, leaving the troubled characters and bleak premise raw and unmitigated.

Music-Only, No Sound Effects

Geoffrey Reggio's groundbreaking series of non-narrative montage films *Koyaanisqatsi* (1982), *Powaqqatsi* (1988), and *Naqoyqatsi* (2002) is accompanied by minimalist music by composer Philip Glass. With very few exceptions, there are no other elements in the soundtrack of the three films. In a non-narrative medium, the notion of diegetic music of course need not apply, although some of the functions ascribed to narrative film music (see Chapter 1) may still be observed to be operating here.

Diegetic Music Becomes Non-Diegetic

This technique, also called "diegetic switch," can be quite effective in linking scenes. A piece of music starts off as diegetic music. As the narrative then progresses to the next scene, music seamlessly segues into a non-diegetic version of the same music. The change will often be noticeable in the sound quality and arrangement of the music.

- The song <u>You'll Be in My Heart</u> in the animated feature *Tarzan* (1999) starts out being sung by Tarzan's adoptive mother Kala (Glenn Close). Then, at the beginning of the second verse, the music shifts to the background and is sung by Phil Collins, off-screen, for the remainder of the sequence.
- In *Ratatouille* (2007), orchestral music accompanies a melodramatic movie playing on Linguini's TV while he is asleep. The character could hear the music if he were awake and so it is diegetic. The music gets louder and then transitions into non-diegetic music as the scene moves on to show little Remy looking dreamily out the window over nighttime Paris.

Diegetic Music Continues across Scenes

A variant of the "diegetic switch" can also be highly effective in linking scenes. A piece of music starts off as diegetic music and then, as the narrative progresses to the next scene, the same diegetic music continues. The sound quality and arrangement of the music will often stay the same and a scene may flexibly cut back to the initial source of the music.

- The television show *Ally McBeal* (1997–2002) made frequent use of this device, cueing a song performed by Vonda Shepard whose lyrics would often be topical for the episode at hand. Shepard would usually be shown performing the song diegetically on stage at some point during the music

46 Different Types of Narrative Media Music

entry, in the bar where the show's characters would end up at the end of each episode.

- In Luc Besson's *The Fifth Element* (1997), the iconic "Diva Dance" aria continues after some establishing shots of the diva whilst the footage subsequently alternates between shots of the singer and a fight happening elsewhere.
- At the end of Neil Jordan's *Interview with the Vampire: The Vampire Chronicles* (1994), Lestat (Tom Cruise) turns on the radio and we hear the Rolling Stones' Sympathy for the Devil. The song carries on into the end credits.
- At the beginning of Damien Chazelle's *La La Land* (2016), diegetic car radios are heard playing various music tracks. The camera zooms in on a woman who starts singing along to the opening of Another Day of Sun, which then turns into a diegetic song and dance number.

Non-Diegetic Music Becomes Diegetic

Revealing what at first appears to be non-diegetic music as diegetic music can be very funny:

- In a scene in *Blazing Saddles* (1974), a spoof Western, the sheriff rides his horse donning fashionable clothes and a Gucci saddlebag. The Vernon Duke jazz standard "April in Paris" accompanies the scene, in itself an odd choice of music for a Western. The moment gets even more absurd when the Count Basie Orchestra is revealed on-screen, as the sheriff passes them in the middle of the prairie.
- In the *Family Guy* (1998–) special "Blue Harvest," a spoof of *Star Wars*, there is a scene set on Tatooine when Luke Skywalker (played here by Chris) is standing outside his uncle's hut, the binary sunset in the background. In the original film, the Force Theme enters non-diegetically, creating a lyrical moment. In "Blue Harvest," Chris-as-Luke instead turns to the camera and introduces "John Williams and the London Symphony Orchestra, everybody!" The camera pans to a cartoon version of John Williams and the LSO playing the Force Theme.
- In the disaster movie spoof *Airplane!* (1980), Ted Striker (Robert Hays) visits a bar where jazz music is playing diegetically, featuring a trombone solo. As he sits at the bar, the legs of a woman appear. We are led to think she may be a pole dancer or stripper. The camera then pans up to reveal that, instead, the woman is playing the trombone.

Different Types of Narrative Media Music **47**

But the reveal of seemingly non-diegetic music as diegetic need not be funny:

- *Iron Man* (2008) opens with several Humvees travelling across a desert plane as the AC/DC song <u>Back in Black</u> plays in the background. Then the scene cuts to the interior of one vehicle in which Tony Stark is riding, revealing that the music is playing on the car stereo.
- Early on in *Star Trek Beyond* (2016), a rock song starts non-diegetically, at the end of a conversation between young Spock (Zachary Quinto) and his father. The track continues as the scene cuts to an exterior establishing shot of a place in Iowa and is, upon the next shot, revealed as diegetic to the interior of a bar that Uhura (Zoe Saldana) is attending.
- In Marvel's *Daredevil* (2015–; season 1, episode 8, "Shadows in the Glass"), Wilson Fisk (Vincent D'Onofrio) is having a flashback to his childhood in the 1970s. The moment starts in the present with a non-diegetic placement of the song <u>Brown Sugar</u> by The Rolling Stones. The next cut takes the viewer to inside the Fisks' apartment, where the song is playing on the radio, and Fisk's mother wants it to be turned down.

Experimental Placement of Music

The pioneers of the French New Wave in the late 1950s and early 1960s experimented with the placement of music to great effect—for example, in *Une femme est une femme* (1961) and *Vivre sa vie* (1962) by Jean-Luc Godard. The abrupt and sometimes purposely strange (by conventional standards) editing of diegetic and non-diegetic music would draw attention to the technical process and artificiality of filmmaking and editing. New German Cinema in the 1970s also experimented with the placement of music in compelling ways.

Blurring Non-Diegetic Boundaries

Some media creators have found compelling ways in which to unsettle the notion of what is diegetic or extra-diegetic music. Careful planning will have been required in all the cases in the following list, but the resulting dramatic and narrative effects are remarkable:

- Near the end of *Amadeus* (1984), Mozart (Tom Hulce) lies on his deathbed and dictates a section of the Sequentia for his Requiem to Antonio

48 Different Types of Narrative Media Music

Salieri (F. Murray Abraham). Music gradually enters in parts and sections as and when Mozart imagines and dictates them. There is a wonderful interplay of dialogue and music here and the audience can really understand the music coming to life, even as the composer is dying.

- In *Lola Rennt* (*Run Lola Run*, 1998), Lola (Franka Potente) runs through Berlin to save her boyfriend's life. The soundtrack comprises driving dance music specially produced for the film. The synergy of fast-paced music and high-speed editing results in a cumulative breathless experience. Potente sings in some of the music tracks, blurring the distinction between diegetic and non-diegetic music. It seems as though the music is in Lola's head all along and the audience is invited to be part of her inner world as she rushes to her boyfriend's side.

- In P.T. Anderson's *Magnolia* (1999) Aimee Mann's song Wise up is one of several songs that accompany this moving narrative. While the other songs remain non-diegetic, "Wise up" sees all the characters breaking into a spontaneous sing-along in their respective places and situations. The song suspends narrative time and captures each character in their current state, which, paired with the matter-of-fact lyrics, makes for a moment of reflection and sadness.

- *Tron: Legacy* (2010) boasts a powerful non-diegetic soundtrack, interspersed with a few diegetic tracks, notably in a nightclub where Daft Punk have a cameo as DJs. Earlier in the film, when Sam Flynn (Garrett Hedlund) visits an armory, before his outing as a contestant in the Games, four women attend to him to get him dressed and equipped. Their high heels click on the glass floor in perfect sync with the music, as though they can hear the music that accompanies the scene. Highly constructed visually and sonically, the filmmaker here toys with conventions of music in relationship to character movement.

- Alejandro González Iñárritu's *Birdman or (The Unexpected Virtue of Ignorance)* (2014) is accompanied by frenzied solo drumming. Antonio Sanchez's music chimes with the main character's chaotic state of mind. The music appears to be non-diegetic for the most part. However, in select moments, the characters suddenly walk past the drummer, whose playing the audience has been hearing all along, sat in a room off the corridor, or on a sidewalk. There is something amusingly self-aware about this choice of music placement. In a more mainstream and commercially driven film such a break with filmic convention may not be possible. Since the film interchangeably places the drummer inside and outside of the diegesis, the placement and positioning of music in relation to the narrative and its protagonists are unsettled, to fascinating dramatic effect.

> **Takeaways**
>
> - You can take liberties with music placement and subvert the notion of music being either *within* or *outside* the narrative.
> - This requires careful planning with the aid of a music supervisor, music editor, and/or a composer.
> - You need to communicate ideas clearly.

2.5 Immersive and Interactive Music

The dichotomy of diegetic / non-diegetic music does not easily fit the realities of gaming. Video game music may be neither diegetic nor non-diegetic: With the player actively shaping the in-game narrative, and controlling one or several characters or objects in the game, can any music the player hears still be considered non-diegetic? Rather than forcing an ill-suited theoretical framework onto the medium, it may be more helpful to focus on what music in linear media (such as films) and games has in common: Both media rely on aural and visual continuity to convey a sense of a consistent diegesis or fictional space.

Video games have adopted many roles and principles for the use of music from linear narrative media. There are clear similarities to the roles and functions of music in gameplay, including aesthetic, stylistic, and cognitive considerations. Gameplay is an immersive and active process that demands agency on the part of the player. Linear media, by contrast, are consumptive and to some degree allow for passive interaction. Video game music enhances the narrative engagement in and experience of gameplay and encourages player immersion in the gameworld. Video game music is often newly composed and recorded to accompany specific characters, locations, situations, or events in the game. Video game music generally speaks the language of film music, borrowing tropes (comedy, horror, romance) and semantics (musical cue structure, scoring devices). In addition to serving traditional musico-dramatic functions, music in video games may also serve to help delineate player status and progress (e.g., reflect how a mission is going). The experiential value of gameplay can be raised significantly by the use of synchronized music. The most medium-specific aspect of video game music is that it must flexibly respond to the players' actions. In addition, whereas the duration of musical cues and overall running time in linear multimedia are fixed, interactive video games may have open-ended playing time.

50 Different Types of Narrative Media Music

Case Study: "Star Wars Battlefront Rogue One: X-wing VR Mission" (2017, Criterion Games, EA Games)

This virtual reality (VR) chapter addition to an established game series is a useful example of immersive music in a VR computer game. Producers James Svensson and Peter Lake, Lead Designer Mark Bridges, and Narrative and Audio Director Jeff Seamster discussed how this VR chapter for "Star Wars™ Battlefront™" was conceived and designed.[1] Criterion Games value collaboration, encouraging their creative team to brainstorm in joint coffee mornings or breakout sessions, using toy modeling (including LEGO bricks) and having sticky notes plastered everywhere in the office. The underlying work ethic is to resist dogma and to embrace disruptive thinking, asking the team members to use their curiosity to challenge convention. The creative dialogue is open and transparent. Creating a VR game, the team was mindful of allowing a sense of agency on the part of the player versus watching someone else. They also realized that, as of 2017, VR was still a relatively new medium, in which visual fidelity and realism were important factors in creating enjoyable experiential gameplay. In devising the players' experience, a judicious balance must be struck between comfort (some players of VR games experience nausea), accessibility, and spectacular action. A captivating narrative premise (the mission) and the lure of flying your own T-65B X-Wing fighter were a compelling starting point. But, beyond that, the team had to devise an immersive narrative that helped propel the action forward without detracting from the players' sense of agency. One device to make this work is the concept of self-voice in VR, whereby the player has a pre-recorded voice that speaks *for* them. Striking a balance between linearity versus true freedom and flexible interaction (making players feel as though they had complete freedom to explore) was necessary to keep the game production manageable. For example, the arrival of a Star Destroyer in the game chapter is heavily constructed. Just prior to the ship's arrival, events in the game discourage players from looking behind them, where they would notice the Star Destroyer's arrival having been fudged visually. Also, the player's spaceship, Red-4, is temporarily disabled when the Star Destroyer arrives, to prevent nausea which players experienced during game testing.

Adding to distinct, spatial, and immersive audio in surround, experiential music is another tool that is used to help structure and segment the interactive gameplay. The creative team worked with composer Gordy Haab to adapt musical themes by John Williams. In the concept stage, the team discussed emotional and gameplay beats. They also used a line graph of intensity for plotting comfort levels, using old-fashioned pen and paper. Music reflects the emotional state of the first-person player, who also expresses her emotional state verbally by use of self-voice, underlining a sense of triumph or defeat depending on how the episode has played out. The orchestral score was recorded at Air Studios with the London Symphony Orchestra, the same orchestra that performed the original *Star Wars* scores. The creative team preferred to have newly composed adaptations of familiar materials rather than just licensing existing music, which was considered artistically valuable. Music serves the various gameplay variables and transitional vignettes in a fairly linear fashion.

Takeaways

- The dichotomy of diegetic/non-diegetic music does not easily fit the realities of gaming.
- Video games have adopted many roles and principles for the use of music from linear narrative media.
- Music in video games must flexibly respond to the players' actions, which may require music cues of flexible structure and duration.

Further Reading

Chion, M. *Audio-Vision: Sound on Screen*. New York: Columbia University Press, 1994.
Diegetic Switch http://tvtropes.org/pmwiki/pmwiki.php/Main/Diegetic Switch
Eisenstein, S. *The Film Sense*. New edition. London: Faber & Faber, 1986.
Interscene Diegetic http://tvtropes.org/pmwiki/pmwiki.php/Main/Inter sceneDiegetic
Jackson, D.M. *Sonic Branding: An Introduction. An Essential Guide to the Art and Science of Sonic Branding*. London and New York: AIAA, 2004.
Kassabian, A. *Hearing Film: Tracking Identifications in Contemporary Hollywood Film Music*. London: Routledge, 2001.
Non-Diegetic to Diegetic http://tvtropes.org/pmwiki/pmwiki.php/Main/ LeftTheBackgroundMusicOn
Winters, B. "The Non-Diegetic Fallacy: Film, Music, and Narrative Space." *Music and Letters* 91(2) (2010): 224–244.

Note

1 BAFTA Crew Games Masterclass—Star Wars Battlefront Rogue One: X-wing VR Mission at the Princess Anne Theatre, BAFTA, 195 Piccadilly, London on 6 March 2017.

How to Think and Talk about Music

3

3.1 Introduction

> Many good directors are bad at giving good directions to composers.[1]
>
> *Rachel Portman, composer*

Creative stakeholders need to **find a shared language** to discuss music. No one expects media creators to be music experts, and there is no need to feel shy or embarrassed if your ability to discuss music is limited by lack of prior experience or knowledge of music terminology. Composers will benefit from a clear brief (more on this in Chapter 7), but they will always welcome an exploratory two-way conversation that leads to that brief. Colorful descriptive language can be a good starting point for a constructive conversation about the general narrative and the dramatic and emotional aims of the project. If you do not (yet) know what music should bring to the project, then it is okay to admit this openly. Acknowledging some degree of uncertainty over music does not lessen your authority. Instead, it will make you a better collaborator, opening the door to a rewarding creative process that leads to the best possible music solutions.

Telling the Story

Creative stakeholders should feel comfortable talking about the general narrative and expressive aims and requirements of the project. Discussing music as a tool in relation to narrative and emotional beats can be helpful. On his first collaboration with Michael Giacchino on *The Incredibles* (2004), director Brad Bird instructed the composer, "You and I have to be 100% hand-in-hand when it comes to storytelling."[2] Director Richard Eyre feels that music must be inseparably wed to the filmic narrative, as was the case, in his opinion, with his film *Iris* (2001, score by James Horner).[3] In order for music to reinforce and amplify storytelling aims, the music supervisor (licenses music, see also Chapter 4) or composer (creates newly commissioned music) also become storytellers. Therefore, as part of the briefing process, any and all aspects of the narrative should be discussed, addressing key "W"s:

- **What** is the central plot, i.e., what is the story about?
- **Who** is the story about and who are the main characters and secondary characters?
- **Where** does the story take place? Geographic setting may or may not be reflected in the music.
- **When** does the story take place? The time period in which the story is set, and which may or may not be reflected in the music.
- **Whose** side is the audience/player on and whose point of view is the story taking? Does the point of view (POV) change from one scene to the next or from one act to another?
- **Why** is the story unfolding the way it does? What motivates narrative development and what motivates the characters? There may be a sense of agency in one character or another. A villain, for example, may pursue a devious scheme unbeknownst to the main character, but known to the audience.

Creative stakeholders may choose to discuss the intended feel of locations, textures, and color schemes. To illustrate what you want to achieve, you may find it helpful to refer to examples from other media (other films, games, visual arts, fashion). Any thoughts on dramatic pacing, flow, and momentum can be addressed. The **structure** and development of the narrative should also be discussed, focusing on the story, plot strand, key scenes, narrative beats, and emotional high points.

Music and Emotions

Discussing the **emotional requirements of a project**, and how these requirements may be served and shaped by music, can be tricky because everyone has a subjective perspective on emotion in music. It may be useful to discuss how an existing piece of music makes us feel and, following on from this, how a piece of music yet to be written for the project *should* make us feel, in the context of a particular scene or segment. Remember that music in conjunction with audiovisual media will first and foremost be perceived *in that context* and not on its own. The resulting combined effect may be quite different from the effect of each component part separately. It is always best to try to describe the intended emotional charge of music in context in language as descriptive and precise as possible. Using everyday language, everyone should feel comfortable to be clear about their intentions. Bearing in mind also that everything can be revised and that the project may evolve in unexpected ways: Sometimes a piece of music that at one point seemed perfect needs to be scaled back because the combined effect of music and the finished footage feels redundant (Figure 3.1).

Writing the Music Brief

Whilst everyone involved in the music planning process may choose to take notes and exchange written comments, a written music brief can sometimes be helpful but is not always required. Written music briefs summarizing the

Figure 3.1 Intended Emotional Effect of Music.

creative requirements of the project are quite common with **commercials** and other projects that require a fast turnaround. Project owners can go into a lot of detail and it is not uncommon for the music brief for a 30-second commercial to be several pages long. In a scenario that leaves little or no time for creative dialogue (the project owners may never meet the music team), a written brief stipulates a top-down working relationship. Sadly, project schedules and industry pressures sometimes dictate this mode of working.

A written project brief is different from a "Scope of the Work" clause in a commissioning contract, which is a clause that determines the amount of music being commissioned, not the creative aims of that music (see also Chapter 6).

Being Too Vague Can Be Unhelpful

Clarity of intent is desirable and what creative stakeholders say should always match what they feel and think. These first discussions are the best opportunity to bring the music supervisor and/or composer up to speed with every aspect of the project, including creative goals, aesthetic aims, and narrative and dramatic intentions. Asking for music to be "experimental" or "fun" or "original" should only ever be the starting point for a meaningful conversation that unpicks these vague and subjective terms. It must be kept in mind that these early conversations between stakeholders are not an audience-facing marketing exercise. Producers and studios may be keen to advertise their film or game with buzzwords ("ground-breaking," "amazing," "you'll-never-see-it-coming"...), but in a creative dialogue this sort of language has no place. It may take some effort for everyone to articulate ideas and understand each other. Referring to existing music by other artists as a point of reference can be useful. Comparing the project to others before it (similarities or differences), including their use of music, can be informative. Discussing works from the past with the music supervisor and/or composer can lead to a better shared understanding of the function of music in those works and help everyone to agree on the best approach to the current project.

Being Too Specific Can Be Limiting

A composer will benefit from detailed input, to a degree, but no composer enjoys being micro-managed. Too much detail can be a hindrance to creativity. For example, if the music brief for a 30-second car commercial is eight pages long, addressing every single cut and every single sound effect and its intended relation to music, this is simply too much detail. It can be very helpful for directors to visit composers in their writing space—Michael Giacchino, for example, insists that directors meet him in his studio, on "home turf" as it were—to listen to a score-in-progress. But it may be less productive if the composer is expected to work on something *while* the director is present. Then again, it is up to the composer and the other creative stakeholders to determine how they feel they can best work together. Danny Elfman, for example, found his musical ideas for *Batman* improvising on piano with Tim Burton present until the director liked something he heard. Ramin Djawadi improvised on the guitar for director John Favreau on *Iron Man* (2008). Other times, a somewhat more hands-off approach by the project owners can give the music team more creative freedom. Clearly setting out and jointly exploring thoughts and ideas for music, seeking agreement and mutual understanding from the composer, and perhaps allowing some creative leeway, will likely produce best results.

Takeaways

- Creative stakeholders need to find a shared language to discuss music.
- Discuss storytelling aims, emotional beats, and narrative structure: What can music contribute?
- Discuss the emotional aims of music in context, not in isolation.
- A written music brief can sometimes be helpful but is not always required.
- When discussing music, honesty and clarity of intent are desirable.
- No creative stakeholder enjoys being micro-managed.

3.2 How to Listen to Music

The following sections offer recommendations on how to listen to music in a focused manner and to encourage media creators to explore nuances and details in music they may not previously have been aware of. Suggestions set out here will enable media creators to listen to select aspects of music, so they may feel more confident in their understanding of music and how they choose to discuss it with others. The chapter then offers guidance as to how to draw on music examples in an informed creative dialogue. **Talking about music** may feel counterintuitive at first and lead to miscommunication. Using

How to Think and Talk about Music **57**

music examples for illustration, the latter part of this chapter explains the **building blocks of music** and **musical attributes** that one may find in a piece of music, offering the vocabulary required to identify and discuss key musical attributes.

When listening to music, it is important that you set aside a time and place for this. Focused listening to music is very different from casual listening one may be used to (in the car, the supermarket, the mall, etc.). Active and attentive listening means to shut out distractions as much as possible and to really concentrate on the music. You should <u>always</u> listen to music with good home stereo or studio monitor **speakers** or a high-quality pair of **headphones**. You should <u>never</u> listen to music on laptop or phone speakers, as these are not capable of reproducing the full frequency range and dynamic depth of recorded music.

Media creators will often have to pass judgment on music:

- music examples selected to aid early creative discussion, found by one of the project owners or provided by the music supervisor or composer;
- different options for licensed music from the music supervisor;
- early demos from the composer;
- work-in-progress cues from the composer;
- final recorded cues for final approval.

Expressing likes and dislikes can be a helpful way to steer the creative process. Evaluating ideas and possibilities may come naturally to some, relying on their gut instinct. Such an instinct is valid, of course, and in day-to-day conversation it is common to give one's opinion quickly and with little explanation (e.g., "I don't like that.") But when it comes to creatively discussing music for a project, you should endeavor to go <u>two</u> steps further:

1. Whether you like or dislike a piece of music, no matter its source or purpose, you should **process** and **understand the reason** for your response. *Why* do I think I like this? What is it that I dislike? "I love this song" expresses a favorable sentiment, but it does not give any indication as to why and how.

2. You should, then, try **to articulate** and explain your feelings in order to brief your collaborators.

Developing a more reasoned and thoughtful attitude towards music is like giving detailed tasting notes on a meal or a good wine: The casual consumer will simply express likes and dislikes. More discerning diners and drinkers will have acquired a more sophisticated palette, spent some time understanding

58 How to Think and Talk about Music

the nature and background of the food or drink they are enjoying (or not enjoying) and then be able to explain their impression upon tasting something. When listening to music, you should:

- remain open and not be too quick to judge;
- be specific and articulate with your observations;
- be as detailed as possible with any comments or feedback.

If the initial feeling is that you like or dislike a piece of music (preferably by reference to the project requirements), ask yourself:

- Why do I like it/not like it?
- What about it, specifically, do I like/dislike?
- How does this piece fit with my project or specific scene/section?

Responding to music, media creators should trust their intuition and gut feeling but they need also to articulate their feelings and thoughts to communicate with the music supervisor and/or composer. Vague and subjective language is best avoided. For example, a piece of music may sound exotic to one listener but familiar to the next, depending on their cultural background. Wherever possible, it is preferable to discuss music in objective and clear terms. If feedback is required on demos or work-in-progress cues, this should be given promptly, as any delay will hold up the composer's progress.

When listening to a piece of music in a focused manner, especially if this is a new experience, taking notes may feel helpful. One may choose to pick up on a wide range of aspects, including, but not limited to:

- style/genre and form;
- melody and harmony;
- instrumentation, ensemble size, and scale;
- timbre, texture, color;
- tempo and rhythm;
- volume and dynamics;
- emotional effect (intended, perceived);
- general tone, mood, feel, vibe, attitude, atmosphere.

If and when one has found **suitable music references** for the project at hand, these should also be shared with the other creative stakeholders, crucially the music supervisor and/or composer, including any notes that help explain how the music might be suitable. "I think I could imagine something along the lines of [name of a piece] in the context of [specific scene in script], because…" is a good starting point.

> ### Takeaways
> - Always use good speakers or headphones to listen to music. Never listen on laptop or phone speakers.
> - Always take time to focus on music examples, demos, work-in-progress cues and final cues.
> - Comments on music should be reasonable and articulate, addressing a range of musical attributes.
> - Feedback on music ideas and demos should be given promptly.
> - Suitable music references should be shared alongside written notes to provide context as to why these references feel useful.

3.3 Existing Music as a Reference

Existing music may be helpful as a reference, informing early conversations about music in a project. This may then lead to the use of existing music, the creation of original music, or a combination of both. Project owners may choose to draw on their own knowledge to start their **search for music examples** and/or immediately delve into a conversation with the music supervisor and/or composer. Some project owners like to **compile playlists** containing music that they think is pointing in the right direction for the project, and share these with the composer and/or music supervisor. Playlists can be a useful shorthand for identifying a desired kind of music, but a **conversation** must follow: Each individual may have a very different perception of the same piece of music, so a conversation is necessary to help all parties align. In this conversation, specific reference may be made to any aspect of the music—for example, instrumentation, tempo, the perceived mood (keeping in mind that this can be highly subjective!), among others.

Finding musical ideas can also be a **collaborative process**, as composer Ramin Djawadi (*Game of Thrones* (2011–), *Westworld* (2016–)) recalls: On *Iron Man* (2008), Djawadi worked with director John Favreau:

> John and I, we would constantly talk. And I actually have to give him credit for the use of guitars, because from day one he said, "You know,

Iron Man, he's a rock'n'roll guy. He's a rock star. And I want guitars."—
And his idea was also to make it different than *Batman* and different than
Spider-Man. So he said, "I wanna go quite different." He really set the
tone of what he wanted and then it was up to me to figure that out, to
make that speak. And that's how we started. So I would start writing, in
the beginning not even to picture. I would just start writing themes and
motifs and he would come over and listen and point out things he liked
and what he didn't and that's how we started the process.[4]

Takeaways

- The music search may be informed by found music examples, perhaps compiled in playlists for sharing, and followed up with a conversation with the composer and/or music supervisor.
- Finding music can also be a collaborative process.

3.4 Categorizing Music: Styles, Genre, Form

Record companies, streaming services, concert venues, the press, and fans use
music style and genre labels to refer to a shared tradition or set of conventions in music, which may include a time period, instrumentation, tone and
rhythm, and cultural context, among others. Genre labels can be broad ("contemporary" or "pop" or "classical") or specific ("deep house") and help communicate with and between audiences who have a shared understanding of
a particular genre or style. On the one hand, genre labels can be convenient:
They help musicians target a sympathetic audience and, in turn, help audiences find music they are inclined to enjoy. As a communication tool, genre
labels can help cut through the huge variety of musical expressions across
different cultures and time periods and pinpoint a particular type of music. If
you search for "EDM" (electronic dance music) on a streaming service, you
are likely to find music that broadly fits the category. On the other hand, genre
labels can be problematic because they are bound to be reductive. Putting a
composer or piece of music in a stylistic drawer potentially risks overlook-
ing nuances that set their music apart. In referring to a notional collection of
music, genre and style labels are vague at best and are easily misunderstood.
Genre labels can also be too broad: "Classical music," for example, is often
used to refer to all traditional Western music, or European art music. Strictly
speaking, however, the "classical" period only lasted from 1750 until 1820.

How to Think and Talk about Music **61**

There are many subdivisions that better describe discrete periods within "classical" music, such as:

- Medieval (500–1400, e.g., Guillaume de Machaut).
- Renaissance (1400–1600, e.g., Claudio Monteverdi).
- Baroque (1600–1750, e.g., Johann Sebastian Bach).
- Classical (1750–1820, e.g., Wolfgang Amadeus Mozart).
- Romantic (1804–1910, e.g., Franz Schubert).

"Jazz" is another extremely broad term. According to their respective record labels, the following pieces are all "jazz." And yet, even laypersons will hear that these four pieces cannot helpfully be considered to be of the same style:

- Come Fly with Me performed by Frank Sinatra from the album "Come Fly with Me" (1958).
- So What performed by Miles Davis from the album "Kind of Blue" (1959).
- Take Five (Live) performed by Al Jarreau from the album "Look to the Rainbow: Live in Europe" (1977).
- Semente performed by the group Snarky Puppy from the album "Culcha Vulcha" (2016).

Finally, genre labels only communicate any sort of meaning if the target audience or conversation partner understands what the label refers to. If you do not know what "deep house" is, for example, then the label is useless. The evolution of music over several millennia has led to an inexhaustibly rich palette of possibilities, just as ongoing developments in the language of film, television, and games (relatively young art forms!) have resulted in even greater diversification.[5] Style and genre labels in music may be a useful starting point to discuss an approach to music. Working past this initial shorthand approach, a more nuanced discussion of music should probe deeper. If one has specific ideas for music, these are better discussed with specific examples, perhaps naming an artist, referencing a specific piece and a specific recording (Figure 3.2).

Takeaways

- Music style and genre labels are reductive and can be misleading.
- It is preferable to discuss music in terms other than style and genre labels.

Figure 3.2 Music Style and Genre Labels.

3.5 Building Blocks of Music: Melody and Harmony

Melody

A **melody** is a series of pitches that form a recognizable line. It is the part of a composition listeners can hum or whistle and are most likely to remember. In songs, the melody is what the lead singer sings, matching lyrics to the notes. The melody need not be, but often is, the top part of the musical arrangement, standing apart from the rest of the surrounding music in terms of pitch and audible volume (foreground). Melodies have powerful expressive potential that media composers may choose to harness at the service of your project. They are a prominent component of a musical composition and are therefore well suited to encode a mood, sentiment, intention, attitude, and tone, affecting the audience's perception of a character or a situation. If used thematically (see also Chapter 6), they can be readily associated with a character, object, or situation and later be used to recall and reference that same character, object, or situation. Although thematic material need not necessarily be melodic, it is tunes that the ear can pick up most readily. Even a layperson can easily detect **melodic themes** in the likes of *Star Wars* (Luke and Leia, Princess Leia's Theme, among many others), the main theme from *The Magnificent Seven* (1960, Main Title and Calvera, Elmer Bernstein), or the Theme from *Dallas* (1978–1991, Jerrold Immel). Whilst there may be other effective ways to fulfill the above functions, using melodies is a proven and efficient way of

How to Think and Talk about Music **63**

serving them. Using well-developed and well-considered melodies in a score unlocks expressive potential and also uplifts the music as something listeners may notice, enjoy, and remember.

You can describe a melody in terms of **register**: Is it high or low in pitch, in relation to the surrounding musical accompaniment? You can also describe the **contour** of a melody as relatively smooth and **connected**, whereby one pitch is followed by another pitch relatively nearby, as, for example, in the Flying Theme from *E.T.: The Extra-Terrestrial* (1982, John Williams). Or a melody can be fairly **disconnected** and full of leaps, whereby pitches leap widely from one to another. In Wayward Sisters, for example, the opening cue from *Nocturnal Animals* (2016, score by Abel Korzeniowski), each phrase starts with a few notes in stepwise motion and then leaps up. Or you may consider the disconnected high French horn melody in Life from *Prometheus* (2012, theme by Harry Gregson-Williams). Most melodies contain a mixture of stepwise pitch motion (which is always easier to sing or play) and leaps.

Some melodies are **memorable** or "catchy," which may be the result of their simple structure and frequent repetition within a piece. Other melodies are more developed, containing a longer series of notes, and are less memorable as a result. For example, Hedwig's Theme from the *Harry Potter* franchise (theme by John Williams) is a long melodic theme of a considerable length and with a few unusual twists and turns. Listeners may remember the beginning of the theme but may struggle to recall and sing the whole tune from memory. Sometimes, a composition draws on very short melodic fragments, which may also be called **motifs**, and these never turn into a longer melody. The well-known five-note aliens communication motif from *Close Encounters of the Third Kind* (1977, Wild Signals by John Williams) is never developed into a longer theme in the film. It is, however, repeated numerous times and ingrains itself in the audience's mind. Hand Covers Bruise from *The Social Network* (2010, Trent Reznor and Atticus Ross) also contains a short six-note motif that repeats numerous times throughout the cue. In longer pieces, parts of the melody or entire passages may repeat identically, becoming even more memorable. Melodies can also develop and evolve throughout a composition, with different instruments taking over the tune. Composers do this for added interest, to provide a range of colors, and to be able to extend a composition without too much literal repetition.

When building longer melodies and themes, composers draw on **phrases**, which can be thought of as short statements that are used to build longer sentences. Several phrases may repeat nearly identically to build a longer melody, for example, retaining the same rhythm each time and only altering the pitch slightly. I'm Forrest…Forrest Gump from *Forrest Gump* (1994, Alan Silvestri), He's a Pirate from the *Pirates of the Caribbean* franchise (Klaus Badelt) and the

64 How to Think and Talk about Music

Main Title Theme from *Westworld* (2016–, Ramin Djawadi) are all built from short melodic phrases. In the *Westworld* theme, the melodic phrases are the bits played by the skeleton on the piano.

One may think of melodies as having a character or mood, deriving from its tonal make-up, i.e., the notes that make up the melody. Composers can draw on different **scales or modes**, which are different series of notes. A non-musician really need not worry too much about the detailed theory behind this. It is enough to be aware that there is such a thing as different scales and modes and that these may be perceived to have different flavors. Some listeners may detect a dark, or sad, or angry quality in a melody with a minor key. A major key may be perceived to be bright, positive, and happy. Without a specific context, these are generalizations, of course. Some musicians even have different feelings about a specific key (F major versus G major, etc.). This perception is highly subjective and will differ from one person to another.

Some well-known film and television music draws on the special flavor of different modes, including:

- Rey's Theme from *The Force Awakens* (2015, John Williams) in Aeolian (or minor).
- American Beauty from *American Beauty* (1999, Thomas Newman) in Dorian.
- The Simpsons Theme (Danny Elfman) in Lydian.
- The Games from *Brave* (2012, Patrick Doyle) in Mixolydian.
- Knight Rider Main Theme (Stu Phillips) in Phrygian.

Melodies may be carried by one instruments or several, in succession or simultaneously. A composer will choose what instruments can best play the melody to balance with other musical elements. They can also determine what instrument may quote the melody at different points, to draw on different flavors as needed. Whenever a composition or song has a melody, that tune can usually be heard clearly. Melodies can exist in isolation or be accompanied by others. On some early games consoles, technical limitations of the sound chip required music to feature prominent tunes and little else, including the music in *Tetris* (Tetris) on the first GameBoy or Nintendo's *Super Mario Land*.

By no means does all music have to contain a melody, let alone a memorable melodic theme. A lot of film and television music since the 1980s has tended to be increasingly non-melodic, favoring instead rich textures, rhythmic patterns, or low-profile drones.[6] Some examples include:

- The Son of Flynn from *TRON: Legacy* (2010, Daft Punk), comprising synthesizer *arpeggios* (chords whose notes are played separately in rising order) and a bass pulse, but no top-line tune.

How to Think and Talk about Music **65**

- River from *Lion* (2016, Dustin O'Halloran and Hauschka), featuring a harp arpeggio and strings.
- Why So Serious from *The Dark Knight* (2008, Hans Zimmer and James Newton Howard), containing a two-note motif and buzzing tone for the Joker that is markedly non-melodic.[7]
- House of Cards Main Title Theme from *House of Cards* (2013–, Jeff Beal), combining a piano arpeggio, bass groove, brass, snare rolls, without a coherent tune.
- Main Title Theme from *Breaking Bad* (2008–2013, Dave Porter), emphasizing visceral contrasting textures in place of a melody.

In recent decades, a noticeable decline in the use of well-developed, high-profile melodies in all media music may at least in part be the result of less than inspired and/or restrictive thinking on the part of the project owners involved. Media creators may sometimes be concerned that melodies will tip the aesthetic balance of a scene in the wrong direction, or that a recognizable tune associated with a character may be predictable or give too much away. These are reasonable concerns, and they should be discussed on a case-by-case basis. But just as it would be wrong to prescribe prominent melodies as the default option for effective narrative scoring, it is unnecessary to rule out this powerful tool altogether. Creative stakeholders should always discuss whether melodies may form part of the musical language for the project at hand, perhaps addressing specific moments in which they can be useful, as well as other moments where different musical solutions will be preferable.

Harmony

The term **harmony** refers to the vertical relationship between musical parts other than the melody that sympathetically sound together to form so-called **chords**. These may provide the accompaniment to a melody. In so-called **tonal music**, the relationship of the melody and harmony is governed by certain rules and conventions that provide a sense of familiarity and expectation, which can be drawn upon to good effect. When the pitches in the melody largely correspond with the pitches contained in the harmony—whereby chord tones are emphasized in the melody and non-chord tones are primarily used for transition between chord tones—the relationship of melody and harmony is considered **consonant** (for example, The Star Shines from *Stardust* (2007), from 2:14). Most tonal music will be predominantly consonant. If the melody and harmonies contain different pitches and largely lack agreement,

66 How to Think and Talk about Music

the result may be considered **dissonant** (for example, Jonny Greenwood's Popcorn Superhet Receiver: Pt. 1. Harmonies in a composition provide texture and color. They can be thought of as a combination of multiple instrumental parts that are linked or stacked and work in harmonic blocks and move in the same rhythm (so-called **homophony**). A lot of music uses relatively simple chords (called **triads** because they consist of three notes). Chords have names such as A major or C minor. These are triads that can be chosen from a set of options available within a given key. The vast majority of European folk music and a lot of popular music use mostly triads.

Just like melodies can be perceived to have a certain flavor, depending on the scale they derive from, so too can harmonies. This derives from the occurrence, order, and hierarchy of major and minor chords within the piece. To be sure, every piece in a minor key (often considered the more subdued or sad type) will contain some major chords, just as every piece in a major key (often considered the brighter and happier type) will contain some minor chords. American film producer Irving Thalberg betrayed his ignorance of music when he wrote in a memo "No music in an MGM film is to contain a minor chord."[8] Demanding that all MGM films should be happy and entertaining, the producer wrongly assumed that minor chords have no place in music in a major key.

Other musical traditions—for example, jazz—use chords that have four notes or more, their sound getting increasingly colored and dense. In some avant-garde music the harmonic language can be highly complex and no longer adheres to the conventions of harmony. Some of this so-called **atonal music** may sound unfamiliar—perhaps unpleasant to some listeners, perhaps fascinating to others. Atonal music can be highly effective in conveying confusion, anger, chaos, or a sense of threat, which is why it has been used in many horror films (such as *A Nightmare on Elm Street* (1984), Boiler Room) and games (such as Jason Graves's terrifying score for *Dead Space 2* (2011), Come Rain or Come Convergence).

A composer will develop the harmonic language of a piece depending on a wide range of factors. Short pieces may use a relatively small set of chords—for clarity and coherence. For example, many pop songs contain only three or four chords throughout. Longer pieces may require a more developed harmonic language—for variety and a sense of forward movement, including more complicated chord structures, inventive progressions from one chord to another, and so-called **modulation** to a different key. Harmonic developmental techniques are part of every media composer's toolset. What particular ideas they choose in each instance is governed by creative intuition but also the context and purpose of a piece. A trained composer spends years studying the theory of harmony. The harmonic language of a composition helps determine its style but also shapes the composition's overall effect. When discussing harmony with a composer, media creators should focus on the desired resulting effect rather than discussing individual chord choices. A composer will certainly be able to offer some alternative options if the harmonic language of a work-in-progress feels somehow lacking.

Homophony is certainly not the only way to build a harmonic structure. In Western music, there have been many different techniques over the centuries. One contrasting approach to homophony is so-called **polyphony**. Having a distinctly more complex and fluid sound than homophonic music, in polyphonic compositions a combination of multiple instrumental lines commence at different points and progress independently, often moving in different simultaneous rhythms and forming a vibrant mesh that does not necessarily result in clearly defined chords. The music of Johann Sebastian Bach (1685–1750) is a prime example of polyphony. Bach's Goldberg Variations, BWV 988: Aria famously features in *The Silence of the Lambs* (1991). Gabriel Yared composed the haunting Mike's Fugue for the film adaptation of Stephen King's *1408* (2007).

Besides more traditional approaches to harmonic accompaniment, there are many examples of film, television, and game music that take different routes. There are examples of music that has **no prominent harmonic accompaniment**, including Main Title from *Terminator 2: Judgment Day* (1991) by Brad Fiedel, which is dominated by heavy percussion and a top-line melodic theme. The harmonic accompaniment of Axel F from *Beverly Hills Cop* (1984, Harold Faltermeyer) is implied by a synth bass-line, but the melodic top-line enters autonomously before drums and bass set in. There are also many film, TV, and game scores that take an atonal approach, often doing away with discernible, let alone memorable, melodies and harmonies altogether. These scores should be understood in the context of the respective project they accompany, of course, as they serve a clear music-narrative purpose. Some examples of largely atonal film scores include:

- There Will Be Blood from *There Will Be Blood* (2007, Jonny Greenwood) uses strings in dense textures, clustered pitch relationships, often dissonant.
- Mr. Turner from *Mr. Turner* (2014, Gary Yershon) employs saxophone quartet and strings in an unusual combination and extreme pitch ranges.
- Main Title from *Planet of the Apes* (1968, Jerry Goldsmith) draws on an eclectic ensemble of woodwinds, piano, synthesizer, and percussion.
- The Beast from *Sicario* (2015, Jóhann Jóhannsson) contains visceral synthesized and other sonically manipulated instrumental parts.

68 How to Think and Talk about Music

Composers will rely on their experience and creative sensibilities to come up with harmonic ideas for a score that suits the narrative and dramatic requirements of a scene or situation, as agreed with the project owners. There is never just one single solution, and, time permitting, composers may come up with a few different options. It is seldom helpful if project owners get too involved in the minute details of harmonic progressions. Instead, one should take in the overall effect of a cue and discuss this. By all means point out concerns regarding harmony where appropriate; all creative stakeholders can then work on closing the gap between the work-in-progress and final outcome.

Takeaways

- Most music comprises a combination of melody and harmony, whereby the melody usually occupies the musical **foreground** and harmonic elements the **background**.
- A **melody** is a series of pitches that form a recognizable line.
- Some melodies as easily **memorable**, others are not.
- Melodic themes can be effective for a character, object, or situation in the narrative.
- Not all music contains melodies.
- The term **harmony** refers to the vertical relationship between musical parts other than the melody that sympathetically work together to form so-called **chords**.
- The relationship between melody and harmony can be consonant or dissonant.
- Some music has no prominent harmonic accompaniment.
- When discussing melody and harmony with a composer, you should focus on the desired resulting effect rather than discussing individual chord choices.
- You may decide to rely on largely **tonal or atonal music** for your score, depending on your dramatic requirements.

3.6 Building Blocks of Music: Instrumentation

Some music is sung, and some music is made by use of non-musical objects (so-called *musique concrète* and other experimental music), but most music is performed on instruments. These instruments may be physical and played by a performer, or they may be virtual and played by a performer or controlled by a computer. Some music is played on a single instrument. Other music is played by a number of instruments together, by a so-called **ensemble**,

How to Think and Talk about Music **69**

sometimes comprising dozens of instruments. A composer and their arranger or orchestrator provide the ensemble with notated parts or give them other instructions (written, verbal) to allow them to play together. Any imaginable combination of instruments may perform the wide spectrum of all media music. Traditionally, film and television music has been orchestral. But, as far back as the 1950s, composers also started incorporating electronic instruments when these first became available. Instruments from non-Western cultures have often been used to allude to specific cultures and to enrich the instrumental palette of the orchestra. Since the 1960s, amplified instruments, including electric guitars, drums, and keyboards have become common in media music. Starting in the 1970s, synthesizers vastly extended the range of sound colors and expressive capabilities of media music. In recent years, it has been relatively rare to find a film score that is purely orchestral (such as Joe Kraemer's score for *Mission: Impossible—Rogue Nation* (2015), e.g., <u>The A400</u>). Sometimes scores are created purely with electronic instruments (for example, the music for *Stranger Things* (2016–) by Kyle Dixon and Michael Stein, e.g., <u>Kids</u>). Most of the time, media music will contain a combination of acoustic and amplified or electronic instruments.

Music is commonly organized in melody (foreground, leader) and harmony (background, accompaniment). Different instruments are assigned roles (or so-called parts) to play melody or harmony. The assigned roles can change in the course of a piece of music. For example, a flute may play part of the accompaniment to start but then become the lead instrument, playing the melody for a while. In the cue <u>Welcome to Jurassic Park</u> from *Jurassic Park* (1993, John Williams), the main melody travels through different instruments of the orchestra, starting with the piano. After the first minute, the tune travels to the flute, and at 1:15 the French horns take over. At 1:30, more brass instruments pick up the same tune, reinforced by strings. The changing instrumentation gives the melody different sound qualities. The ever-growing instrumentation (number of instruments playing) and the change in dynamics (getting louder) evoke a rousing sensation, culminating in a big cymbal hit just before the two-minute mark. Williams has written a relatively simple tune and aptly shapes it into a theme that in the context of the film generates a sense of awe and grandeur in the audience (who are watching CGI dinosaurs roam about).

It is not necessary for you to become a specialist of musical instruments in order to have a meaningful conversation about the music for a project. No one expects non-musicians to know the names of all the instruments in the orchestra, for example. But it is helpful to be aware that musical instruments will be playing the music that is recorded or licensed for a project. These instruments have different sound qualities, are capable of different

70 How to Think and Talk about Music

techniques, and are played by highly skilled specialists. Many expressive possibilities arise from the use of real instruments and musicians and the amazing range of different sounds musical instruments can make. Those less than familiar with musical instruments are not alone: Many media creators have not had a musical upbringing, never played an instrument in school, let alone learnt to read notation.

The good news is that it is never too late to learn more about instruments. Reading this chapter and listening to the music examples listed in the chapter is a good starting point. You may try to pay a little more attention to the different instruments that are playing next time a song plays on the radio or music accompanies a commercial on TV. In the beginning, it does not matter whether you can identify *all* the instruments that are playing. Beginning to pay closer, conscious attention is enough. Much of today's music, especially in pop and dance music, is heavily processed so that it can be difficult to hear what exact instruments are playing. Noticing this is an achievement in itself. If you are intrigued to learn more about the sound of musical instruments, you may also choose to go to concerts to watch an orchestra play and gain new impressions. You may initially not recognize the difference between a violin and a viola, but it may be enough if you can tell a string instrument apart from a woodwind or brass or percussion instrument.

Instrumentation: Listening Examples

Benjamin Britten's <u>Young Person's Guide to the Orchestra</u> is a fun piece to listen to. The narrator actually introduces the different instruments before they are played. Here are some music examples that might also be helpful:

Woodwinds

Piccolo Flute

• Top-line tune in <u>Soul Bossa Nova</u> (Quincy Jones).

Flute

• Melody in <u>Main Title</u> from *To Kill A Mockingbird* (1962, Elmer Bernstein).

How to Think and Talk about Music **71**

- Rey's Theme from *Star Wars—The Force Awakens* (2015, John Williams).
- Beginning of Luke and Leia from *Star Wars, Episode VI: Return of the Jedi* (1983, John Williams).

Pan Flute

- Main tune in Leaving Wallbrook/On the Road from *Rain Man* (1989, Hans Zimmer).

Oboe

- Main tune in Ripley from *The Talented Mr. Ripley* (1999, Gabriel Yared).

Clarinet

- Lead instrument in Sonatina lyrico: II. Ballad (Vasco Hexel).
- Tune in Driving from *Driving Miss Daisy* (1989, Hans Zimmer).

English Horn (Cor anglais)

- Theme from *Six Feet under* (2001–2005, Thomas Newman).
- Top-line tune from 0:25 in This is Berk from *How to Train Your Dragon* (2010, John Powell).
- Melody from 0:05 in the ballet Cinderella, Op. 87: 43, Oriental Dance by Sergei Prokofiev.

Bassoon

- The lowest-pitched member of the woodwinds family.
- Beautiful solo in Rimsky-Korsakov's Scheherazade Op. 35, 2nd movement II. Lento at ca. 0:45.
- As accompaniment in Tchaikovsky's The Nutcracker Op. 71, Act II, No. 12c, Divertissement. Tea (Chinese Dance).
- Also Vivaldi's elegant Bassoon Concerto in B-Flat major, RV501 (La Notte).

72 How to Think and Talk about Music

WOODWINDS (WHOLE SECTION)

- Scherzo for Motorcycle and Orchestra from *Indiana Jones and the Last Crusade* (1989, John Williams).

FRENCH HORN

- Tune in Luke and Leia from ca. 0:25, from *Star Wars, Episode VI: Return of the Jedi* (1983, John Williams).

Brass

TRUMPET

- Top-line in Main Title Theme from *Star Wars* franchise (John Williams).
- Bugler's Dream/Olympic Fanfare at 0:45 (John Williams).
- Raiders March from *Indiana Jones* franchise (John Williams).
- Twentieth Century Fox Fanfare (Alfred Newman).

FLUGELHORN

- This is a larger trumpet-style instrument, with a deeper, rounded sound.
- Solo in Red Arrow Inn from *The Black Dahlia* (2006, Mark Isham).

SAXOPHONE

- Main Title from *Taxi Driver* (1976, Bernard Herrmann) from 0:42.
- Tune in The Pink Panther Theme (Henry Mancini).
- Love Theme in *Blade Runner* (1982, Tangelos).

TROMBONES

- Can be difficult to find in isolation but often underpin trumpets in the brass section.
- Opening chords of The Man Who Knew Too Much from the film of the same title (1956, Bernard Herrmann).

How to Think and Talk about Music **73**

BRASS (WHOLE SECTION)

- Overture from *Dancer in the Dark* (2000, Björk).
- Scherzo for X-Wings from *Star Wars—The Force Awakens* (2015, John Williams).
- The Batman Theme from *Tim Burton's Batman* (1989, Danny Elfman).
- Avengers Unite from *Avengers: Age of Ultron* (2015, Danny Elfman).
- Opening of This is Berk from *How to Train Your Dragon* (2010, John Powell).

Percussion

SNARE DRUM

- Twentieth Century Fox Fanfare (Alfred Newman).

CYMBALS

- Back to the Future from *Back to the Future* (1985, Alan Silvestri).

TIMPANI

- Prelude from *North by Northwest* (1956, Bernard Herrmann).
- Beginning of Bugler's Dream / Olympic Fanfare (John Williams).

MARIMBA

- Dead Already from *American Beauty* (1999, Thomas Newman).

XYLOPHONE

- Carnival of the Animals, XII. Fossils (Saint-Saëns).

CELESTA

- Hedwig's Theme from the *Harry Potter* franchise (John Williams).

74 How to Think and Talk about Music

Harp and Piano

PIANO

- I'm Forrest ... Forrest Gump from *Forrest Gump* (1994, Alan Silvestri).
- Cellar Door from *Donnie Darko* (2001, Michael Andrews).
- Welcome to Lunar Industries from *Moon* (2009, Clint Mansell) also features drum set and electric guitars.
- American Beauty from *American Beauty* (1999, Thomas Newman).

HARP

- Accompaniment to viola at the Anakin's Dream from *Star Wars: Revenge of the Sith* (2005, John Williams).
- Accompaniment in the ballet Cinderella, Op. 87: 43, Oriental Dance by Sergei Prokofiev.

Strings

SOLO VIOLIN

- Theme from *Schindler's List* (1993, John Williams).
- Main Menu—And Ever We Fight on from *Killzone 3* (2011, Joris de Man).
- A River Runs through It from *A River Runs through It* (1992, Mark Isham).

VIOLINS

- Wayward Sisters from *Nocturnal Animals* (2016, Abel Korzeniowksi).
- Murder from *Psycho* (1960, Bernard Herrmann).
- Love Scene from *Vertigo* (1958, Bernard Herrmann).

CELLO

- Desert Music from *Sicario* (2015, Jóhann Jóhannsson).
- Ghost of Things to Come from *Requiem for a Dream* (2000, Clint Mansell).
- Sayuri's Theme from *Memoirs of a Geisha* (2005, John Williams).

How to Think and Talk about Music **75**

Double Bass

- Concerto for Double Bass and Orchestra in A minor, I. Allegro agitato (Edvard Grieg).
- Main tune (over piano) in Carnival of the Animals: V. The Elephant (Saint-Saëns).

Cello and Double Bass

- Main Title and First Victim from *Jaws* (1975, John Williams).

Strings (whole section)

- Scotty Trails Madeleine from *Vertigo* (1958, Bernard Herrmann).
- Beginning of Journey to the Island from *Jurassic Park* (1993, John Williams).
- George's Waltz (I) from *A Single Man* (2009, Shigeru Umebayashi).
- Psycho Suite from *Psycho* (1960, Bernard Herrmann).
- Temptation from *Psycho* (1960, Bernard Herrmann).

Some Eclectic/Unusual Instruments

- Bagpipes in The Games from *Brave* (2012, Patrick Doyle).
- Mandolin in Lara's Theme from *Doctor Zhivago* (1965, Maurice Jarre).
- Vibraphone, metals, and synthesizers in Arose from *American Beauty* (1999, Thomas Newman).
- Dulcimer in opening and the doubling tune in Discombobulate from *Sherlock Holmes* (2009, Hans Zimmer).

Listening to these music examples and beginning to recognize the sound of individual instruments can help you communicate more confidently about instrumentation in the music for your next project. Having a basic grasp and general appreciation for the musical possibilities that arise from different musical instruments will improve your creative dialogue with the music team. When discussing music in the abstract, or by reference to existing music, or on the basis of demos made by the composer, you may sometimes choose to point out specific instruments. If you are unsure what instrument(s) they are hearing, it is perfectly fine to *describe* the sound you are hearing, as

76 How to Think and Talk about Music

best as you can, using language you are comfortable with. There is no shame in asking, "That sound there, is that a harp?" Bear in mind also that composers will often use unusual instruments, or effects, or electronic sounds that do not sound anything like an instrument you have heard before. Again, simply asking, "What is that amazing sound?" or, "What is that piercing tone?" will be a good way of addressing specific aspects of the instrumentation and facilitate the creative dialogue. If necessary, the composer can make changes to the instrumentation based on these discussions.

There are cost implications to using instruments in music recording: Performers need to be paid at a rate commensurate with their level of experience. In many countries, there are musicians' union regulations that govern these pay scales and also working hours. If project owners have a general understanding of the role of instruments in their music, they will be in a better position to understand why they may need to allow for a music-recording budget (more on this in Chapter 6). Most of the time, the composer will be working with computers to plan the music and create demos. Nearer the end, however, depending on budgets and timelines, they will need to record real instruments to replace virtual instrument parts. Project owners should listen to their composer when they ask for a recording budget, weighing their creative demands against other project considerations (overall budget, timelines, prospective income streams, etc.). Real instruments will always sound better and more musically expressive than a demo made at the computer. The musical qualities that live instruments offer can truly uplift your score. If you are unsure about the benefit of live recording, discuss your hesitation with the composer.

Takeaways

- Most music is performed on instruments, which may be physical and played by a performer, or virtual and played by a performer or controlled by a computer.
- Different instruments may play the melody and harmony accompaniment.
- Varied instrumentation brings added color and interest to music.
- The symphony orchestra normally consists of woodwinds, brass, percussion, and strings. Other instruments may be added.
- It is okay not to know or be able to recognize some instruments.
- Recording live instruments requires a budget for recording sessions.
- Real instruments will always sound better, be more expressive, and musically more rewarding than virtual instruments.

3.7 Musical Attributes: Tempo and Rhythm

Tempo

Tempo in music, which can be thought of as "slow" or "fast," refers to the speed of the underlying pulse of a piece around which other musical elements are measured and organized. Most people can count out a beat intuitively, such as 1-2-3-4 or 1-2-3. Beats in music are an underlying pulse, not to be confused with the rhythm in which a melody is sung or a drum patter is played (see next section). These rhythms are often varied, whereas the underlying beat is constant. As humans, we have no internal organ to measure time accurately and thus are poorly equipped to judge tempo in absolute terms. Just as our heart rate varies (in itself a pulse that beats in different tempos), so too does our perception of time and the speed at which it elapses. An hour can fly by when we are with friends and engaged in conversation, or an hour can seem like an eternity when we are bored. Accordingly, our perception of tempo is subjective. We may speak of a "fast" piece of music or a "slow" tempo, but without further details this is fairly vague. Composers have included tempo instructions with their compositions for centuries, such as *Allegro* (fast) or *Andante* (slow). To indicate a specific tempo unambiguously, composers and musicians nowadays measure tempo in beats per minute (bpm), which can be written down and recalled by use of a metronome (which beats in time for the performers to play to). Media composers will assign an exact tempo marking to ensure accurate synchronization of their music with the moving image. "Fast" (which could be moderate, rapid, rushed, frantic, etc.) will be followed by an indication of 130 bpm or 140 bpm or more. Slow (regal, sedate, dragging, etc.) can mean 65 bpm or 50 bpm or 70 bpm.

When discussing music for a project, you may prefer not to speak about tempo in terms of beats per minute but rather in general terms, remembering that a composer and/or music supervisor may have a different idea of "fast" and "slow." There will always be room to adjust a tempo up or down later on in the process. Besides an absolute tempo setting, you may also consider, and in turn discuss, whether the tempo of the music should be steady (marching, strident, assured, etc.) or changing (varied, or so-called *rubato*, which is a form of musically expressive slowing down and speeding up akin to an expressive spoken recitation). "Getting faster" is also referred to as *accelerando*. Likewise, "slowing down" translates to *ritardando*. These musical nuances only need to be discussed if they feel pertinent to a narrative end.

78 How to Think and Talk about Music

Rhythm

A sense of rhythm in music arises from subdivision of the underlying beats, by melodic parts, the harmonic accompaniment, and percussive elements. Different styles of music may have rhythmic idiosyncrasies (such as samba, swing, a waltz, etc.) Rhythmic elements in a piece may be more or less pronounced but few pieces are free from any sense of rhythm. Rhythmic elements may be called upon to good effect in media music and they can influence the **listener's perception of tempo**. For example, the track <u>Titel</u> from *Das Boot* (1981, Klaus Doldinger) is performed roughly in the same tempo as the <u>Main Theme</u> from *Crimson Tide* (1995, Hans Zimmer), but the busier rhythmic subdivisions and more pronounced percussion part in the latter makes this piece *seem* faster. A sense of increased or decreased tempo can also result from the **rhythmic interrelationship between music and visuals**, both of which have an underlying tempo, pace, movement, and structure. The way the picture editing speed (cuts per minute or frames) relates to the speed of the music (beats per minute) affects whether the audience subjectively perceives the cumulative result as moving faster or slower. One can undertake a simple experiment by choosing a segment of footage, preferably silent and visually abstract (to minimize distractions). One may experiment with synchronizing music of different tempos and observe the different resulting effect. What happens when we choose music whose tempo is faster than the film's editing speed and/or inner movement? What happens when we choose music that is slower? Whether a picture edit falls on a musical beat or in between beats, if a cut coincides with the start of a music phrase, if the flow of the edit largely corresponds with or works against the flow of the music: These are all determining factors for the resulting viewing experience and perceived tempo. Editors will often use music to help shape the flow and tempo of an edit-in-progress. Countless chase sequences, horror films, first-person shooters draw on the subliminal benefits of pairing quickening music with an increasingly faster visual pace.

Many music videos have been cut to the musical beat, and the close link between cuts and musical beats has a striking effect. *Koyaanisqatsi: Life out of Balance* (1982) was a groundbreaking non-narrative film that provided a powerful audiovisual experience, pairing minimalist music with time-lapse photography. Narrative films including *Lola Rennt* (*Run Lola Run*, 1998), *Drive* (2011), and *Baby Driver* (2017) are fast-paced examples of the breathless synergistic interplay between fast music and rapid picture cuts.

Rhythmic patterns, or **grooves**, can flavor a piece. The sleek and reverberant drum pattern in <u>Top Gun Anthem</u> from *Top Gun* (1986, Harold Faltermeyer) may sound dated now but using drum computers was certainly in vogue at the time. The cool and understated sound of <u>Woke up This Morning</u> (Alabama 3), the title song of *The Sopranos*, results from its rhythmic foundation, a combination of a low pulsing electric bass and drum kit. <u>Driving with the Top Down</u> from *Iron Man* (2008, Ramin Djawadi) is basically a rock song with the vocals omitted. The strong driving guitars and heavy metal drums deliver a cue that is full of energy. Some rhythmic elements in film music are so powerful and effective that they take on a representative function for the film as a whole. This was the case with the aggressive metallic drum pattern in the *Terminator* franchise (score by Brad Fiedel), heavily emphasized in the main title of *Terminator 2: Judgment Day* (1991).

It is not always necessary or practicable for you to micro-manage all tempo and rhythm considerations for the music in a project but giving some general pointers and expressing their views as to how fast a cue should be, whether it should be fast or slow, highly rhythmic or less so, remain in a steady tempo or speed up or slow down, may form part of a constructive discussion with the music team. You may choose to discuss the rhythmic aspects of a melody, perhaps working towards a tune that is of a steady, flowing pace, or highly rhythmic, pushing and pulling against the underlying beat. Some melodies are calm and measured, others rushed and agitated. Discussing the rhythmic drive of a cue, or rhythmic patterns therein, can be part of a broader discussion of tone, style, and surface appeal of a cue.

> **Takeaways**
>
> - Tempo describes the speed of the underlying pulse of a piece of music, measured in beats per minute.
> - Tempo in a piece of music may remain steady or change over time.
> - A sense of rhythm arises from subdivision of the underlying beats, by melodic parts, the harmonic accompaniment, and percussive elements.
> - The rhythmic interrelationship between music and visuals is affected by tempo in the music and the picture editing speed.
> - Tempo and rhythm can be used to dramatic effect.

3.8 Musical Attributes: Volume and Dynamics

A discussion of volume in music needs to differentiate between **absolute or relative volume**. A rock band may play loudly inside a sports arena (i.e., at a high volume in absolute terms), but standing in line at the concessions stand outside punters are hearing that loud band *relatively* quietly. When listening

80 How to Think and Talk about Music

to recorded music on a home stereo or on headphones, listeners have control over the playback volume whereas the volume at which the recording was made never changes. To add yet another variable, when music is placed in the soundtrack of a project, decisions are made by the editor or sound mixer as to the *relative* volume of that music against other soundtrack elements, independent of the volume at which the music was originally played and recorded. Therefore, when discussing volume and music, it is useful to first clarify whether you are referring to volume within the music and/or as against other soundtrack components. There are no hard and fast rules about absolute and relative volume levels in media music except that intelligible dialogue, when present, almost always takes priority (think of the countless scene in which characters converse in normal speaking voices in a noisy nightclub).

Changing volume levels *within* a piece of music are so-called **dynamics**. These are performance instructions given to the players. These are not absolute values (unlike absolute volume, which can be measured in decibels), but they indicate relative relationships:

> *pianissimo* (very quiet)
> *piano* (quiet)
> *mezzo piano* (somewhat quiet)
> *mezzo forte* (somewhat loud)
> *forte* (loud)
> *fortissimo* (very loud).

These terms are used by musicians and composers to communicate in scores and instrumental parts, to inform a live performance on stage or in the recording studio. A conductor will often work with larger ensembles to help balance the different parts. Media creators do not need to feel obliged to speak in these terms if it feels forced or unnatural to them. It is perfectly acceptable to use the English equivalent (or whichever is the preferred language by the creative team). Dynamics in music are often associated with a performance sentiment or attitude as well, somewhat similar to different volume levels in day-to-day speaking. We speak loudly (*forte*) when we need to be heard, or want to assert ourselves. We shout (*fortissimo*) when we are angry. We speak somewhat quietly (*mezzo-piano*) when we are among friends having a casual conversation, and we may whisper (*pianissimo*) to a loved one. Dynamic changes can also result from changing instrumentation. In an orchestral piece, sections with fewer instruments playing will usually be quieter than sections where the whole orchestra is playing. Besides these underlying dynamics, music can also get louder (*crescendo*) and get softer (*descrescendo* or *diminuendo*), either

How to Think and Talk about Music **81**

across a passage where the whole ensemble gets louder or quieter or in individual parts (e.g., a single note on a violin getting louder). The overture of Back to the Future (1985, Alan Silvestri) is a nice example of a piece of film music that has many dynamic changes, both from one section to another but also in instrumental parts. One may observe, for example, the dynamic swells in the cymbal rolls and held brass notes.

Since the mixing and dubbing process mitigates the playback dynamics of media music (see Chapter 8), dynamic changes cannot always be heard in the final product. A lot of dubbed audio, especially in television, is heavily compressed and the dynamic range of the signal is greatly diminished. On a soundtrack album, where music can be heard on its own, we can hear dynamic changes within that music more clearly. During the creative process, you may choose to discuss the volume levels *in* the music (performance) separately from the volume *of* the music (when mixed in with other soundtrack elements). If music should be "louder," you need to be clear whether you are seeking a more passionate performance or if you just want to raise the volume of music in the overall soundtrack mix.

> **Takeaways**
>
> - When discussing music, you must clearly differentiate between absolute and relative volume.
> - Changing volume levels *within* a piece of music are called dynamics, which are communicated to performers with performance instructions.
> - The absolute volume of music against the other soundtrack elements and the dynamic range of the music recording are often heavily processed in dubbing.

3.9 Musical Attributes: Timbre

In music, sound quality may also be called "timbre," referring to distinguishable characteristics of a tone, which may be produced by a single instrument or several at once. Timbre can be thought of in terms of everyday **materials** such as wood, metal, glass, stone, fabric, etc. Timbre can also be described in terms of **texture** (e.g., rough, soft, hard, wooly), **density** (e.g., light, dense, diffuse), **weight** (heavy, light, oppressive, volatile), or **temperature** (warm, hot, burning, cold). Musical instruments produce sounds of different timbres

82 How to Think and Talk about Music

depending on the materials they are made of as well as the different playing techniques (so-called articulations). For example:

- The vibrating strings inside a **piano** are made of metal and struck by hammers covered in felt. A piano may sometimes have a metallic sound, a wooden or mellow timbre, at other times a glassy quality. This depends on the particular piano being used, the way the performer is playing, the room in which the piano is placed and, in media music, how it is being recorded.
- A **violin** is made of wood, its strings of metal or sheep intestines or synthetic materials. The bow used to play a violin is made of wood and hair or synthetic materials. Depending on the articulation used by the player, the resulting sound will vary widely in timbre, ranging from hushed to mellow to brilliant to piercing.

It is not necessary for you to know what each and every articulation is called (in the case of a violin, including *arco, pizzicato, col legno*, etc.). Instead, it is more helpful to try to open your ears to different sonic possibilities and discuss these. For example, if you tell a composer that for a particular scene you are looking for a warm and soothing, light and soft sound in the music, they may perhaps use strings, or a flute, or a synthesized sound.

When a composition contains more than one instrument, the cumulative timbre of a piece is determined by the instrumentation and orchestration. Experienced listeners may be able to identify individual instruments within a texture, but this is not essential in order to discuss the resulting overall timbre. Some pieces have a relatively steady, unchanging timbre, whereas others change quite significantly, either gradually or suddenly. Time from *Inception* (2010, Hans Zimmer) is a good example of a piece that gradually evolves and shifts in timbre.

Thinking of a musical sound in terms of material, texture, density, weight, or temperature can inform the creative dialogue. For the purpose of discussing music, it really does not matter whether you can correctly associate a specific instrument with a resulting timbre—whether you have heard it in a piece or are hoping to instruct the use of that timbre in a piece yet to be written. Being as descriptive as possible, perhaps referring to existing music examples where appropriate, you can begin to work towards musical solutions that have a timbre that works well for a particular moment in the project. Listen to the music examples in the list below and pay close attention to timbre. The descriptors given here for each track should only serve as starting points, rather than an exhaustive list.

- <u>Dead Space Theme</u> from *Dead Space* (2008, Jason Graves)—full orchestral texture, deep, dark, eerie, scratchy, metallic.
- <u>Come Rain or Convergence</u> from *Dead Space 2* (2011, Jason Graves)—massive, visceral, busy, overpowering.
- <u>Dawn of a New Time</u> from *Battlefield 1* (Johan Söderqvist and Patrik Andrén)—warm, soothing strings, deep, soft.
- <u>Light is Green</u> from *Halo 5: Guardians* (2015, Kazuma Jinnouchi)—gradually building from mellow and soothing to bright and impactful.
- <u>Advanced Soldier Overture</u> from *Call of Duty: Advanced Warfare* (2014, Harry Gregson-Williams)—high piercing strings underpinned with low rumbling percussion, brass, and low strings that are warm and weighty.
- <u>Shooter Main Title</u> from *Shooter* (2007, Mark Mancina)—busy texture, low boiling, undulating drones.
- <u>War Opening Titles</u> from *War* (2007, Brian Tyler)—edgy, distorted, claustrophobic.
- <u>Avengers Unite</u> from *Avengers: Age of Ultron* (2015, Danny Elfman)—bright metallic brass, heavy, earthy percussion.
- <u>The Beast</u> from *Sicario* (2015, Jóhann Jóhannsson)—gradually morphs from smooth, warm, almost soothing, to harsh aggressive percussion slaps.

Takeaways

- Timbre in music refers to sound qualities that can be described in terms of texture, density, weight, or temperature.
- Instruments produce different timbres depending on the materials they are made of as well as the way they are played.
- The cumulative timbre of a piece is determined by the instrumentation and orchestration.
- Changes in timbre can have powerful expressive potential.

Further Reading

Bazelon, I. *Knowing the Score: Notes on Film Music.* New York: Van Nostrand Reinhold, 1975.

Copland, A. *What to Listen For in Music.* New York and London: Signet Classics, 2011.

Edward, K.H. *How to Listen to Music: Hints and Suggestions to Untaught Lovers of the Art.* 7th edn. HardPress Publishing, 2016.

Gioia, T. *How to Listen to Jazz.* New York: Basic Books, 2016.

Greenberg, R.. *How to Listen to Great Music: A Guide to Its History, Culture, and Heart.* New York: Plume, 2011.

Ockelford, A. *Comparing Notes: How We Make Sense of Music.* London: Profile Books, 2017.

Previn, A. *No Minor Chords: My Days in Hollywood.* 2nd edn. London and New York: Bantam Books, 1993 (includes the Irving Thalberg anecdote).

Ratliff, B. *Every Song Ever: Twenty Ways to Listen to Music Now.* London and New York: Penguin, 2017.

Notes

1 Portman in a talk at the Royal College of Music on 2 October 2012.
2 Giacchino in a talk at the Royal College of Music, hosted by the Royal Albert Hall in the Elgar Room on 18 October 2017.
3 In a video clip shown during "James Horner: A Life in Music" at the Royal Albert Hall on 24 October 2017.
4 Djawadi in a personal interview via Skype on 3 August 2010.
5 Altman discusses the fluidity of genre labeling of films in his fascinating book R. Altman. *Film/Genre.* London: British Film Institute, 1999.
6 See also Vasco Hexel. "Understanding Contextual Agents and Their Impact on Recent Hollywood Film Music Practice." Ph.D., Royal College of Music, 2014. http://ethos.bl.uk/OrderDetails.do?uin=uk.bl.ethos.606560.
7 See also Vasco Hexel. *Hans Zimmer and James Newton Howard's* The Dark Knight: *A Film Score Guide.* Lanham, MD: Rowman & Littlefield, 2016.
8 A. Previn. *No Minor Chords: My Days in Hollywood.* 2nd edn. London and New York: Bantam Books, 1993, p. 152.

When to Think and Talk about Music

4

4.1 Introduction

In the past, film and TV music was not a priority for project owners until well into post-production. Films in the Hollywood studio system, up until the early 1960s, were basically made in an assembly line: A director, employed by the studio, would direct a film, then pass it on to a picture editor, also employed by the studio. The studio composer (in those days, called music director) would score the film once the edit was finished and "locked," spending perhaps four to six weeks on a project. While the composer was scoring the film, the director had already moved on to the next project. It is not surprising that many Hollywood filmmakers used to treat music as a condiment that was added to taste at the end, as seasoning rather than a main ingredient, and that creatively they would feel fairly disassociated from the scoring process.

Nowadays, emerging modes of media production, enabled by digital technology, have given rise to new creative opportunities and different approaches. Expensive film stock is now largely obsolete and digital media encourage overshooting (see also Chapter 8). Films and other visual media are increasingly assembled in the editing suite rather than minutely planned in pre-shoot. Picture editors are able to change an edit more easily and quickly, and all digital editing is non-destructive, with unlimited undo/redo. The "locked" picture is also a thing of the past so that composers and other members of the music team no longer have the certainty of a fixed picture cut (timings, pacing, etc.), nor can they afford to wait with their work until editing is finished: It simply *may not* finish until shortly before a project's release.

86 When to Think and Talk about Music

All the more reason, therefore, to start thinking about music earlier in the creative process.

Project owners will be juggling a million different things, with many issues and problems vying for their attention. It is not helpful to add music to their post-production worries. If discussions about music are left until that late phase, lack of vision and forethought for music can lead to rushed discussions, a wasteful creative process, and lazy or cowardly decisions. For example, a student director once sent the same script to three student composers to pitch music for a work-in-progress short film. He did not provide any input as to what he wanted music to achieve. When the three pitches were in, the picture editor then tried out all three pitches as temp tracks against a working edit. The director and the editor took a view on each score and finally settled on one of them. In the absence of a music brief and a discussion with the composers, the three pitches were naturally speculative. This must have been frustrating for composers who would have found guidance in a clear brief. It was also wasteful to ask *three* composers to throw their music in the mix, especially since the pitch was unpaid. The director lost the opportunity to discuss his vision for music with a skilled collaborator, ending up with a score that the composers created in isolation. The director might instead have opted to sit down with *one* composer to have a meaningful conversation about the music, before a single note was written. The subsequent compositional process would have been informed by the director's input. (More on briefing the composer in Chapter 7.)

In other areas of media production, onboarding creative departments early on is commonplace. One may consider, for example, set design, which has been firmly established as a pre-production step. Informed by the script, a team of people starts working on ideas and then creates the look and feel of the set(s), the costumes, props, etc. Christopher Nolan worked closely with his location scout and sound design team to find suitable locations in which to shoot and sound record scenes for *The Dark Knight* (2008), favoring real locations over studio sets in his pursuit of heightened realism.[1] The Ray Kroc biopic *The Founder* (2016) recreated the very first McDonald's restaurant of 1954 as realistically as possible, based on historical architectural sketches of actual McDonald's restaurants.[2] The HBO show *Westworld* (2016–) drew inspiration for its costumes from historical sources and costume designers then 3-D printed accurate replicas of vintage fabrics, in line with the shows futuristic premise and setting.[3] Mostly a CGI-enhanced studio-shoot, Bill Condon's live-action adaptation of Disney's *Beauty and the Beast* (2017) drew inspiration from a wide range of sources for its lavish costumes and dazzling set design.[4] Much time and effort are spent, sometimes well in excess of what might seem

When to Think and Talk about Music **87**

necessary to please the casual viewer, on creating a look and feel that best serves the respective script and delivers a compelling result. Many viewers will never realize that none of the White House-based shows *West Wing*, *House of Cards* (2013–), *Veep* 2012–, and *Designated Survivor* (2016–2018) is shot in the actual White House (there are some exterior establishing shots of the real thing).[5] The four shows do not even share sets. Each show had its own team devise a version of the White House that suited the respective tone and style.

Thinking about Music Early On

So, if production and set design happen early on, why not think about music early on as well? One can consider music planning part of the fabric-making of a project, just like set design or lighting or sound recording. As early as during script stage you can consider what role music should be assigned and what status it is given in your project. At this early stage, things can be fluid and need to be set in stone. Considering music during pre-production may give you a chance to onboard key creatives and enfranchise them to your creative process towards a shared goal. This can also enhance scheduling and planning: Once a general music concept has been implemented, the creation and/or sourcing of that music can coincide with pre-production (it is a devolved task) and then continue throughout production and post-production. Granted, one can shoot material without having a score ready. But creative stakeholders may feel more motivated, even inspired during production if music creation is already underway. Walt Disney placed such high importance on music that in the 1930s he and his team devised a story-boarding system that showed music notation underneath each picture card. Contemplating music alongside the gestational timeline of the project is something that may fit naturally with the creative workflow of video game design: Here, the product being worked towards is to varying degrees interactive and must accommodate player behavior. Since actual gameplay—as opposed to narrative vignettes in between—are designed to be flexible and of different playing time, there is less of a natural point at which music might be composed to "locked picture."

If the music team is in place and work underway early on, music choices and creation can fluidly take shape as audiovisual material is delivered downstream. Ben Salisbury and Portishead's Geoff Barrow crafted a potent and unsettling score for Alex Garland's *Ex Machina* (2014). "We read the script before they'd even started shooting," says Salisbury. "We saw it develop and we were right in there with the narrative journey that the film took, every

88 When to Think and Talk about Music

change that was made editorially we were part of."[6] Many contemporary media composers draw on a technologically enabled process (computers, sequencers, digital recording) to create scoring demos in a cost-effective and expedient manner (see also Chapter 7). If composers are involved in a project early on, they can spend more time experimenting with musical ideas, which can inspire an ongoing dialogue between creative stakeholders. This process can produce a score that will ultimately better serve the project. Composer Hans Zimmer has been at the pioneering forefront of advanced music technology and new scoring methods. He describes a dialectical process that he maintains throughout a project: "I create problems for directors on a daily basis. I provoke. I ask 'what if we did something entirely different here?'" Christopher Nolan has said of Zimmer, "I have never worked with someone so dedicated to the idea that the real risk is in playing it safe."[7] The composer need not actively provide music to the project owners while they are preoccupied with other priorities. They may instead wait until an opportune moment arises to discuss music. The larger the scale of a project, the more likely it is that the picture editor may start cutting some material while elsewhere the shoot is ongoing. In these instances, it can be helpful to have some early music ideas ready to use in the picture-edit-in-progress.

Many composers prefer to get involved in a project as early as possible to help media creators develop a vision for music in their project. Composer Klaus Badelt (*Pirates of the Caribbean: The Curse of the Black Pearl* (2003), *Constantine* (2005)) cherishes team spirit:

> I have a specific separate mobile study to move wherever the director is. If he's editing at Warner Brothers, let me move in there too, have my studio next to the cutting room. So I can hang with them, sit next to them, not talk about music at all maybe. Just get a feel for what's important, how the director feels. I go to the set if I can. How does he direct his actors? What's important to him? And nothing can replace that feel. [...] Music is part of the process. I play them early stuff and I love to make mistakes and to learn from them. I might often be more critical than the director.—I had this once, where they were happy with what I played to them. And [it was only when I played my music to them] that I stopped before it was finished [and asked,] "please let me make changes." My background was in filmmaking. I remember saving a lot of money as a twelve-year-old to buy a super-8 film camera to do short films [...] That's what I loved to do before I had my first keyboard. I love film. I love film and the function of music in film—I just happen to be a composer and write music.[8]

Takeaways

- For best results, consider and discuss music early on.
- Onboard your composer and/or music supervisor in pre-production.

Introducing: The Music Supervisor

Does Your Project Need One?

Probably. Regardless of the scope of the project, onboarding a music supervisor is always a good idea, especially, but not only, when licensed music is to be used. Music supervisors have a broad technical, managerial, and musical skill set that they will use to help with all music-related matters during development, pre-production, production, post-production, and delivery. If they are onboarded during pre-production, they can embed themselves within the creative team and maximize their positive effect on the project. Music supervisors will charge a per-project fee that is commensurate with their experience and the scope of the project, but this is a worthwhile investment. One can enquire about going rates from one's own professional network and/or the music supervisor's rep.

What Do They Do?

Music supervisors are qualified and specialized professionals who can help with all music-related aspects of film, television, advertising, video games, and any other media formats. As your creative allies, they can help with music-spotting decisions, find suitable music for sync, secure the rights and permissions required to use that music, and oversee the production and implementation of music in the project. If the project will rely predominantly on newly composed music, a music supervisor can facilitate communication and logistics between the composer and other creative stakeholders.

Sourcing Music

Music supervisors have up-to-date knowledge of many styles of music and have established connections with the music industry. Understanding the

90 When to Think and Talk about Music

requirements of the project at hand, a music supervisor will actively look for music that serves project-specific needs. Music supervisors will regularly receive materials from major record labels, independent labels, artistic managers, directly from bands and solo performers, and directly from composers. They often have vast categorized playlists of music that they can readily put to work on a project.

Licensing Music

Music supervisors secure the rights of new and existing recordings, and clear synchronization and master use licenses of pre-existing music (see also Chapter 5). They will negotiate with rights holders and talent, discussing terms and costs for a license. In undertaking these negotiations on the project owners' behalf, they shoulder the hassle and prevent potentially costly mistakes. For example, they will determine the legal framework applicable to the project at hand, any applicable obstacles to specific music usages (including different distribution platforms and territories), and ensure all rights holders are contacted before a music sync can proceed. Music supervisors can also source cheaper alternatives for music that is proving too difficult or costly to license. For example, a re-recording of a well-known song can prove cost-effective if the original version of a particular track is too expensive to sync.

Pricing Music

Music supervisors have current knowledge of all costs associated with music. They will know going sync rates for different media formats. They will know about more obscure issues, such as current musicians' union fees for licenses where this might become relevant (mostly on US recordings). They can highlight liabilities arising from sync and advise on a reasonable music budget with respect to all music-related costs. This includes obtaining quotes for sync licenses. They will, then, also ensure that all required music elements are delivered within the agreed budget.

Monetizing Music

Music supervisors can help explore possibilities for additional music uses, perhaps external to the project itself, to maximize ancillary revenue streams such as soundtrack album sales, promotional tie-ins, etc.

How Do They Interface with the Project Owners?

Music supervisors are key partners in determining the use of music in a project. They have a thorough understanding of the role and function of media music. As part of a creative dialogue, they can advise the project owners on the musical vision, tone, and style that best suits the project. They will also liaise with the production and post-production teams, communicating about music requirements at every stage of the project. They can, for example, advise on the exact length of a song placement, depending on how a scene evolves, but also gauging cost implications. During editing, they can provide two or three alternative tracks, offering options whilst starting tentative sync negotiations behind the scenes. On projects that require little or no sync of existing music, a music supervisor can oversee and support the music team, which may include a composer and his or her team, songwriters, recording artists, on-screen music performers, and recording engineers.

Where and How Do You Find a Music Supervisor?

Is there a project comparable in scope and budget to the one you are currently working on? Is there a recent film, TV show, video game where you thought the use of music was interesting and compelling? You should approach the music supervisor of that project. Are they available? If not, they may be able to recommend someone who is. Other members of your creative team, the producers, the commissioning body or investors, your wider support circle will likely have contacts too. Since a music supervisor can be such a key asset, it is essential that whoever you hire is qualified, has up-to-date experience, and is well connected within the music industry, as evidenced by their prior track record. They also need to be compatible with the project owners, professionally and personally. Failing all else, there are always search engines (you can try typing "music supervisor" and add one's local area into the search field). There are countless individuals and companies that will readily offer their services. Beware of search engine results that look like general directories but are in fact private companies pandering their services. Some of the more established music supervisors do have representation so you can reach them via their respective agencies.

Music Supervisors in Their Own Words

I've heard people talk about how they think that music supervisors just do clearances or think that music supervisors work for labels or publishers, that they're just placing music for companies they work for, which is not true […] Our job is really to be able to essentially identify with the creative leads on a project what the vision of the music will be, what the role of music will be.

Thomas Golubić, music supervisor for Better Call Saul *and* Halt and Catch Fire[9]

Music supervisors are part of [the] creative team—the costumer, the production designer, the hair stylist, we all sort of come together to try to tell the stories that the creator wants to tell.

Alex Patsavas music supervisor for The O.C., Mad Men, The Twilight *series, and others.*[10]

Every single thing involving music filters through us somehow. It's overseeing all the production, mixing, and also working with the choreographers and actors, and getting all the recordings ready for the shoot. And that's just the tip of the iceberg.

Steven Gizicki, music supervisor for La La Land[11]

Introducing: The Music Editor

Does Your Project Need One?

Most likely. The music editor is to music what the picture editor is to the footage. Depending on the scale of a project, one or several music editors may be required. If you have onboarded a composer, the music editor(s) will usually be part of their team.

What Do They Do?

Music editors are often trained musicians who understand the music needs of a project and are able to provide a range of creative, technical, and clerical tasks:

- **Spotting Session**—Music editors may attend the spotting session (see also Chapter 7) for note taking, marking the beginning and end points of all music entries and what type of music is required (source, score, sync, composed, etc.). They share these notes with the music supervisor and composer, as applicable. Composers may also require more detailed notes for each separate music cue, which the music editor will create.

- **Temp Tracks**—Music editors can source music for temp tracks (see also later in the chapter) and edit these into something resembling a composed score, cut to picture. Temp tracks may serve a range of purposes, including giving the picture editor a better sense of pace, to inform discussions between creative stakeholders, and test screenings.

- **Score Preparation and Conforming**—Music editors can work with the composer to create so-called click tracks that are used in the scoring session to help the ensemble keep in-sync with the picture. During the scoring session, music editors facilitate timing and picture sync, and they can help with last-minute changes. If changes are made to footage *after* the scoring sessions, music editors communicate these changes to the composer and their team and/or conform the recorded music themselves, to fit the revised picture edit.

- **Formats, Mixing, and Dubbing**—In preparation for the final dub, music editors ensure music is delivered in the correct audio format and sounds the way the composer intended. Music editors will deliver all music to the dub, and attend to help with the final mix. Original music is commonly delivered to the dub in so-called stems (or stripes) and, often working as the composer's representative on the dubbing stage, music editors will be on hand to make any and all changes to the music as required.

- **Logging Music Usage**—Once all music has been dubbed (i.e., placed in the final project), music editors will prepare a final cue sheet or so-called master cue list. This is a detailed breakdown of all the music featured in the project, including duration and type of usage (source, underscore, song, etc.). This master cue list is used by royalty collection societies to calculate performance royalties for their members (see also Chapter 8).

How Do They Interface with the Project Owners?

The role of music editors sits in between the production team and the composer's team. Although they are commonly chosen and hired by the composer, music editors are likely to deal directly with directors, picture editors, and producers. Music editors will also be an asset to creative stakeholders besides the composer when they wish to make last-minute changes to music on the dubbing stage.

94 When to Think and Talk about Music

Where and How Do you Find a Music Editor?

Music editors may be hired by the composer, the production company of your project, or any of the project owners. There are companies that provide music editing services as part of their service portfolio, as well as freelance music editors. If the project uses only existing, licensed music, the music editor will work with the post-production team to place this music in the project. A production company or broadcaster may also have a number of in-house music editors or go-to freelancers.

Music Editors in Their Own Words

> For temping, we look at the film, decide where music should start and stop, figure out a musical direction, and compile a library of soundtracks that we think will work. We loosely sync up various cuts of each soundtrack to the picture and make note of which cuts work best. Then, we start editing the music to fit various sequences. [...] *Red Dragon*, directed by Brett Ratner, was memorable because I got to create a temp score for a truly twisted character. An amateur critic attended one of the previews and gave Danny Elfman a glowing review without realizing it was all my temp music. That was pretty sweet.
>
> *Charles Martin Inouye, music editor on* Red Dragon,
> About a Boy, The Jungle Book[12]

> In post-production, I conform the music to any picture changes. I choose some of the source cues, and I craft transitions (and sometimes marriages) between them and the score. On the mix stage, I deliver the full music Pro Tools session to the re-recording mixer, and then serve as an ambassador for the music.
>
> *Ethan Stoller, music editor on* Sense8[13]

> After scoring, all of the best recordings and performances have to be edited together. Often, I'm called in to align musical performances that were recorded at different times. They're playing to a click track, but everyone has his or her own definition of where the beat is. They're not playing to each other. It's my job to make it sound as if they were all in the same room together. *The Departed* was like this, really layering parts of the score in Pro Tools.
>
> *Tim Starnes, music editor on* The Hurt Locker,
> The Lord of the Rings *trilogy*[14]

4.2 Season to Taste: Adding Music at the End

If the music team joins the project early on, they can select, to use a food metaphor, rich ingredients for the project that will come together harmoniously, rather than smothering everything in salt and fat before serving, to make it palatable. Filmmakers may sometimes want to call upon music to help fix a bad scene, a clumsy edit, and an actor's awkward performance. Music cannot do that. Whilst music can add gloss to an otherwise bad picture, it cannot remedy underlying flaws in the project. Yes, music can *help* make a film funny or sad or scary, but music alone is unlikely to succeed if the script, acting, or editing are lacking. A poorly conceived score will not be as impactful, narratively cohesive, or conducive to the great dramatic potential that music holds.

To be sure, for best dramatic effect, there are times when music needs to be composed at a later stage. But this does not mean that music should not have been considered well in advance. In fact, music that is close-scored to a locked picture is often at its most effective if planning in advance has flagged to the director and editor that the footage should leave room for music:

- In Alfred Hitchcock's *Vertigo* (1958) there is a prolonged "chase" sequence (actually a rather leisurely pursuit) when Scotty follows Madeleine through San Francisco; Bernard Herrmann's accompaniment is carefully paced to fit the scene.
- Henry Mancini's music for the "heist" in Blake Edward's *Breakfast at Tiffany's* (1961) is lighthearted and tongue-in-cheek, but clearly composed to picture (one may notice the starting and stopping of the music to match the actor's movement).
- In the *Better Call Saul* (2015–) episode "Witness" (season 3, episode 2), directed by show-runner Vince Gilligan, composer Dave Porter provides a long sustained action cue that starts and stops in close-sync with the on-screen action. Mike Ehrmantraut is following a possible target. The music builds to a big climax when the "Los Pollos Hermanos" sign is revealed, which is a rewarding signal for invested fans who were waiting for Gustavo "Gus" Fring to join the show.

Takeaways

- If the role, tone, status, and placement of music are considered early on, the planning and creation of that music can holistically evolve alongside the project, and be used to the best effect.
- Close-scoring to a locked picture can be at its most effective if the picture cut leaves room for music (time, space, pace).

96 When to Think and Talk about Music

4.3 The Mixed Blessing of Temp Tracks

Sourcing and Placement

Before final music decisions are made (original music composed or existing music licensed), temporary music may be chosen as placeholders. So-called temp tracks are a tool that allows the creative stakeholders to gauge the feel of a scene, the pacing of a segment, different stylistic approaches, etc. Temp tracks may also be used for internal studio screenings, test audience screenings, or video game demos that take place before the final music has been licensed and/or created. Temp tracks may be sourced from a wide range of sources, including, but not limited to, existing film and game scores, pieces of concert music, and popular music. Since temp tracks are not normally intended for public release, there is no need to clear temp music for licensing.

Editors may select and put temp music in a scene because it can help them better judge the flow and speed of a passage. For example, editor Christopher Rouse used John Powell cues from previous *Jason Bourne* films when editing *The Bourne Ultimatum* (2007). A chase sequence will be much more exciting with fast-paced music under it. A horror thriller in editing may not feel spooky without some eerie music. Sound effects and Foley are not yet ready at this early stage, so temp music can become doubly helpful in creating a sense of cohesions and completeness in the soundtrack. There is nothing wrong with an editor placing some music in a scene temporarily if this facilitates his or her work. Editors are in a unique position during post-production to mold the visual language of a project. If using temp tracks aids their progress, then this should be encouraged. However, it should be kept in mind that editors' music choices are fairly arbitrary, informed by their intuitive outlook on the project, respective knowledge of music, and the availability of music at the time of editing. Furthermore, editors' subjective music choices may not be coordinated with the director, producers, let alone a composer. Therefore, when reviewing an edit-in-progress that has temp music, it is important to remember where that music came from, who has selected it, and what purpose it serves. Although it is likely the editor will have selected something that serves their needs at a particular juncture, nothing suggests that the temp music chosen is the best possible solution. That said, lucky accidents do happen: Lisa Gerrard's CD fell into the hands of an editor on *Gladiator* (2000) and this fortuitous (but random) choice led Hans Zimmer to collaborate with Gerrard on what became an iconic and award-winning score. Most of the time, however, temp music chosen by an editor should be acknowledged for what it is: a utilitarian placeholder, to be supplanted by different, carefully chosen or crafted music later on.

Directors may choose to use these temp tracks in an edit-in-progress for producers and other creative partners to get a feel what they are aiming for. In choosing temp music, directors are likely to resort to material they are familiar with. Composers and music supervisors are keenly aware of trends whereby certain pieces or composers are used frequently for temp music, including:

- Hans Zimmer (*The Thin Red Line* (1998), *Inception* (2010), *The Dark Knight* (2008)).
- Danny Elfman (*Edward Scissorhands* (1990), *A Nightmare before Christmas* (1993)).
- Thomas Newman (*American Beauty* (1999), *Wall-E* (2008)).
- Alexandre Desplat (*Syriana* (2005), *Grand Budapest Hotel* (2014)).
- Max Richter (*Waltz with Bashir* (2008), "On the Nature of Daylight").

Limitations

Although temp tracks can be a useful tool, there are intricacies they cannot deliver. Since these tracks may be found by a number of different people and sourced from a range of different places, a temp score will not have the **musical unity** and cohesion of a composed score. The moment-by-moment architecture of a scene or segment may not be served well by existing music, unless a scene or segment has been structured *around* that music. **Thematic material** cannot be developed organically and closely matched to the narrative in ways a skilled media composer might when working on the same project. And new musical themes by definition cannot be found when using existing music as temp tracks.

Replacing the Temp

Temp tracks are destined to be replaced by newly commissioned or licensed existing music. Depending on who has chosen temp tracks and when, original music and/or music licensing may be well underway while a temp score is used as placeholder. Conversations about original or licensed music will to varying degrees be influenced by temp music choices. Understanding what existing music the director and other stakeholders feel works well for the project at hand can facilitate communication and cut out time-consuming trial and error. So, on the one hand, temp tracks can facilitate collaboration.

98 When to Think and Talk about Music

Some composers support the use of temp tracks as a communication tool: Marco Beltrami recalls temp tracks comprising snippets from his own previous scores being helpful when working with director Jonathan Mostow on *Terminator 3: Rise of the Machines* (2003). He recalls that the working edit was "about seventy percent temped with my music."[15]

When replacing temp tracks, all parties involved should allow for some creative freedom and flexibility. Temp music can usefully inform the initial music brief and conceptual approach, but they should not rigidly dictate the creative direction for music. It is advisable that the creative team discusses what, specifically, the temp score does well, and whether there is anything in the temp music (the style, the tone, dynamic, pace) that should be retained in the newly composed score. If certain aspects of the temp work less well, this should be discussed also, so that the composer can try to solve that music cue differently. In a tension-fraught restaurant scene in Doug Liman's *Mr. & Mrs. Smith* (2005), a generic "needle-drop" tango was used as temp music to accompany the dialogue and dance between a married couple of spies (Angelina Jolie and Brad Pitt). Realizing that the temp music did not evolve to best suit the gradually rising tension in the scene (nor to fit the couple's dancing), Liman eventually asked composer John Powell to compose a bespoke tango.[16]

Temp Love

Director John Amiel (*Somersby, Entrapment*) feels that temp tracks are an "essential tool" for communication but only "provided that the director enfranchises the composer to take the intention of the music rather than the notes of the music."[17] Temp music inevitably ends up influencing, even prejudicing everyone's perception of what comes after it, which is human nature: As post-production progresses, everyone involved gets used to seeing and hearing the edit-in-progress with temp music over and over again. So-called temp love sees creatives fall in love with the temp, so used to it that they find it difficult to accept anything else. Composer John Powell recalls that the opening of *Antz* (1998) was temped with music from Alan Silvestri's *Mousehunt* (1997), which seemed to fit the scene perfectly. Powell, who says he reveres Silvestri, found it difficult to compose new music that could live up to the temp.[18] Composer Mychael Danna (*The Ice Storm* (1997), *Life of Pi* (2012)) feels that using temp tracks "screws up the whole composing process because a lot of your choices seem to be made before you even come on to the film, and half of your work as a film-score composer is getting people to stop listening to the temp score."[19] Music supervisor and owner of Air Edel, Maggie Rodford, voices the collective feeling that temp tracks are the "bane of composers."[20] Composer Basil Poledouris (*The Hunt for Red October* (1990)) feels that temp tracks are "a crutch. I think it's an unnecessary tool that's used too early in the making of the motion picture. It doesn't allow the film to develop its own life."[21] Temp tracks can preclude a meaningful and rewarding creative collaboration between directors and composers.

Since many stakeholders get to hear the temp throughout post-production, and since the temp is indicative of what creative stakeholders consider a workable, even good, solution for the project, it is not uncommon for composers to be asked to create what amounts to a near **soundalike** of the temp track. In media composer circles, creating a soundalike without getting sued is a skill all too often called upon. Advertising campaigns and TV commercials are notorious for seeking soundalikes, most commonly because the project at hand lacks sufficient funds to license the original that is being copied. When project owners ask a composer to emulate a temp track as closely as possible, they prevent an exploration of the expressive possibilities that might arise from the use of original music on a project. The individual voice of the composer is rendered irrelevant if they are merely asked to copy something.

Composers can feel straitjacketed even when their *own* music is being used as a temp. Director Paul Greengrass threw out a lot of John Powell's original music for *The Bourne Ultimatum* (2007), instead resorting back to the temp tracks, which happened to be Powell's own music for the previous two installments in the franchise. The score for the Waterloo action sequence, for example, is compiled from temp tracks that Powell merely tidied up and re-recorded for the new film (to ensure smooth music transitions). Asked about this sequence, he admits that he had absolutely nothing to do with *scoring* it, in the sense that none of his new music for this sequence made it into the final cut.[22] Would he have preferred to have his own, new ideas used in the film? Of course. But he acknowledges that the director made some creative choices that were his to make. Other composers feel more protective of their original work: Danny Elfman fell out with director Sam Raimi over *Spider-Man 3* (2007), and actually quit the project, frustrated by having to repeatedly re-score temp cues of his own music from the previous *Spider-Man 2* (2004) film.

Taken to an extreme, temp love can squeeze out original music altogether. Working on *2001: A Space Odyssey* (1968) for over a decade, Stanley Kubrick placed a selection of concert pieces in his edit-in-progress. He used Richard Strauss's <u>Also Sprach Zarathustra, Op. 30</u> for the iconic opening passage and Johann Strauss's <u>On the Beautiful Blue Danube</u> for the beautiful exterior shots of Space Station V. He used the <u>Kyrie</u> from György

100 When to Think and Talk about Music

Ligeti's Requiem and Lux Aeterna by the same composer in several places, editing the two pieces together for the "Encounter with the Monolith" scene. This was an act considered blasphemous by classical music purists and which drew Ligeti's scorn and an eventual lawsuit. Today, *2001: A Space Odyssey* is widely revered as a masterpiece. The film arguably gave rise to the mainstream popularity of "Zarathustra" and the compilation score is widely admired. What most people do not know is that Kubrick's music choices started out being temp tracks. In choosing existing pieces from different time periods and musical styles, Kubrick perhaps focused on surface characteristics. He may have felt that "Zarathustra" lent an air of pomp and grandeur to "Dawn of Man"; that the waltz of "Blue Danube" highlighted the dignified dance-like movement of the space station; and that Ligeti's micro-polyphony, eerie and atonal to the average listener, may work well towards a sense of foreignness and alienation, with underlying tension and trajectory. Nevertheless, the intention from the start was that original music should be commissioned. Acclaimed composer Alex North (*A Streetcar Named Desire, Cleopatra*) was hired to replace the temp tracks with an original score. There is only anecdotal evidence as to what the collaboration between North and Kubrick was like. The outcome, however, is well documented: None of North's music made it into the final cut. Allegedly, the composer only found this out when he attend the film's premiere and heard only the temp tracks he had worked hard to replace.

Several things went wrong here: Having clearly fallen in love with temp music, the director nevertheless chose to work with a composer towards newly composed, original music. Although there may have been some pressure from studio bosses at MGM (at the time, having an original score was the thing to do), Kubrick could have simply insisted on his music choices, saving North a lot of work and hurt feelings. Having, however, agreed to work with North, Kubrick might have found a way to reconcile his musical choices with the input from the composer, possibly raising the film to yet a higher expressive level. Finally, having decided that North's complete score was not to his liking, Kubrick might have honestly told the composer before the premiere... There were also legal implications to Kubrick's use of the temp score in the final film. Composer Ligeti sued and there were various licensing disputes over other pieces too. This just highlights the fact that whilst no permissions are required to use music as unpublished temp tracks, as soon as that same music is to be used in the final project, the requisite licenses must be sought prior to release.

If and when you find yourself insisting that a temp score should be emulated, it is worth taking a step back and asking yourself: Why? What is so great

When to Think and Talk about Music **101**

about this temp track? What is it about it that is working particularly well? If it is so perfect, why not (try to) license that music? If the cost of licensing is prohibitive for the project at hand, is a soundalike really the best way to go?

Temp Tracks Are Unoriginal

If temp tracks have been sourced from existing sources, then that music has probably has been heard and used previously elsewhere. Every time existing music ends up in a project, at least part of the audience will be familiar with that music, and their experience be influenced by their prior encounters with that music. For example, composer Yann Tiersen's evocative score for *Amélie* (2001) has been reused widely, notably in advertising. But when the cue Comptine d'un autre été, l'après-midi from *Amélie* appears in *Good Bye Lenin!* (2003) the effect is distracting for audiences familiar with both films, especially as the music's original setting is so well judged. To be sure, fascinating creative opportunities *can* arise from placing familiar music in new contexts—for example, Richard Wagner's Ride of the Valkyries in Francis Ford Coppola's *Apocalypse Now* (1979). Arguably, the use of existing music in a new context provides scope for originality of expression. The use of Wagner's pompous piece in a war movie picks up on the visual beauty of helicopters in a sun-soaked setting, provocatively and controversially brushing aside the atrocities of war, if only momentarily. Lovers of Wagner, however, may have been offended by the appropriation of Wagner's music. If such usages of existing tracks are deemed ideal for the project, then a music supervisor can be called in to work out licensing agreements. When working with a composer towards an original score, there is a unique opportunity to create something completely new and bespoke. It is up to the creative stakeholders whether they wish to cease and cherish that opportunity, and not be too quick to cage your composer in by dictating the terms of their creativity with a temp track whose emulation they insist upon.

Media composers and their scores are sometimes accused of being derivative, but in assessing recent media music it is important to keep in mind that this music has had to pass media creators' judgment, too often influenced by temp tracks. The use of temp tracks and a creative team's insistent attachment to them result in the regurgitation of familiar material. Hans Zimmer complains that after he had scored Terrence Malick's *The Thin Red Line* (1998), working on subsequent projects, he would for the longest time be shown edits-in-progress with his musical theme for that film (Journey to the Line).[23] The theme became Zimmer's quasi template for many scores that followed, including *The Da Vinci*

102 When to Think and Talk about Music

Code (2006, the cue <u>Chevaliers de Sangreal</u>), and the closing scene of Christopher Nolan's *Inception* (2010, the cue <u>Time</u>), with noticeably similar results.

Outliers

There are directors who do not use any temp tracks, mindful of the fact that these may limit the composer. Remembering his experience of working with Denis Villeneuve on *Sicario* (2015), composer Jóhann Jóhannsson recalled that "Denis edits free of temp music. It's a totally fresh approach so I have this clean slate to work with. We tried this when working on Prisoners, and it works."[24] Villeneuve and editor Joe Walker sent Jóhannsson an early cut of *Sicario*, for which the composer sent back a few demos with the sound of helicopter blades slowly getting louder. That early composition was pivotal in setting the tone. "Denis is not afraid of letting the film breathe," says Jóhannsson. "He doesn't like to carpet the whole film with music and I love this minimal approach. When the music is there, it serves a purpose."

Best Practice

Composer Michael Giacchino (*Lost* (2004–2010), *The Incredibles* (2004), *Star Trek* franchise) prefers never to listen to temp tracks, as he feels this would unduly influence or limit his approach.[25] He stresses that temp tracks are useful tools for editing and internal studio purposes (including screenings for executives and test audiences), but that temp tracks should never be seen as an end in themselves. If all creative stakeholders are to feel enfranchised and meaningfully involved in working towards a scoring solution that best serves the creative vision and needs of the project at hand, temp music can help illustrate initial ideas. This need not happen in a prescriptive manner but should instead be informative, helpful, and with a shared goal in mind.

When starting a new project, consider your options with regards to music selection and placement: Will licensed music be required? If so, why not start a dialogue with a music supervisor early on, putting creative heads together and multiplying music knowledge. The music supervisor will be able to gauge up front what licensing options are available. They can also prevent disappointment that may ensue if other stakeholders (including editors) choose a temp track that everyone falls in love with but that later cannot be cleared for licensing. Will you involve a composer, as well as or instead of licensed music? If so, invite them early on to provide or recommend some music that the editor can use. Composers are often happy to collate some material of their own existing music for the editor to use before new music is subsequently composed. Some composers even like to compose some new tracks or suites specifically for the project, giving editors a "goody bag" of material to play with (see later in the chapter). If the editor also has some music ideas, or feels they need a certain type of music, they should be in touch with the music supervisor and/or composer directly, so they can help each other out and keep each other in the loop. Knowing about the editor's ideas, the composer is then able to create something that is better tailored to the specific scene at hand.

> **Takeaways**
>
> - Temp tracks are utilitarian placeholders that may serve a purpose during production and post-production.
> - Temp tracks do not have the musical unity and cohesion of a newly composed score, nor can they provide the moment-by-moment architecture of original music, including themes, etc.
> - Temp tracks are destined to be replaced by newly commissioned or licensed existing music.
> - Temp tracks are unoriginal.
> - Temp tracks may inform but should not dictate the direction of the commissioned or compiled score.

4.4 You Cannot "Temp" Originality

If project owners can retain a healthy level of detachment from temp tracks, they may allow scope for exciting possibilities that arise from unexpected, innovative music uses. It takes the bold vision of an invested composer or music supervisor to imagine a fresh approach. Freed from the creative straitjacket that, in the worst case, temp tracks impose, composers and music supervisors stand a chance to pursue novel ways in which music and visuals interrelate.

Inventing the Language of Classical Hollywood Film Music

When Max Steiner was called in to score Merian C. Cooper and Ernest B. Schoedsack's *King Kong* (1933), the film was in trouble: The directors were concerned that the elaborate special effects, on which the film drew heavily, looked silly and unconvincing. Steiner was tasked to compose a score that

104 When to Think and Talk about Music

could help complete the film, to instill in the audience a sense of the foreign
locale (Skull Island), to increase the drama, make Kong seem more menacing,
and to sell the unlikely emotional bond between the ape and Ann Darrow
(Fay Wray). Despite severe budgetary constraints, Steiner nevertheless composed an ambitious symphonic score. He devised recognizable and recurring
musical themes (The Adventure Begins (King Kong/Jungle Dance)) to such
striking effect that his score became the de facto scoring template for Classical
Hollywood film scores. For decades to follow, film scores would be largely
orchestral and thematic.

The Compilation Song Score

Mike Nichols's *The Graduate* (1967) forever changed the role of popular songs
in (Hollywood) films. Alongside a score by Dave Grusin, the film was the
first to feature a compilation of pop songs by Simon & Garfunkel, both old
and new. The hit song Mrs. Robinson was written specially for the film. The
songs reflected the film's themes of coming-of-age angst and rebellion, whilst
also jibing aesthetically with the film's contemporary edge. At the time of its
release, the film became the third-highest grossing film of all time.

The Renaissance of the Symphonic Film Score

Following a period of pop, jazz, and compilation scores, Steven Spielberg's *Jaws*
(1975, Main Title and First Victim) brought about a renaissance of the symphonic film score. John Williams opted to score this understated horror film
with utmost economy, his shark motif comprising a mere two alternating notes.
In the absence of elaborate visual effects (we do not even see the shark until late
into the film), music ably characterizes and represents the threat forever looming off the shores of Amityville. The ensuing resurgence of symphonic scores
is a perfect example of a hit inspiring imitators. Williams himself, of course,
perpetuated the use of orchestra with his scores for *Star Wars*, *Indiana Jones*, etc.,
most of which were musically more developed and elaborate that *Jaws*.

Film Music Becomes Cool

Martin Brest's comedy *Beverly Hills Cop* (1984) struck a chord with audiences.
Composer, arranger, and music producer Harold Faltermeyer composed and

produced the score using synthesizers and electronic instruments, notably the now iconic Roland TR-808 drum machine. Synths were commonly used in pop music at the time, giving the score a contemporary and commercial sound that appealed to audiences. Rarely had a film score sounded so fresh and of its time, attested also by how dated it may sound today. Faltermeyer's theme Axel F for main character Axel Foley (Eddie Murphy) became a hit single in its own right. In the words of Hunter Stephenson, "Axel F" "hopped into bed with America's zeitgeist like few songs before or since."[26]

Composed Synth Pop Scores

Barry Levinson's *Rain Man* (1989), starring Dustin Hoffman and Tom Cruise, was Hans Zimmer's first Hollywood film score. Newly arrived in Los Angeles and without any standing in the industry, Zimmer composed and programmed the entire score in Levinson's production office on a Fairlight synthesizer that offered only sixteen simultaneous notes (so-called voices, for example, in the cue Leaving Wallbrook / On the Road). The technological constraint must have influenced his compositional technique and style at the time, as did his previous work in bands and in 1980s British film and TV. The result was a compelling score that had the sound and flair of late-eighties popular music, with gentle grooves and a catchy melodic theme on synthetic pan flute. *Rain Man*'s critical acclaim amplified its star-powered popular appeal, and the mellow and sympathetic score earned Zimmer an Academy Award nomination.

Zero Excess: Irreducible Musical Expression

Having proven with the Joker theme in *The Dark Knight* (2008, beginning of Why So Serious) that a single sound can represent a character, for Nolan's *Inception* (2010) Hans Zimmer devised a musical gesture of hard drum hits and low brass stabs (think aggressive fog horns with drums), what later came to be called the *Inception* "bwaaah."[27] There was nothing original in the musical gesture as such. But distilling a sense of foreboding, threat, and imminent danger into a singular musical strike, which in the context of *Inception* is used to great dramatic effect, was a successful invention. The idea was later copied in countless films, film trailers, commercials, and computer games. Emulation being perhaps the best form of flattery, the widespread use of the "bwaaah" sound, in film trailers and other movies, proves just how successful the invention was perceived to be and how influential it became as a result.

106 When to Think and Talk about Music

Nothing "original" has creative currency for long. Zimmer himself has spoken about innovation getting used up and his ongoing pursuit of innovation and re-inventing himself, because he is so readily copied.

> **Takeaways**
>
> - Temp tracks are not conducive of original music solutions.
> - Giving composer and music supervisor freedom to innovate can lead to new forms of expression, be it in music alone or in the combination of music and visuals.

4.5 Reversing the Workflow: Music-First

There are times and circumstances when thinking about music early on is essential and where having music composed or compiled during pre-production may be necessary.

On-Screen Performances

On-screen performances are the most obvious opportunity for music to be planned and recorded in advance. Noisy sets are not ideal for recording music during the shoot, so music should be pre-recorded in a music studio. Performers may actually sing or play an instrument during the shoot, but their performance will be mimed or post-synced with pre-recorded sound. This is simply to ensure the best possible audio quality, which live sound on set cannot provide. Whilst in the final edit a performance may look and sound live, sound is usually post-synced, as are many sound and Foley sound effects.

- In Alfred Hitchcock's *Rope* (1948), Phillip Morgan (Farley Granger) plays Mouvement Perpétuel No. 1 by Francis Poulenc on the piano and, later, a short original piece by composer David Buttolph, which is also used during the main title. Phillip's hands are visible when he plays Poulenc.
- Ryan Gosling learned the piano to play jazz pianist Sebastian in Damien Chazelle's quasi-musical *La La Land* (2016), and he is shown playing various pieces throughout the film. Just because we see him playing does not mean we actually hear what he is playing. Sound may well have been pre-recorded and post-synced.

- Singer-songwriter Vonda Shephard sings topically chosen songs onscreen in *Ally McBeal* (1997–2002). The music we hear was not recorded on set.
- In Damien Chazelle's *Whiplash* (2014), protagonist Andrew (Miles Teller) is a drummer. Justin Hurwitz composed and recorded a number of big band ensemble pieces in advance for the cast to be able to perform seemingly live during rehearsal and in the competition/concert near the end of the film.
- An eclectic range of performers take to the stage in a Harlem nightclub in season 1 of Marvel's *Luke Cage* (2016–).

Musicals

In musicals, songs will by definition have to be written, and usually pre-recorded, ahead of production. There are a few well-documented cases in which actors sang live on-set, notably Tim Burton's *Sweeney Todd—The Demon Barber of Fleet Street* (2007), Tom Hooper's *Les Misérables* (2012), and Bill Condon's live-action adaptation of Disney's *Beauty and the Beast* (2017). Some directors feel they can get a more believable performance out of their actors if they ask them to sing live on-set. However, a cleaner recording of the vocal will invariably be obtained in a music studio. In a film musical, it is far more common to have actors mime to pre-recorded tracks. In the past, actors would sometimes even have a voice-double (pre-recorded by default)—for example, Richard Beymer as Tony in Jerome Robbins and Robert Wise's movie adaption of Leonard Bernstein's *West Side Story* (1961) and Audrey Hepburn as Eliza Doolittle in George Cukor's *My Fair Lady* (1964).

Theme Songs (That Are Performed in The Film)

Composer Henry Mancini wrote the theme song "Moon River" for Blake Edwards's *Breakfast at Tiffany's* (1961) and in a key scene Holly Golightly (Audrey Hepburn) is singing the song whilst accompanying herself on guitar. In the ensuing romantic exchange of "hi"s between her and Paul Varjak (George Peppard) the music then segues into composed underscore, picking up on the tune of the song. Mancini also composed the song "Meglio stasera" for *The Pink Panther* (1963), which is performed live in the film, the singer oddly facing the camera throughout.

108 When to Think and Talk about Music

Shooting to Final Music

- Ramin Djawadi was closely involved in the planning of the use of The Rolling Stones' Paint It Black in the pilot episode of HBO's *Westworld* (2016–). Djawadi's new instrumental arrangement of the 1971 hit song accompanies the arrival of a band of bandits. The placement of the song will have involved a music supervisor to secure the licensing, the composer's contribution to ensure scoring continuity (style and instrumentation) for this underscore usage, and directorial forethought and input for having the actors' movements and attitude jibe with the rock and roll accompaniment.
- For Godfrey Reggio's experimental film *Koyaanisqatsi* (1982), minimalist composer Philip Glass composed and recorded his music in advance. Reggio played recordings of Glass's minimalist music during filming to inform his approach to the aesthetic feel of the film.
- Daft Punk provided a collection of finished tracks to Joseph Kosinski before he started shooting his sleek *TRON: Legacy* (2010). He then played the music on-set during production. There are several scenes, notably in the Armoury and Derezzed segments, in which the actors clearly move in time with the music, to good dramatic effect.
- For his international break-through film *Lola Rennt* (*Run Lola Run*, 1998), director and composer Tom Tykwer's translated his acute creative vision into a synergistic music-film. He closely collaborated with composers Reinhold Heil and Johnny Klimek, creating the music for the film in tandem with the shoot and, later, post-production. Lola (Franka Potente) did not actually run to the music during shooting, but the director's vision informed the pace and flow of every scene.

Subverting the Notion of Source Music

One of the more unusual uses of music composed and recorded in pre-production can be found in Alejandro G. Iñárritu's *Birdman or (The Unexpected Virtue of Ignorance)* (2014): Improvisatory jazz drumming accompanies the film as underscore. The chaotic nature of the drums mirrors the main character's sense of confusion and struggle for control of his environment. In a rewarding and self-aware twist, and a complete break with conventional narrative logic, on several occasions the drummer is shown on-screen. The resulting effect makes for a richer viewing experience. Careful planning went into the shooting of this film, with the cast rehearsing for several weeks before filming in a Broadway theater.[28] Revealing the drummer in select moments, and thus toying with the dichotomy of diegetic and non-diegetic music, was possible due to the thorough advance planning, including that of music.

"Goody Bag" Approach

Here, the composer starts writing music by choice, not out of necessity. They may also choose to compose different pieces of music inspired by the project but not yet in close-sync with the moving image, leaving the actual placement of the music for later. This approach to music composition can be helpful, firstly, for the project owners because it gives them range of ideas and expressive options to choose from. Secondly, "goody bags" can free up the composers' creative energies because they does not have to worry about the various constraints that come with fitting music to specific visuals: goody bag music will simply need to be flexibly adapted to the project downstream. See also Chapter 8.

- Composer John Powell took this approach when working on the animated feature *Ferdinand* (2017). He recalls coming up with different themes and tunes up front and labeling them as "hero," or "action," or "matador," etc. Later, when the film was being assembled, Powell tried out different placements of his ideas throughout the film, re-assigning and/or re-naming cues accordingly.
- Daft Punk composed much of their score for *TRON: Legacy* (2010) ahead of shooting and left it up to the director to place their music in the film as he saw fit.
- Michael Semanick describes a flexible scoring process for *There Will Be Blood* (2007), in which composer Jonny Greenwood sent over various pieces of recorded music for the music editor and director then to adapt and place as they saw fit: "Jonny gives music editor Paul Rabjohns his stuff and then he'll take this part and move it here. Then he might trim the pitch or change a cue altogether. They send him a palette of stuff and it's 'Oh that's great! And parts of this are great; what if I put these two things together and this together…' etc. The tone is set and P. T. [Anderson] pretty much guides it all the way; lets you run with it and then pulls you back in."[29]

Takeaways
- On-screen performances usually require a music-first workflow, where music is pre-recorded in a recording studio.
- Shooting to music can inspire the filming process and guide actors.
- The "goody bag" approach can offer composers added creative freedom and also give media creators more options for music selection and placement.

110 When to Think and Talk about Music

Further Reading

Gorbman, C. *Unheard Melodies: Narrative Film Music.* London: BFI Publishing, 1987. Contains a detailed analysis of the score for the 1933 *King Kong.*

Harris, M. *Pictures at a Revolution: Five Movies and the Birth of the New Hollywood.* New York: Penguin Books, 2009. Includes a fascinating discussion of *The Graduate.*

Saltzman, S. *Music Editing for Film and Television: The Art and the Process.* London: CRC Press, 2014.

Notes

1 See also Vasco Hexel. *Hans Zimmer and James Newton Howard's* The Dark Knight: *A Film Score Guide.* Lanham, MD: Rowman & Littlefield Publishers, 2016.

2 Laura Morgan. "See What the First McDonald's Burger Joint Looked like in 1954." Architectural Digest. Accessed 4 April 2017. www.architecturaldigest.com/story/the-founder-set-design-see-what-the-first-mcdonalds-burger-joint-looked-like, accessed 1 February 2018.

3 Elena Fishman. "Of Course Westworld's Costumes Are 3D-Printed, Too." Racked, 27 October 2016. www.racked.com/2016/10/27/13408436/westworld-costumes, accessed 1 February 2018.

4 Elizabeth Stamp. "How Beauty and the Beast's Magnificent Sets Came to Life." Architectural Digest. Accessed 4 April 2017. www.architecturaldigest.com/gallery/beauty-and-the-beast-set-design, accessed 1 February 2018.

5 Elizabeth Stamp. "House of Cards Set Design and Filming Locations." www.architecturaldigest.com/story/house-of-cards-set-design-locations, accessed 4 April 2017. and Elizabeth Stamp. "Behind the Scenes of ABC's Designated Survivor." Architectural Digest. www.architecturaldigest.com/story/designated-survivor-set-design, accessed 4 April 2017.

6 www.rollingstone.com/music/premieres/hear-the-ex-machina-score-by-portisheads-geoff-barrow-and-ben-salisbury-20150403, accessed 17 March 2017.

7 Jon Burlingame, "20 Billion-Dollar Composer: For Hans Zimmer, 'The Real Risk Is Playing It Safe,'" Variety, http://variety.com/2014/music/features/ 20-billion-dollar-composer-for-hans-zimmer-the-real-risk-is-playing-it-safe-1201173698/, accessed 27 February 2018.

8 Badelt in a personal interview via Skype on 10 November 2011.

9 www.avclub.com/article/how-tvs-best-music-supervisors-picked-their-emmys-257270, accessed 1 February 2018.

10 www.stereogum.com/1808743/qa-tv-film-music-supervisor-alex-patsavas-on-soundtracking-the-o-c-mad-men-the-twilight-series-the-astronaut-wives-club-and-more/franchises/interview/, accessed 1 February 2018.

11 http://variety.com/2017/music/news/guild-of-music-supervisors-awards-steven-gizicki-1201990816/, accessed 1 February 2018.

12 https://www.editorsguild.com/About/What-Do-Our-Members-Do/Past-Featured-Members/ArticleID/245/charles-martin-inouye-music-editor, accessed 2 February 2018.

13 https://www.editorsguild.com/About/What-Do-Our-Members-Do/Past-Featured-Members/ArticleID/275/ethan-stoller-music-editor, accessed 2 February 2018.

14 https://www.editorsguild.com/About/What-Do-Our-Members-Do/Past-Featured-Members/ArticleID/166/tim-starnes-music-editor, accessed 2 February 2018.

15 Christian DesJardins. *Inside Film Music: Composers Speak*. Los Angeles: Silman-James Press, 2006, p. 22.

16 John Powell in "BAFTA Conversations with Screen Composers" on 10 July 2017 at the Elgar Room, Royal Albert Hall, London.

17 DesJardins, op. cit., pp. 336–337.

18 Powell, op. cit.

19 DesJardins, op. cit, p. 55.

20 Rodford in a talk on music supervision on 7 August 2013 at the Transatlantyk International Film Festival, Poznań, Poland.

21 DesJardins, op. cit, pp. 178–179

22 Powell, op. cit.

23 Zimmer in a talk at the Royal College of Music on 3 October 2013.

24 https://www.screendaily.com/awards/composers-johann-johannsson-sicario/5098958.article, accessed 6 February 2018.

25 Giacchino in a talk at the Royal College of Music, hosted by the Royal Albert Hall in the Elgar Room, 18 October 2017.

26 www.slashfilm.com/interview-harold-faltermeyer-creator-of-soundtrack-themes-to-fletch-beverly-hills-cop-top-gun-and-kevin-smiths-cop-out/, accessed 18 July 2017.

27 https://inception.davepedu.com, accessed 5 March 2018.

28 www.latimes.com/entertainment/envelope/la-et-mn-birdman-creators-rehearsing-labyrinth-20150213-story.html and www.businessinsider.com/birdman-how-it-was-filmed-2014-10?IR=T, accessed 17 July 2017.

29 Interview with re-recording mixer Michael Semanick and sound designer Chris Scarabosio by J. Riehle, 13 January 2008. http://designingsound.org/2008/01/there-will-be-blood-exclusive-interview-with-re-recording-mixer-michael-semanick-and-sound-designer-chris-scarabosio/, accessed 7 February 2017.

Licensing Existing Music   5

5.1 Introduction

This chapter addresses key considerations that pertain to the use of existing music in a project, be it instrumental music or songs. There may be any number of reasons why you prefer existing music to newly composed music, and pros and cons should be considered carefully:

Pros

- Existing music is readily available and thus requires zero creative lead-time.
- Costs will be known in advance, pending licensing negotiations.
- Using existing music offers the potentially bankable association with an established star, popular piece of music, etc.
- What you hear is what you get.

Cons

- Existing music may come with an audience's prior associations.
- Existing music cannot be customized to the project in ways bespoke music can.
- Licensing negotiations can be difficult and protracted.
- Cost of licensing can be substantial.
- Lack of originality.

The music search must be informed by the project requirements. Accessing existing music in this digital age has become exceedingly easy, but finding the *right* music can take some time. YouTube, Apple Music, Spotify, Tidal, and Google Play are just a few of a growing number of platforms for legal streaming or downloading of music. Listening to the radio, you might happen upon a piece of music that feels right for the project at hand. Services such as SoundCloud are a useful repository of music by emerging artists. Live concerts and shows such as Cirque du Soleil may be inspiring, or music may be found accidentally in a public place—for example, a bar or a restaurant. A busker in the street may play a song that happens to suit the current project. This happened to composer Harry Gregson-Williams who heard a young boy singing in the streets of Dublin and ended up recording the kid for the powerful closing cue of *Veronica Guerin* (2003). Family, friends, and colleagues may have ideas and suggestions for music. Paying attention to television and cinema can be useful, perhaps to find artists rather than a specific piece of music. Record labels readily interface with studios and other content creators because having their catalogue placed in projects is a lucrative part of their revenue stream. Labels may proactively pitch for sync to push their catalogue. Many young artists are actively vying for attention, trying to cut through the noise on social media, search platforms, festivals, etc. If and when you work on larger projects, music will be more likely to actively come to you: Numerous companies and individual musicians are tracking the moves of the industry and will readily offer you their work for sync when they learn about a specific opportunity. Many companies provide online platforms and searchable databases of so-called **production music** that is being offered specifically for the purpose of affordable synchronization licenses.

Some media creators are highly knowledgeable about music and they draw on this knowledge when considering sync options: Director and writer Quentin Tarantino, for example, famously makes great music sync choices for his films, informed in part by his own interest in music. It is said that director and writer Martin Scorsese listens to stacks of CDs to search for music that he feels works for the respective film he is working on. But there is a potentially overwhelming abundance of choice out there. The first stages of the music search, where choices may be filtered and whittled down, can be delegated. It may be useful to onboard a **music researcher** who can help source suitable existing music. A relatively junior member of the creative team, they will be expected to closely follow a set brief and source music accordingly. They will not normally be expected to make creative choices or to get involved in licensing negotiations. **Music supervisors** can also facilitate the search for existing music. They will have a number of trusted sources and leads for music that

114 Licensing Existing Music

they can call upon. Music supervisors also have expert knowledge of the music industry and musical styles. As a more senior member of the creative team, the music supervisor may act as a stakeholder with vested creative interest and initiative to serve the project. They will supervise the music researcher's work and partake in reviews of the existing music that has been sourced.

Synchronization licenses and a license for use of the master recording (called **master use license**) will be required for all existing music to be used in the project (see later in the chapter). The music supervisor can lead negotiations and manage the music budget allocated to sync fees. With smaller music budgets, it can be preferable to consider cheaper alternatives that the music supervisor can advise on.

Takeaways

- Weigh up the pros and cons of licensing existing music for the project at hand.
- The music search must be informed by the project requirements.
- Accessing existing music is easy, but finding the *right* music can take time.
- A music researcher and music supervisor can facilitate the music search.
- Synchronization licenses and master use licenses will be required for all existing music to be used in the project.

Introducing: The Music Researcher

Does the Project Need One?

Perhaps. Regardless of the scope of the project, onboarding a music researcher can be helpful when existing music is to be used. Onboarding them during pre-production will enable them to undertake music searches without having to rush.

What Do They Do?

The music researcher is a qualified professional who can help with all music searches for film, television, advertising, video games, and any other media formats. Working to set parameters and perhaps a music brief, deploying research and organizational skills, the music researcher will identify and source suitable music for the project. The music researcher has up-to-date knowledge of many styles of music and may have academic knowledge of music (history, ethnomusicology) and/or have established connections with the music industry. Understanding the requirements of the project, the music researcher will actively look for tracks that serve project-specific needs.

How Do They Interface with the Project Owners?

The music researcher will liaise with the production and post-production teams and, working to set parameters, feed music options into the creative workflow. The final choice of specific tracks ultimately lies with the project owners, possibly also with input from the music supervisor.

Where and How Does One Find a Music Researcher?

Music researchers may work in-house with music agencies or they may be freelancers. Depending on the project needs, a music researcher may come from a record label, a broadcaster, a music production company, an advertising agency, or a university music department. The qualifications of the music researcher must match the project needs at hand, depending on what type of music is being sought. For example, for a dramatized documentary on Mozart, an expert classical musicologist may need to advise on music choices.

5.2 Obtaining a Synchronization License for a Piece of Music

There are legal and contractual differences between, on the one hand, obtaining a synchronization license to use an existing piece of music that has previously been published versus, on the other hand, commissioning a new, bespoke composition (including songs), which is covered in Chapter 6. If a piece of existing music has been selected for use in the project at hand, the rights holders of that piece will have to be identified, contacted, and asked for permission to use the piece (i.e., synchronize it with the visuals). In some rare cases, a synchronization license may be granted free of charge. Most of the time, however, a licensing fee will be due, which is negotiable (except for

116 Licensing Existing Music

production music; see later in the chapter). There are **two types of copyright** associated with *every* recorded piece of music:

1 The **publishing rights to a composition** (which includes all types of music, including songs). The composition is composed and written by one or several composer(s) or songwriter(s) and owned by those individuals. If a composition has been released commercially, it is usually owned jointly by a music publisher and the composer.
2 The rights to an actual studio audio recording of that composition (or song), the so-called "**master.**" The **master sound recording** is usually owned by a record label.

Duration of Copyright

Even if a composer is dead or a band has split up, their music remains covered by copyright for a set duration. Different rules apply in different geographic territories regarding the duration of a copyright, commonly determined by the lifespan of the author and the date of publication. At the time of writing, the **duration of copyright** on a composition is:

- the lifetime of the author +70 years in the **European Union**, and 70 years from publication (or, if unpublished, 70 years from creation), whichever is longer;
- the lifetime of the author +70 years in the **US**, and 95 years from publication (or 120(!) years from creation), whichever is shorter.

Determining whether a composition is in or out of copyright can be tricky and confusing. The bottom line is, however, that you cannot simply use a piece of music without first obtaining the requisite permissions. To **obtain permission** to use an existing recording of an existing composition, the project owners (or someone representing the project) must contact both the **owner of the composition** *and* the **owner of the sound recording** and negotiate synchronization licenses. In order to do this, the author/composer/writer, the music publisher, and the record label attached to the composition and recording need to be identified. All the vested parties must be consulted and give their consent before a sync can proceed. One must **never assume** that licensing will be possible, so the rights holders should be contacted **early on** in the creative process to prevent problems down the line.

Licensing Cost Factors

Many factors determine the cost of licensing. Not all of these considerations may be clear when negotiations first start, so it is always better to approach rights holders early to explore the feasibility of licensing. The rights holders may refuse to grant a license for any reason, or demand fees that are too high for the project at hand, and so alternative music solutions may need to be pursued. Whether or not a particular piece is available for license in a project will always depend on the specific circumstances.

- In most cases, a **non-exclusive license** will be sought, whereby the composition and recording at hand may be synchronized with other projects, previously, currently, or in future.
- Occasionally a project may seek an **exclusive license** (whereby the composition is married to this project exclusively). This is quite rare, however, when licensing existing music. One scenario may involve a non-exclusive license for a song (the composition) paired with an exclusive license for a newly commissioned recording of that song (for example, for a TV commercial). Otherwise, exclusive licenses are common when commissioning original music (see Chapter 6).
- The music rights holders will want to know what is the intended use for their composition / recording: What is the nature of the project? In which context will the music be used?
- Will the music be in the **background**, for example, on a radio in a car while characters are talking? Or will the music **feature prominently**? For example, a character may point out a song by name as it comes on in a club, saying, "I love this song," and then start dancing to it.
- What is the intended **duration of the usage** (in minutes and seconds)?
- And how **long is the term of the license**, i.e., will the license be indefinite or limited to a certain time frame?
- In what **territories** will the project be distributed: Worldwide or in selected markets only?
- In what **formats** will the project be distributed? With feature films, it is often desirable to cover a number of different formats: theatrical release, physical discs (DVD / Blu-ray), digital download, streaming, pay-per-view broadcast, and terrestrial broadcast.

The music sync license should ideally cover all formats, present and future, to avoid problems down the line: The comedy *Shag* (1989) featured many licensed pop songs. Following its theatrical release, the film was first released on VHS tape. The VHS release contained the same music as the theatrical release. The music sync licenses will have covered both release formats. A DVD version of the same film, released later in the 1990s, contains *some* of the songs from the theatrical release, but also many substitutions. It is possible that the sync licenses for the songs did not cover subsequent releases in new formats, and sync licenses were not successfully renewed for the DVD release. Likewise, the original soundtrack album CD contains the songs of the DVD version, not the theatrical/VHS version. For fans of the film and its compilation score, the music substitutions in the new format may have been a disappointment. It is also counter to good creative practice to have to revise music sync decisions in new-format releases due to licensing constrictions. It is, therefore, advisable to negotiate sync licenses that cover the widest foreseeable release of a project, including future formats yet to be invented.

Unlicensed Music Uses Are Illegal

Obtaining the correct licenses from all rights holders and completing the required paperwork can be time-consuming, but it is necessary. Copyright infringement is a crime in most countries. Just because music is exceedingly easy to find, and just because it is technically possible to drop just about any track into a project, this does not make it legal. No distributor will screen your film, no network air your program, and no games platform stream your game if the requisite paperwork for your music clearance is not in place. Sometimes rights holders are difficult to identify and reach. In those cases, having tried hard to find and contact them ("due diligence") is <u>not</u> enough to substitute an actual synchronization license. Applicable licenses must be negotiated and paperwork must be completed. Luckily, the task of identifying the rights holders and exploring the feasibility of a sync can be delegated. A **licensing manager** can join the project to look after these aspects of the music. They will have solid working knowledge of the music industry and be able to identify respective rights holders. They may also draw on an existing professional network to speed up the licensing process for specific pieces. A **music supervisor** can oversee all the licensing needs, within established parameters (project music requirements, budgets, negotiations with rights holders).

Costs and Budgets

Any production that uses music should have a music budget, regardless of whether that music will be predominantly licensed existing or newly

Licensing Existing Music **119**

commissioned music. Industry veterans may recall a rule of thumb that said 10 percent of a production's budget should go to music. These days, it is more likely that **2 percent to 5 percent of the overall production budget** goes to music. However, a music budget depends on many variables, especially when sync licenses are involved, so percentages are only indicative. Also, there is a certain bare minimum: If a student film only has an overall budget of $2,000, for example, 2 percent of that budget will not to be enough for music. Some productions spend proportionately more money on music than others—for example, if licensing a particular song is felt to be creatively important for the project. However, it is important to be realistic when planning music licenses for a new project. Licenses can cost relatively little, or they may require huge sums. It is impossible to predict in the abstract how much money will be needed to secure your sync licenses, or even what a reasonable budget might be. Music rights holders will determine the sync fee based on the nature and scope of the project, the type of composition or song in question, and their own status and that of the composition or song in question (obscure, well-known?). Licensing costs are negotiable and the cost of a sync license is informed by the aforementioned factors. Licensing a song by a relatively unknown artist released on a small label will be cheaper than licensing a big hit.

Scenario 1

In a script it says, "Marlene sings 'I'm Every Woman' in the shower." An experienced producer or music supervisor will immediately think, "No, Marlene is probably *not* singing that song because we don't have the budget." Written by Nickolas Ashford and Valerie Simpson, the song was first released by Chaka Khan in 1978, on her debut album "Chaka," and was a chart success. Whitney Houston recorded the same song in 1992 for *The Bodyguard* soundtrack and in 1993 the single was an even greater commercial success. The publishing rights for "I'm Every Woman," required so that the actress playing Marlene can sing the song in the shower, will be too expensive. Is it really important for the narrative that Marlene sings this specific song? If so, maybe the expense is justified? Otherwise, why not have Marlene hum some nondescript tune instead? That would be free, so long as it does not sound too similar to "I'm Every Woman."

Scenario 2

A major brand launches a new ad campaign. They can afford to hire a fancy ad agency and use the music of a major act. For example, in 2010, the Virgin

Atlantic airline launched a £6 million global TV commercial using a new cover version of the Nina Simone song "Feeling Good." They hired the rock band Muse to cut the cover. The publishing license for the hit song was surely expensive. Hiring Muse was probably not cheap either. Getting a new master sound recording made added to the cost: Studio time, paying staff and performers.

Licensing fees change, so to get an up-to-date overview of going rates it is best to liaise with experienced producers and/or a music supervisor currently working in the field. Whether a project is crowd-funded or financed by a broadcaster, a games studio, or a film production company: The financiers will take a view on any and all expenditure, including music. This should not deter you from pursuing the music you want, no matter its source. But keep in mind that the project's financial backers may veto certain choices on grounds of cost. Music budgets for licensing are best approached flexibly and with an open mind. Always endeavor to focus on your creative intentions, pursuing music solutions that best serve the needs of the project. Working closely with experienced producers and a music supervisor will lead to the best results within the available budget.

Blanket Licenses

All major television networks in Europe and the US have so-called **blanket licenses** that allow them to place just about any music they wish in their programs without having to negotiate a separate sync license (covering both the publishing and master rights). This is why one may hear the latest Adele song in an episode of MasterChef. To obtain a blanket license, networks pay very large one-off fees to the respective royalty collection society of their home territory. In return, all music covered by the agreement is pre-cleared for use in programs produced and broadcast by the networks in that specified territory. These blanket licenses are an attestation to terrestrial networks' long legacy in the broadcasting industry and are a rare and convenient commodity. As soon as a program is sold to be broadcast *outside* the home territory, or released on another medium (including cinemas or global streaming), appropriate music sync licenses need to be negotiated. This is due to "geo-blocking" of copyrighted materials, which is also the reason why services like Netflix offer different content in different countries. **International productions** such as *Top Gear* (BBC Studios) would in the past have had to strip out all the well-known music used in their UK broadcast and replace it with different, separately licensed tracks in respective territories. Not an easy task for a show that at one point reached 600 million viewers in dozens of countries worldwide. Nowadays, production companies **anticipate music licensing requirements** that may arise from international distribution of their shows: They pursue licensing solutions that will allow them global use of that music sync. For expensively produced shows such as *Downton Abbey* (2010–2015, ITV, UK), *Peaky Blinders* (2013–, BBC, UK), or *Mad Men* (2007–2015, AMC, US), international distribution is essential to recoup expenditure. Certain cable and pay-per-view operators may <u>not</u> have blanket licenses to start with and therefore are required to negotiate music usages on a per-project basis, often at a significant cost. The same applies to films with intended cinema release, straight-to-DVD or streaming contents, computer games, etc.

When working on a project that requires licensed music, you need to bear in mind that sync costs may prove prohibitive to certain music uses. Other times, you may feel that a particular song is essential for your project and work with the other project owners to allocate the requisite music budget.

Case Study: American Graffiti (1973)

> George Lucas's second feature film, *American Graffiti*, follows four friends over the course of one summer night on their last night together in town, providing a snapshot of teen culture in the early 1960s. Instead of a conventional, composed underscore, the soundtrack comprises 43 popular songs of the 1950s and 1960s, ever-present in the film (playing on the radios of cruising cars, or the P.A. at the school dance). Source music plays a crucial role in painting a nostalgic picture, defining the emotions of the protagonists, who struggle with their respective aspirations and anxieties. Recognizing that popular music would play a crucial role in his film, Lucas paid close attention to the song selection. In his biography of Lucas, author Brian Jay Jones recalls the challenges the filmmakers faced when sourcing the music Lucas envisioned:
>
>> Lucas had made up an extensive song list, selecting at least three songs for each scene in the event he couldn't clear one or two of them. When [co-producer Gary] Kurtz ran the list by executives at Universal, they "practically had a heart attack," said Kurt, and urged Lucas to record the songs with an orchestra or a cover band instead. Kurtz blanched. "We can't do that," he said. "We have to use the original records." Executives eventually agreed, but warned Kurtz that if clearances exceeded 10 percent of the budget the difference was coming out of [producer Francis Ford] Coppola's pocket. Lucas wasn't going to be able to afford about half of the songs he wanted anyway. Right away, Elvis's music was out: the rights were too expensive, and the King's label refused to negotiate. Kurtz had better luck with the Beach Boys

> [and] secured a number of Beach Boys songs, including "Surfin' Safari" and "All Summer Long," for a reasonable fee—and once Kurtz and Lucas could point to the involvement of the Beach Boys, clearing song rights became much easier. Eventually Lucas would clear forty-three songs for the movie, including hits by Buddy Holly, Chuck Berry, Fats Domino, the Del-Vikings, and Booker T. & the M.G.'s. Lucas had just secured the sound track that would make the film—and he and Kurtz had brought the clearances in for around $90,000. Right on target.[1]

The anecdote shows that where the story stipulates a specific type of music, careful planning, paired with perseverance and a bit of goodwill, can lead to great results. *American Graffiti* captured the mood and spirit of a generation and was nominated for five Academy Awards, including "Best Picture." The film was a box office success and energized a trend in Hollywood to target younger audiences.

Takeaways

- There are **two types of copyright** associated with *every* recorded piece of music: the **publishing rights to a composition** and the **master sound recording rights**.
- You must obtain all applicable licenses and permissions for music usages.
- You cannot use a piece of music without first obtaining the requisite permissions.
- Copyright infringement is a crime in most countries.
- Rights holders of a piece of music chosen for sync have to be identified, contacted, and asked for permission to use the piece.
- Never assume that licensing will be possible.
- Many factors affect the cost of licensing.
- Major television networks have blanket licenses for music.

5.3 Getting Your Head around Music Royalties

What Are Music Royalties?

Just like actors, directors, and other creatives involved in film and media production, media composers earn **performance royalties** (also called residuals). These accrue when music is placed in a film or TV show and then distributed, screened, or broadcast. Performance royalties are *not* payable on cinema screenings in the US, but they are payable on cinema screenings in other territories. Royalties are usually split between the composer and the publisher of a composition or song. Besides performance royalties, composers may also earn so-called **mechanical royalties**, due as a percentage share of the sales revenue of physical or digital copies of a composition or song, including in a broadcast. There are also **sheet music royalties** (on the sale of printed music), **foreign royalties**, and **synchronization royalties**. On large projects such as big-budget feature films, secondary revenue streams such as soundtrack albums may results in significant revenue and an agreement may be put in place that splits royalties between the composer and the film studio. At the time of writing, music royalties for video games were non-existent, but rights holders are actively pushing for this to change.

Composers join a performing rights organization (PRO), which collects royalties on their behalf. The American Society of Composers, Authors and Publishers (ASCAP) is the largest PRO in the US and there are smaller organizations such as BMI and SESAC. There are local PROs in all major countries. These organizations have reciprocal agreements for royalty collection to cover international performance. PROs agree music license fees with the users of music (broadcasters, radio, online, live venues, and others), collect these fees, and then distribute them to writers and music publishers. Mechanical royalties are handled by different organizations such as the Harry Fox Agency in the US and the Mechanical Copyright Protection Society (MCPS) in the UK.

What You Should Remember about Music Royalties

Royalties are really not something you need to worry about during the creative process: They are payable as a percentage share of sales revenue. They do not add to your production cost at the point of creation. If your project is a success, royalties will become due as a small fraction of your turnover. The higher the sales revenue, the higher the royalties. Everybody wins. Performing rights organizations use cue sheets to track the use of music in radio, TV, feature films, and web streaming to ensure composers and publishers are compensated for the use of their work. It is your responsibility to file a cue sheet with the respective PRO, depending on which PRO the composer and publisher(s) are members of. No additional cost arises from filing a cue sheet. Filling in the cue sheet does *not* mean you immediately owe royalties, as these only become due later, once your project has been screened or broadcast. Once the project has been finalized, the music editor, music supervisor, or a producer will prepare the music cue sheet (see also Chapter 8).

Further Information

American Society of Composers, Authors and Publishers (ASCAP) www.ascap.com
Harry Fox Agency www.harryfox.com
Performing Right Society (PRS) & Mechanical-Copyright Protection Society (MCPS) www.prsformusic.com

5.4 Using Licensed Music

The following section (of which Table 5.1 provides an overview, starting on the next page) addresses pertinent licensing considerations for different categories of music, focusing on commercially released popular music, so-called classical music, jazz, and traditional/folk music (sometimes called world music). For each category, a guide to key concerns and idiosyncratic issues that may arise from using that music is followed by a selection of common usages.

Commercial Pop Music

What Is It?

Popular music is accessible to and appreciated by a mass audience. Using pop music that has previously been released commercially can be desirable for use in media for a range of reasons (see later in the chapter). There is a long tradition for the use of songs in feature films, for example, including theme songs that were specially written for a film. Pop music has also been used extensively in television and video games.

Buyer Beware

There are many vested interests in commercial pop music, especially if a song has been a chart success. On the one hand, artists are aware of their brand and their image, and tightly control the context in which their music is used. On the other hand, record labels and publishers want to maximize revenue from their catalogue whilst at the same time upholding certain standards. Obtaining a **sync license** can get very expensive, as sync fees for a well-known song by an

Table 5.1 Overview: Licensed Music Categories

	Popular Music	Classical Music	Jazz	Traditional and Folk Music
What Is It?	Commercially oriented music aimed to be accessible to and appreciated by a wide audience	An umbrella term that is often used to refer to all traditional Western music, or European art music.	A type of music of American origin that first emerged in the early twentieth century. Characterized by improvisation. Sub-styles include swing, bebop, and free jazz.	Music that is native to a chosen cultural sphere and normally passed down through generations in oral tradition. Sometimes referred to as World Music or ethnic music.
Buyer Beware...	There are many commercial interests vested in commercial pop music (the artist, the publisher, the record label) and these will dictate whether a sync is possible and at what cost. Sometimes sync licenses are refused flat out, sometimes they prove too expensive for the project at hand.	There are numerous recordings of most classical works and they can sound quite different in terms of recording quality, musical interpretation, and tempo. Licensing costs will vary depending on the respective label, ensemble, conductor, etc. A specialist music researcher or music supervisor can help source suitable versions.	There is a strong performance and improvisation component to jazz. Different renditions by different artists can vary drastically in instrumentation, style, and tempo.	The source culture and its music should be researched properly and any music usages informed by this research.

(continued)

Table 5.1   **Continued**

	Popular Music	Classical Music	Jazz	Traditional and Folk Music
Licensing	There will always be costs involved in using the recording of a song that is in copyright, regardless of how commercially successful or well known that song is. Re-recordings or "covers" can help reduce licensing costs if master recording rights prove too expensive	A lot of classical music is in the public domain (composition out of copyright) but the vast majority of recordings are in copyright. Master use licenses will almost certainly be required for whichever recording has been found, even if the composition (e.g., Beethoven) is in the public domain.	Jazz standards may or may not be in copyright. Always check. Newer jazz compositions are in copyright. Master use licenses are required for most jazz recordings, with the exception of some very early material held in public archives (which provide information on licensing on their respective websites).	Due diligence is required when vetting the origin of a piece of music: Is it in copyright? When working with local performers towards a new recording, the master recording will be owned by the project owners, but musicians should be compensated for their work. If their contribution constitutes authorship, they should be credited as composers.

(continued)

Table 5.1 **Continued**

	Popular Music	Classical Music	Jazz	Traditional and Folk Music
Dos and Don'ts	**Do** remain mindful of pop music's cultural connotations. **Don't** request soundalikes, which are artistically bankrupt and almost always motivated poorly.	**Do** beware of the cultural baggage that comes with classical music. **Do** keep in mind that some audience members will object to the re-purposing of classical music. **Do** be respectful of how the composer intended his or her music to be heard. **Don't** cut up and edit classical music, unless you have good reasons.	**Do** always pre-record jazz music if it is to be used as source music during a shoot (for example, an ensemble playing on-screen) to facilitate continuity and consistency in the musicians' performance.	**Do** check whether it acceptable to take the music out of its local context. **Don't** misappropriate or misquote traditional music in different contexts. **Don't** resort to clichés when adapting/ borrowing from this music.

128 Licensing Existing Music

established artist can easily reach six figures. Everything is negotiable, but, generally speaking, the bigger the hit, the higher the sync fees. Sometimes obtaining a sync license may be impossible because the rights holders simply refuse to grant a license. For example, until 2016, original recordings by the Beatles had *never* been synced. Only then was one single license issue for "Hey Jude," used in the Chinese feature film *Yesterday Once More* (2016) by director Yao Tingting.

Licensing

There will *always* be costs involved in using the recording of a song that is in copyright, regardless of how commercially successful or well-known that song is. There are two types of copyright that may apply, one covering the **composition**, the other covering the **master recording** (see earlier discussion). The cost of licensing will vary depending on:

- the **type of usage** (featured, background);
- the **specific context** (feature film, television episode, trailer, commercial);
- the **release formats** (cinema, broadcast, streaming only);
- **territories covered** (Europe only, worldwide, term of license, e.g., one year, three years, or in perpetuity;
- **duration of usage** (number of minutes and seconds).

Example 1: Recording and Composition in Copyright

The 1975 hit song "Bohemian Rhapsody" by Queen was featured prominently (and famously) in *Wayne's World* (1992) when Wayne (Mike Myers) and Garth (Dana Carvey) rock out to the tape in their car. The sync fee in this instance may not actually have been very expensive, considering that by the early 1990s Queen had been somewhat forgotten by American audiences (they had not toured the country in over a decade).[2] The film was a massive success and the scene featuring "Bohemian Rhapsody" instantly became iconic. The song even climbed back into the US singles charts and put Queen back on the map. By the time the same song was used in a trailer for *Suicide Squad* (2016),[3] a hefty sync fee will have been payable. The whole trailer is structured and edited around a shortened version of the song. Contrarily, in *The Good Wife* (2009–2016; season 7, episode 12, "Tracks"), the lawyer Lucca Quinn (Cush Jumbo) quizzes a witness on hooks in "Bohemian Rhapsody," but the song is never played: It had become so well-known, and commercially

Licensing Existing Music **129**

successful, that sync fees were probably prohibitive for the music budget of *The Good Wife*.

Example 2: Recording Out of Copyright, Composition in Copyright

Even if the recording of a particular song is no longer in copyright, or if a new recording is specially made for the project at hand, the composition may still be protected and thus requires licensing. Until a legal dispute pushed the song into the public domain in 2016, music publisher Warner/Chappell was collecting licensing fees for the song "Happy Birthday" on behalf of the composers, sisters Patty Smith Hill and Mildred Hill. This quirk in copyright law was humorously picked in Tina Fey's *30 Rock* (2006–2013; season 5, episode 4, "Live Show") when the characters are about to break into the song and then stop just short of singing it, flagging that it is under copyright. Had the characters actually sung the song, a sync license for the composition would have been required for the composition, at a cost.

Re-recordings and Covers

Occasionally, project owners pursue the use of a specific popular song but are unable to secure the requisite master use license. Costs and limited budgets are almost always the problem. Other times, the rights holders of the original recording simply refuse to grant a license. When a sync license for a composition (in this case a pop song) can be obtained but not the master use license, a new recording may be a viable option. Re-recordings or "covers" may already exist, as some popular songs have been covered by a number of artists. If the recording by the original artist is not available, the master use license of an existing cover version may be significantly cheaper. Especially with commercials, where post-production turnaround can be tight, sourcing an existing cover can be a cost-effective and expedient route. Sometimes a newly recorded cover may be preferable. For *Back to the Future* (1985), the song "Earth Angel," originally recorded in 1954 by The Penguins, was covered by Harry Waters Jr. who appeared in the film as Marvin Berry & The Starlighters. The new recording proved doubly useful, serving as source music: Berry appears in the film, performing on-stage during the Enchantment Under the Sea Dance. There may also be aesthetic considerations that stipulate the use of a cover version: The official trailer for *Justice League* (2017) featured a version of the Beatles'

130 Licensing Existing Music

Come Together, recorded by Godsmack in 2012, in close sync with film footage. The Beatles' original would have lacked the requisite heaviness and gritty flair. There may also be structural concerns that require a new arrangement and recording of an existing song: For the opening reel of *The Royal Tenenbaums* (2002), composer Mark Mothersbaugh adapted and re-orchestrated the Beatles' "Hey Jude." The new version is an instrumental, which sits comfortably under the introductory voice-over, and Motherbaugh adapts the duration and order of song sections to fit closely with the structure of the opening.

Dos and Don'ts

Do remain mindful of pop music's cultural connotations. As with any existing music, audiences will have different prior experiences and associations with popular music. Cultural references may not be universal across different markets and territories. Project owners should discuss with their music supervisor what intended purpose licensed pop music should serve, and agree what music will best serve this purpose.

Don't request soundalikes. Temp tracks are commonly used as placeholders and for reference (see Chapter 4). It is one thing to use an existing track to inform and inspire a creative process: **Soundalikes**, however, aim to copy the original as closely as possible, to the point of being identical, but just different enough not to infringe copyright ("copy without getting sued"). Soundalikes are the musical equivalent of knock-off Gucci handbags. They are creatively bankrupt and lack artistic integrity. Trying to subvert or circumvent the licensing process can attract all kinds of legal trouble as well. If the project does not have the budget required to sync a specific piece, and if a cover version is not good enough, then a different piece of music should be found. Working with a music supervisor and/or composer, a different music can be sought, or a new composition commissioned.

Commercial Pop Music in Sync

Establishing a Time Period and/or Geographic Setting

Compiling songs that were popular in a particular time period or come from a chosen region or country can be useful. A skilled music supervisor can help choose affordable songs and/or allocate more of the music budget to key scenes and associated music sync while economizing elsewhere. There are many films whose compilation scores were exceedingly effective in capturing the spirit of a time and place:

- *Easy Rider* (1969) struck a chord with a generation of young audiences, the songs used very much of their time (notably Steppenwolf's Born to Be Wild).
- *Forrest Gump* (1994) makes extensive use of pop songs as historical markers, effectively tracing years of Forrest's amazing journey through the 1960s to the 1980s.
- Besides newly composed music, the game *Call of Duty: Black Ops* (2010), set in the 1960s Cold War, used commercial pop songs to help set the time period and also the tone for key segments. The 1968 hit song Sympathy for the Devil by The Rolling Stones is featured in a jungle battle scene.
- In François Ozon's *Water Drops on Burning Rocks* [*Gouttes d'eau sur pierres brûlantes*] (1999), the use of the German hit song Tanze Samba mit mir (Tony Holiday, 1977) effectively places the film in 1970s Germany. Ozon breaks with narrative logic, and creates a brilliant comedic moment, when his cast spontaneously breaks into a choreographed dance to the song.

Establishing a Socio-Cultural Setting

Pop music can help establish a social or cultural setting: What music the characters listen to, are surrounded by, or associated with, can help denote their class, social *milieu*, etc. For example, the use of electronic dance music in *Trainspotting* (1996) and *Lola Rennt* (*Run Lola Run*, 1998) was reflective of the respective characters (although, admittedly, in both cases the tracks were newly written and produced for the film). The use of hip-hop in *Dangerous Minds* (1995), *8 Mile* (2002), and *Moonlight* (2016) is another example of the use of pop music as a socio-cultural marker.

Pop Music as Source Music

Since pop music commonly accompanies everyday live, it is likely to be heard in media whenever a commonplace setting is being depicted: a bar, a café, a diner, a shopping mall, etc. Shopping malls and elevators tend to play easy-listening

132 Licensing Existing Music

music, so-called Muzak (which is actually a branded product owned by Mood Media), to enhance the customer and user experience. It is unlikely that much of the music budget will be spent on source music sync where it is only background filler. Production music (see later in the chapter), which can mimic commercial pop music, may suffice here. Everything changes if a character is to actively engage with the music. For example, in *Modern Family* (2009–; season 2, episode 8, "Manny Get Your Gun"), Mitchell (Jesse Tyler Ferguson) unexpectedly takes part in a flash mob in a shopping mall to the 1992 En Vogue song "Free Your Mind." This featured usage required a well-known danceable song. The sync may have been very expensive. To maximize screen time, the flash mob is recapped during the credits sequence. Another common example: A character walks over to a jukebox in a 1950s diner, inserts a coin and chooses her favorite track. In this case, the music choice needs to be carefully considered.

Other source usages involve characters singing (along to) pop songs. In a pivotal scene in *Blue Velvet* (1986), Ben (Dean Stockwell) lip syncs to Roy Orbison's <u>In Dreams</u> for Frank. The choice of the specific song was made to suit the moment in the film. There are several prominent song placements in *Top Gun* (1986): In a light-hearted moment, Maverick (Tom Cruise) and Goose (Anthony Edwards) perform Jerry Lee Lewis's "Great Balls of Fire" together. The chosen song had to be well known to feel accessible to the audience. It also needed to be a blues that is easy enough to play on the piano and sing together. The scene shows the characters as close friends having fun, which heightens the feeling of loss experienced later when Goose dies.

Packaging and Audience Buy-In

Project owners may conceive of the use of commercially released pop tracks simply because they are familiar with them. Incidentally, using commercially released pop songs can bring a familiar and likeable quality to a scene, a setting, and a project as a whole.

- *The Graduate* (1967) was among the first feature film to make extensive use of licensed songs that had previously been released. Director Mike Nichols remembers working on the famous montage sequence: "It wasn't until we laid Simon & Garfunkel's 'The Sound of Silence' over it that we knew the scene worked. I'd been listening to their album every morning in the shower before I'd go to work, and then one morning it just hit me: 'Schmuck! This is your soundtrack!' [Film editor] Sam O'Steen worked on weekends, so the next Saturday I brought the track over and it was like, Holy shit, this fits exactly and it's twice as powerful! It's one of those miraculous moments you get when you're making a movie, where everything somehow comes together."[4] The film struck a chord with audiences at the time and became a big commercial success, and so too its compilation soundtrack album.

- The animated feature *Happy Feet* (2006) is a jukebox musical that draws on existing pop songs. Some of the songs were re-recorded for the film. Stevie Wonder's 1976 hit "I Wish" (from the album "Songs in the Key of Life") featured in the iconic dance sequence by the adorable penguin Mumble. The sync proved so effective that the scene was used in the cinema trailer, probably at great expense for the additional music sync license.
- The comedy series "Ally McBeal" (1997–2002) used a mix of original and cover songs performed by singer-songwriter Vonda Shepard to accompany each episode. The licensed songs were selected to reflect the theme and mood of each respective episode.
- The pilot episode of *Westworld* (2016–) surprised with the use of the 1966 hit <u>Paint it Black</u> by The Rolling Stones. The song was adapted by series composer Ramin Djawadi as an instrumental and performed on orchestral instruments. The use of a familiar song whose lyrics furthermore jibe with the setting of the scene (an army of bandits arrives in town, their leader dressed in black) makes for a salient and stylish moment.
- Computer games may also draw on well-known songs. For example, *Gears of War 3* (2011) used the moody hit song "Mad World" by Gary Jules in its opening trailer and in-game. The song had originally been written for the film *Donnie Darko* (2001).
- *BioShock* (2007) used Django Reinhardt's 1952 version of "Beyond the Sea (La Mer)," heard after the game's protagonist has survived a plane crash.
- *Grand Theft Auto: Vice City* (2002) used an unprecedented 100+ pop songs from different genres, a music licensing coup. Critics and players praised the game for its ingenious use of music (for example, players could change radio stations in cars they stole), recorded dialogue and open world design.

Montages

Music has proven highly effective in accompanying montage sequences. Particularly in the 1980s and 1990s, using licensed pop songs in a montage

134 Licensing Existing Music

sequence was commonplace (*Baywatch*, anyone!?). Montages may feature newly written and recorded songs—for example, <u>Gonna Fly Now</u> by Bill Conti (aka "The Rocky Theme Song") in *Rocky* (1976) or <u>Maniac</u> by Michael Sembello in *Flashdance* (1983). Montages may instead feature pop song previously released (and possibly quite well known)—for example, <u>Oh, Pretty Woman</u> by Roy Orbison in *Pretty Woman* (1990), <u>Mama Told Me</u> by Three Dog Night in *G.I. Jane* (1997), and <u>She's a Lady</u> by Tom Jones in *Bend It like Beckham* (2002). In the early 2000s, pop song montages somewhat fell out of favor, perhaps in part because they had become a cliché with which audience no longer engaged. No small thanks to the self-mocking montage sequence in the spoof comedy *Team America* (2005).

Commercial Synergy: Compilation Soundtrack Albums

Pop songs can become lucrative commercial successes as a result of music syncs. The entertainment industry eagerly exploited commercial synergies between feature films and soundtrack albums, especially in the 1980s and 1990s. Sometimes, record labels would eagerly push their catalogue into films just to have their songs featured on the soundtrack album. For example, the 1984 song "I Can Wait Forever" by Air Supply can be found on the soundtrack album of *Ghostbusters* (1984), even though the song only features in the film for the briefest of moments, when a workman listens to it on his Walkman. The music video for the song comprises footage from the film to melodramatic effect. At their peak, compilation soundtrack albums were big business. Some of the biggest-selling soundtrack albums include *The Big Chill* (1983, featuring "I Heard It through the Grapevine" by Marvin Gaye, "A Whiter Shade of Pale" by Procol Harum, and others), *Space Jam* (1996, featuring "I Believe I Can Fly" by R. Kelly, and others), the aforementioned *Forrest Gump* (1994), and *Wayne's World* (1992). In more recent years, the rise of digital streaming has caused album sales to fall and compilation soundtrack albums have somewhat fallen out of favor. Nevertheless, some more recent films have had commercially successful soundtrack album releases, including *The Great Gatsby* (2013), whose compilation soundtrack was curated by rapper Jay-Z. Marvel's *Guardians of the Galaxy* (2014) featured a mix tape as a central plot device. The accompanying compilation soundtrack album, "Guardians of the Galaxy: Awesome Mix Vol. 1," featured hits by artists ranging from The Jackson 5 to David Bowie, and was a hit with both critics and audiences. The soundtrack peaked at number one in the US Billboard 200 and the Canadian Album Chart, selling over 500,000 copies in the US alone.

Licensing Existing Music **135**

Cinematic Television

The 2010s saw a rise in high-quality television and streaming content. A number of shows emerged across a range of platforms that used commercial pop music to great effect. The relatively high cost of licensing well-known popular music can be justified by the resulting added aesthetic and dramatic impact and overall production value. Shows with compelling uses of licensed songs, either in their original version, as re-recordings, or as instrumental arrangements, include:

- *Better Call Saul* (2015–, AMC)—Music supervisor: Thomas Golubić.
- *Fargo* (2014–, FX)—Marguerite Phillips.
- *Luke Cage* (2016–, Netflix)—Gabe Hilfer, Season Kent.
- *Peaky Blinders* (2013–, BBC)—Amelia Hartley.
- *Mr. Robot* (2015–, US)—Amie Bond and Charlie Haggard.
- *Westworld* (2016–, HBO)—Evyen Klean, Jennifer Reeve.
- *Stranger Things* (2016–, Netflix)—Nora Felder.
- *The Handmaid's Tale* (2017–, Hulu)—Michael Perlmutter.

Classical Music

What Is It?

"Classical music" is an umbrella term that is often used to refer to all traditional Western music, or European art music. Strictly speaking, however, the "classical" period only lasted from 1750 until 1820. There are many subdivisions that better describe discrete periods within "classical" music, such as the Medieval (500–1400), Renaissance (1400–1600), Baroque (1600–1750), Classical (1750–1820), and Romantic (1804–1910) eras, with overlaps and transitory phenomena therein. Twentieth-century contemporary classical music encompasses new music such as minimalist, serial, and avant-garde. There are many different forms that describe the structure of a composition, including sonata, lieder, fugue, symphony, opera. There is a large repertoire that is frequently performed around the world, by small ensembles, orchestras, ballets, and opera companies. No one expects media creators to be well versed in the terminology and repertoire of classical music, although there are of course avid music lovers among media creators. Making reference to a composer and their work, a specific composition, perhaps even a particular recording of that composition, is usually the best way to have a conversation about classical music during project planning.

Buyer Beware

There are numerous recordings of most classical works, by different ensembles, with different conductors, soloists, singers, etc. Depending on when a recording was made, the sound quality will be noticeably different. These can differ greatly in their interpretation. Some conductors tend to take tempos faster, some conductors interpret them more slowly. Some performances are more energetic, others more reserved. Different orchestras have very different sounds. Compare, for example, three different recordings of Beethoven's Symphony No. 7 in A major, Op. 92, II. Allegretto:

- II. Allegretto performed by the Vienna Philharmonic Orchestra, conducted by Carlos Klein, recorded in 1976.
- II. Allegretto performed by the New York Philharmonic Orchestra, conducted by Leonard Bernstein, 1968.
- II. Allegretto performed by the London Symphony Orchestra, conducted by Bernard Haitink, 2006.

These differences will have an effect on how the respective recording fits in sync, so they should be carefully considered. A specialized music supervisor or music researcher can advise on these differences, which may sometimes be subtle. The availability and sync cost for recording over another will differ. Famous orchestras, famous conductors, and newer recordings will likely cost more to sync than lower-profile equivalents. A skilled researcher may be able to find cheaper alternative recordings of the same composition that work equally well for the project at hand. Sometimes a sync license may simply not be available at a reasonable cost or for other reasons. For "Also Sprach Zarathustra" in *2001: A Space Odyssey* (1968), Kubrick originally wanted (and got) Herbert von Karajan's recording with the Vienna Philharmonic, released by Decca (UK), but Decca executives refused to have the conductor and orchestra named in the film's credits. As a result, the soundtrack album, where the conductor and orchestra would have to be listed, featured a different recording, with Karl Böhm conducting the Berlin Philharmonic.

Licensing

A lot of classical music is in the public domain, meaning the composition is out of copyright. However, the vast majority of recordings of classical music are in copyright. Master use licenses will almost certainly be required for whichever recording has been found, even if the composition (e.g., Beethoven's 7th) is in the public domain. No master use is needed if a new recording is to be made for the project, but then a suitable ensemble will have to be found as well as a recording venue. Most classical music is performed from notated scores and parts, which can be hired from publishers, for a fee. The cumulative cost of studio + orchestra + music hire + conductor can quickly spiral out of control. It will often be cheaper to seek the master use rights for an existing recording than commissioning a new recording.

Dos and Don'ts

Do remain mindful of classical music's cultural connotations. As with any existing music, audiences will have different prior experience and associations with classical music. Cultural references may not be universal across different markets and territories. When using classical repertoire, **do** be respectful of how the composer intended their music to be heard.

Don't re-purpose classical music without compelling creative reasons. Purists may take issue with re-purposing and using classical music in the context of audiovisual media as anything other than straightforward source music, feeling that the "application" of that music cheapens it. **Don't** edit classical music without good creative reasons. Classical music lovers may object to the editing of classical music and disengage with the project if edited music offends their sensibilities.

- Audience members familiar with Ligeti are pained by the scene in Kubrick's *2001: A Space Odyssey* (1968) where the auteur spliced together two different compositions by Ligeti ("Atmospheres" and "Lux Aeterna"), when the astronauts approach the monolith on a barren lunar landscape. Kubrick seems to have chosen his music editing point based on surface qualities in the music and the aesthetic and dramatic requirements of the scene, all the while disrespecting the structural integrity of both compositions.
- Disney committed a similar "crime" in *Fantasia* (1941) when he edited Stravinsky's "Rite of Spring," which was newly re-recorded for the film.
- In *Quantum of Solace* (2008), Puccini's opera "Tosca" is completely cut up and out of order during an action segment. This was potentially distracting for audience members who know the opera and so realized that chronological order in the music was not maintained.

138 Licensing Existing Music

It is advisable that you consult with a music supervisor and/or composer before cutting up and editing a piece of classical music. If such editing feels necessary for reasons of structure, there may be subtle ways of solving the issue. Sometimes a new composition, perhaps inspired by the classical piece at hand, may be the better option.

Classical Music in Sync

Used for Cultural References

Pandering to well-worn clichés, classical music is often used to give characters an air of sophistication and wealth. In *The Dark Knight* (2008), in the restaurant where Bruce Wayne (Christian Bale) and his Russian ballerina girlfriend crash Harvey Dent and Rachel Dawes's dinner, classy surroundings are complemented by an off-screen string quartet performing Schubert's String Quartet No. 13 in A minor, D. 804. Classical music has commonly been used to suggest intellectual prowess in a character and villains always seem to love classical music. In *A Clockwork Orange* (1972), protagonist Alex's favorite composer is Ludwig van Beethoven, whose 9th Symphony features heavily in the film. In a key scene of *Silence of the Lambs* (1991), Hannibal Lecter (Anthony Hopkins) enjoys a piano version of Johann Sebastian Bach's Goldberg Variations, BWV 988 (originally written for harpsichord). Alexandra (Sigourney Weaver) receives a private performance of Brahms's String Quartet No. 1 in C minor, Op. 51, No. 1 in Marvel's *Defenders* (2017; season 1, episode 2).

Used for Character Association

Classical music can help refine a character and paint them in a sympathetic light. In *Philadelphia* (1993), terminally ill Andrew Beckett (Tom Hanks) welcomes his lawyer Joe Miller (Denzel Washington) to his home. He plays him a recording of Maria Callas singing "La mamma morta" ("They killed my mother"), an aria from act 3 of the 1896 opera "Andrea Chénier" by Umberto Giordano. Beckett knows the aria very well and becomes increasingly emotional as the recording progresses. In the eyes of the audience, he is made to look frail and deserving of sympathy. To Miller, the moment adds to visible alienation, sharpening the contrast of beauty and high culture in the music versus down-to-earth, no-nonsense prejudice in the lawyer. The episode "Take Shelter" from Marvel's *Defenders* (2017; season 1, episode 2) begins with an

Licensing Existing Music **139**

opening fight montage during the Hand's attack on the Royal Dragon restaurant, underscored with Brahms's Symphony No. 1 in C minor, Op. 68. The rousing piece of music at once amplifies the visceral intensity of this opening montage, and also brings a degree of polish and elegance to the overall experience.

Choice of Music Motivated by the Story

- *Shine* (1996) is a biopic of pianist David Helfgott (Geoffrey Rush), who suffered a mental breakdown and spent years in institutions. The compilation score contains a potpourri of different classical pieces.
- In *La tourneuse de pages* (*The Page Turner*, 2006), Mélanie (Déborah François) takes revenge on Ariane (Catherine Frot), a classical pianist who overcomes performance anxiety. There are some inspired music choices that highlight Mélanie's anxiety.
- In *Mission: Impossible—Rogue Nation* (2015), the aria "Nessun Dorma" ("None Shall Sleep") from the final act of Giacomo Puccini's opera "Turandot" features heavily. There is an extended segment in the Wiener Staatsoper (Vienna State Opera) in which Ethan Hunt (Tom Cruise) stops an assassination from taking place during the aria. This particular music usage and plot device was almost certainly inspired by:
- Hitchcock's *The Man Who Knew Too Much* (1956), in which an assassination is also about to take place during a concert. The climactic scene at the end of the film takes place at the Royal Albert Hall during a performance of Arthur Benjamin's "Storm Clouds Cantata," conducted by Bernard Herrmann. Herrmann, who also composed the original score for the film, extended Benjamin's work to make it fit the 12-minute sequence. Remarkably, this entire segment takes place without dialogue, from the beginning of the performance until the climax, when Doris Day screams to distract the assassin. Watch out for the timpani player miming.

New Arrangement of Classical Music to Better Serve the Project

- *Amadeus* (1984) depicts the rivalry between Wolfgang Amadeus Mozart (Tom Hulce) and Antonio Salieri (F. Murray Abraham). Mozart's music was adapted to fit the narrative and dramatic requirements of the film.
- For *Die Hard* (1988), composer Michael Kamen chose to adapt the "Ode to Joy," the main tune from Beethoven's 9th Symphony in D minor,

140 Licensing Existing Music

Op. 125 ("Choral") as a theme for German villain Hans Gruber (Alan Rickman) (another villain who loves classical music!), highlighting the character's eloquence and sophistication.

Original Music Posing as "Classical Music"

Newly composed music can sometimes better serve the moment-to-moment narrative requirements of a project. If narrative logic and other aesthetic considerations nevertheless require classical music, original scores sometimes take on the guise of classical music:

- For *The Red Violin* (1999), John Corigliano's Academy Award winning score, featuring soloist Joshua Bell, stands in as traditional/classical music through the ages.
- *Pride & Prejudice* (2005) features original music by Dario Marianelli, notably piano pieces that have a purist classical flavor.
- For *The Soloist* (2009), Dario Marianelli composed original music in the place of classical music the talented cellist might play.

Jazz

What Is It?

By some considered the only "truly American" art form, jazz notionally encompasses a hugely diverse set of musical traditions, now so broad it may be verging on unhelpful. There are numerous sub-genres (ragtime, swing, bebop, Latin jazz, free jazz, etc.) that are more or less clearly defined. There are also different types of ensembles that perform jazz, including solo instruments, trios, quartets, big band, with or without a vocalist, and *a cappella* vocal groups. Rather than thinking of jazz as a style, during a creative conversation regarding "jazz" music, it will be more helpful to refer to specific artists and their work.

Buyer Beware

There is a strong performance and interpretative component to jazz, so different renditions by different artists can vary drastically in instrumentation, style, and tempo. Improvisation is also a big part of jazz performance, and a soloist will play something different every time. Therefore, with jazz standards, it is often useful to try to identify a specific recording rather than just the name of a piece or even an artist.

Licensing

In traditional jazz, one often refers to "standards" which have been performed and recorded by numerous artists over the years (<u>Autumn Leaves</u>—listen to the three different versions in the Listening Companion—<u>All of Me</u>, <u>Mack the Knife</u>, and many others). These are widely known tunes that may or may not be under copyright (it is important to check). For licensing, clearances must be sought for the composition (where applicable) and the master audio recording of a particular rendition. Some very early jazz recordings, often on wax cylinders or shellac, are no longer protected by copyright. There are several public archives, notably in the US, that look after these recordings and make them available to the public. These archives provide information on the terms of usage, including synchronization licenses, on their respective websites. It should be noted that the sound quality of these very early recordings is not always very good.

Dos and Don'ts

If jazz is to be used as source music and performed on-screen, then only the composition must be licensed and a new recording subsequently created for the project. **Do** pre-record jazz tunes (including any improvised solos, where applicable) and then have musicians mime on set. If you let jazz musicians play and improvise live on set, recording clean audio can be a problem, as well as music continuity between different improvised takes.

Jazz in Sync

There are times when the use of jazz is clearly implied, even required by the underlying story. **Biopics** of jazz musicians are one obvious example, including *Miles Ahead* (2015), which explores the life and music of trumpet legend Miles Davis (played by Don Cheadle, who also directed the film); *Born to Be Blue* (2015) about the trumpeter, singer, and style icon Chet Baker (Ethan Hawke); and *Bird* (1988) about saxophonist Charlie Parker (Clint Eastwood, also directing).

142 Licensing Existing Music

Other films deal with **jazz as an historical and cultural phenomenon**, including *The Cotton Club* (1984), about a famous night club in Harlem; *Round Midnight* (1986), set in 1950s New York and focusing on the fictional character Dale Turner (Dexter Gordon), a saxophone player struggling with alcoholism and drug abuse; and *Swing Kids* (1993), in which a group of youths in Nazi Germany listen to banned American swing music. For *Whiplash* (2014), composer Justin Hurwitz adapted existing pieces and wrote some new music for big band in a jazz idiom.

The 2011 video game *L.A. Noir* draws on jazz as an **effective tone-setter** for a plot set in 1947 Los Angeles. The original jazz score by Andrew Hale and Simon Hale is complemented by over 30 licensed jazz pieces by Louis Armstrong, Ella Fitzgerald, Billie Holiday, and others.

Characterization and Cultural References

As with classical music, jazz may be used to portray and frame a character in a certain way. In *The Talented Mr. Ripley* (1999), Tom Ripley (Matt Damon) pretends to love jazz in order to befriend Dickie Greenleaf (Jude Law) and Marge Sherwood (Gwyneth Paltrow). In Disney's animated feature *Aristocats* (1970), laid-back alley cat Thomas O'Malley (Phil Harris) is a passionate jazz musician. Living a musician's life without rules and responsibilities, his laid-back character is in stark contrast with the posh Duchess and her three kittens. In *Jerry Maguire* (1996), Chad the Nanny (Todd Louiso) lectures Jerry Maguire (Tom Cruise) on jazz and comes across as pretentious, snobbish, perhaps somewhat psychotic. In *As Good As It Gets* (1998), Melvin Udall (Jack Nicholson) performs a jazzy rendition of Eric Idle's "Always Look on the Bright Side of Life" (from *Monty Python's Life of Brian* (1979)) at the piano. The fact that Melvin plays the piano so well adds depth to his character, the quirky choice of song at the same time suggesting a sense of humor that has not yet been apparent in him and making for a light-hearted moment of bonding between him and the neighbor's dog (for which he is performing in the first place).

Traditional and Folk Music of Different Cultures

What Is It?

Depending on the home culture of a project, there may be cultural references, including with music, that will feel "local" or "foreign." The term "world music" in the Western cultural sphere is often associated with a notional collection of non-Western music cultures. In a globalized world and with increasingly internationalized media production, this vague and wholesale outlook on global music traditions is no longer useful. It is better to make specific reference to music of countries, cultures, tribes, etc.

Buyer Beware

Media creators have long drawn inspiration from music cultures other than their own. When a project is set in a particular country or cultural sphere, music will often be expected to reflect this. Thorough research, perhaps supported by a music researcher, the music supervisor and/or the composer should inform the use of existing music or the creation of newly composed music that adapts or borrows from the respective musical culture at hand. In past practice, project owners have too often neglected musical integrity and truthfulness when it comes to musical references and quotations. In a globalized world, this is no longer good enough. Regardless of whether audiences will notice the difference, a project will demonstrate greater creative integrity if the use of traditional and folk music (licensed or adapted) evidences understanding of the source musical culture and its musical idiosyncrasies.

Licensing

A lot of traditional and folk music is centuries old so that copyright and other concepts of authorship and ownership may not apply. Due diligence is required when vetting the origin of a piece of music. In some cases, the absence of a structured music industry means establishing authorship and copyright ownership is not always easy. Obtaining a synchronization license for existing recordings may prove impossible for lack of reliable contacts. Nevertheless, this does not excuse you from trying. Always set aside appropriate resources to pay for clearances in due course. Local performers may perform traditional pieces that have been passed down through generations. Recording and incorporating this music can enrich a project in the right circumstances. Obtaining existing recordings of traditional and folk music may not always be easy, as a recording industry may not exist in the particular locality. A new recording may be the only way to capture that music. Local musicians need to be found, hired, and recorded. The reward for the project will be a pristine recording of a desired piece of traditional music. Any musicians that are involved in providing newly recorded music need to be compensated appropriately. Occasionally, their work may constitute a new

144 Licensing Existing Music

composition of which they are the authors. A composer credit and synchronization license will be necessary in this case. In film and games production, there has conventionally been a tendency to adapt and emulate traditional music for a project rather than using actual traditional music. There may be many reasons for this, including lack of access to local musicians, or lack of time and resources to obtain usable recordings.

Dos and Don'ts

Do respect local traditions and try to understand the background of a musical culture: Is it appropriate to record this music? Will local musicians be happy to have their music featured in a multimedia project? Are there cultural or religious considerations that might restrict the use of that particular music in a different context?

Don't misappropriate or misquote traditional or folk music (e.g., playing funeral music during a party scene). Any musical adaptation should avoid clichés (think, for example, of the poor imitations of Native American music in the past).

Traditional and Folk Music in Sync

There are many films whose scores draw on traditional music influences and make inspired choices when implementing these influences in an original score:

- *The Year of Living Dangerously* (1982)—Maurice Jarre's score incorporates Javanese gamelan (Djakarta and Poverty and Misery).
- *Kundun* (1997)—Philip Glass's minimalist score alludes to Tibetan gongs and throat singing (Sand Mandala).
- *The Motorcycle Diaries* (2004)—Gustavo Santaolalla's guitar scores jibes with the South American road trip setting.
- *The Darjeeling Limited* (2007)—The compilation score comprises recordings by several Indian recording artists such as Satyajit Ray and Ali Akbar Khan, including songs from Bollywood and Merchant Ivory films.
- *Love in the Time of Cholera* (2007)—composer Antonio Pinto taps in to Columbian musical traditions for this love story (Hay Amores).
- *Hotel Rwanda* (2005)—Besides newly composed underscore, the film also features music by African artists Dorothee & Ben Munyaneza (Rwanda), Yvonne Chaka Chaka (South Africa), and Bernard Kabanda Ssalongo (Uganda).

- *Vicky Cristina Barcelona* (2008)—The compilation score for this film features a number of Spanish artists, including the song Barcelona by Giulia y los Tellarini.
- *Babel* (2006)—This film contains an eclectic array of music: Gustavo Santaolalla's Academy Award winning score, a number of tracks by Japanese composer Ryuichi Sakamoto (notably his minimalist Bibo No Aozora in the closing segment), and further pieces to indicate the different geographic settings of the multiple plot strands.
- *The Throne* (*Sado*, 2015)—Jun-seok Bang's original score for this historical drama was in part inspired by Korean traditional music—for example, the recurring recitative and drumming that punctuate the narrative structure.

5.5 Using Production Music

Production Music, also called stock music or **library music**, is recorded music produced and owned by production music companies, available for licensing to customers for use in film, television, radio, advertising, and any other recorded media. Clients can browse through extensive and comprehensive catalogues that contain music of just about any style, instrumentation, duration, etc. These catalogues are indexed and cross-referenced to allow clients to search for music without requiring expert knowledge. For example, searching for "romantic piano" will readily produce a selection of relevant recordings. Finding production music is very easy. Universal Publishing Production Music, EMI Production Music, De Wolfe Music, Warner/Chappell Production Music, WestOne, and Audio Network are just a few of the many established companies. These companies all employ large teams that will assist prospective clients with **music searches**, interfacing with music researchers, music supervisors, and other creative personnel on the client side. An unlimited number of tracks may be downloaded and previewed in full-quality audio and often in variations (full length, cut-downs, stems, different instrumentations). Only once the right track is found does the client pay, and for that track only.

Fast, Easy, and Cheap

Clients may choose to use production music because it is easy to access and available immediately. Cutting the lead-time for music can make the difference of meeting a post-production deadline or not. The huge variety of styles available, paired with the high production value of library music, means clients get music tracks that sound as good as, if not better than, anything they could have specially commissioned. The relatively low cost of licensing means less pressure on the music budget. When using library music, clients pay a fixed and **non-negotiable synchronization fee**. The price is determined by the type of usage, territory, duration of music used, length of license agreement, etc. Licensing production music for a student short film may cost only a few dollars. Licensing a track for use in a feature film or film trailer can cost several thousand dollars. However, licensing fees are significantly lower than negotiable synchronization fees for commercially released tracks. Furthermore, compared to bespoke music, library tracks are almost always cheaper because the client will not incur added costs for commissioning or music recording. The use of library tracks is economical and good value for money. In some circumstances, using production music makes plain sense—for example, if a film with a very low post-production budget requires a source cue playing on a radio that would otherwise be expensive to produce. Aiming for 1940s jazz, say, using a library track is almost certainly the easiest and cheapest way to get a usable track in place. The alternative would be to find a composer or jazz ensemble to write, arrange, perform, and record a track that emulates a 1940s style: All of which takes time and costs much more than the statutory sync license for the use of a non-exclusive library track. Sometimes even Hollywood blockbusters will use production music: In *The Dark Knight* (2008), when Lucius Fox meets Bruce Wayne in a public pedestrian passageway in Hong Kong, the innocuous music in the background is "Bamboo Rafting" by Miklosh, a track published by JW Media Music, a London-based production music company.

Value-for-Money

Great skill and care are invested in production music and the quality and production value of these library tracks is exceedingly high. Production music companies hire some of the best composers in the field, the best session musicians, record in the best studios, and work with eminent recording and mastering engineers.

Ready-Made and Off-the-Rack

One of the reasons production music companies can offer music at relatively low licensing rates is that production music is licensed on a strictly **non-exclusive** basis. The same track may be used by any number of clients, for a wide range of projects, globally, and at the same time. There is nothing bespoke or unique about using production music, because the same library track can and will be used in dozens if not hundreds of projects. A purchasable commodity, production music should be used only when there is a good creative reason or compelling budgetary concerns. An experienced music supervisor can help find suitable production music tracks for a project, ensuring the music fits the requirements agreed by the creative stakeholders. Licensed production music tracks may complement other licensed tracks, or be placed among newly composed cues. It is up to the creative team to carefully judge whether the use of production music is the best way to go, for each project. Cost will always be a factor, but there are creative, narrative, and dramatic considerations to be taken into account also. Just because a solution is quick and cheap, it may not be the best solution, or one of creative integrity. Using production music can cut out the voice of a composer who would bring to a project their creative intuition and sensibilities. An original score will be more than the sum of its individual tracks. Music that is composed specially for a project can work towards a greater sense of unity, character, or any other attribute that the creative stakeholders agree to pursue. Using ready-made tracks precludes collaborative creativity that might lead to unexpected results.

Takeaways

- Production Music is recorded music produced and owned by production music companies, available for licensing on a non-exclusive basis.
- When using library music, clients pay an affordable, fixed, and non-negotiable synchronization fee.
- Production music is easy to access and available immediately.
- There is nothing bespoke or unique about using production music.
- A purchasable commodity, production music should be used only when there is a good creative reason or compelling budgetary concerns.

Further Reading

Jeongwon, J. *Opera as Soundtrack*. London: Ashgate, 2013.
Jones, B.J. *George Lucas—A Life*. London: Hachette UK, 2016. Includes further details about the making o f *American Graffiti*.

Notes

1 Brian Jay Jones. *George Lucas—A Life*. London: Hachette UK, 2016. Kindle edition, Part I: Hope 1944–1973, 5. American Graffiti 1971–1973.
2 See also https://www.rollingstone.com/music/news/the-oral-history-of-the-wayne-s-world-bohemian-rhapsody-scene-20151130, accessed 5 March 2018.
3 https://www.youtube.com/watch?v=CmRih_VtVAs, accessed 8 February 2018.
4 https://www.timeout.com/newyork/film/mike-nichols-on-the-graduate, accessed 8 February 2018.

Commissioning Original Music **6**

6.1 Introduction

This chapter addresses key considerations that pertain to the use of original music in a project, be it instrumental music or songs. There may be any number of reasons why project owners prefer original music to existing music, and pros and cons should be weighed up carefully:

Pros

- Commissioning original music leads to a new creative asset that is bespoke.
- Exciting creative possibilities arise from commissioning original music and collaboratively working with a composer towards the finished score.
- Original music can be tailored flexibly to serve the project needs.
- Original music may bring added benefits for branding of the project and audience buy-in.

Cons

- Original music is not available immediately.
- Original music may sometimes require a substantial budget.
- Commissioning original music can be more expensive than licensing existing music.

150 Commissioning Original Music

- Using original music may not offer the potentially bankable association with an established star or well-known piece of music.

There are key benefits to commissioning original media music, including potential for collaborative creativity and the possibility of arriving at unique scoring solutions. Having original music versus licensed existing music in a project is akin to ordering custom-tailored couture versus off-the rack ready-to-wear clothing. Although commissioning original music can be relatively more expensive than licensing existing music, the creative rewards of bespoke scoring choices will make the expenditure worthwhile. Creative lead-times may be longer than with existing music, but this gestational period allows you to experiment and can lead to compelling outcomes (see also Chapter 7). Some filmmakers think of original music as a purchasable commodity, much like licensed music. This is a misconception. Media composers are creative artisans, not servants. Anyone hoping for a creative one-way street, where requirements are spelled out and music then licensed to spec, should opt for existing music. Allowing the media composer to contribute as a storyteller brings creative potential and risks, which bold media creators will embrace and celebrate. Exciting opportunities arise from "the new," creating something that was not there before. Collaboratively seeking out expressive possibilities, you may sometimes choose the obvious, or opt not to do the obvious. The inherently referential nature of media music means that, if it is to be effective, it can only be so "original" (see also Chapter 1). It is always advisable to recognize industry conventions, local traditions, and audience tastes. But, with these in mind, you can, then, choose to pursue new modes of expression. These may be found in:

- new approaches to audiovisual storytelling paired with conventional music (new filming technique, editing style);
- new approaches to music itself (innovative compositional technique, instrumentation, form);
- new approaches to the combination of music with audiovisual media (e.g., an unexpected pairing of styles, incongruous juxtaposition of fast/ slow materials, interplay of music and sound design, etc.).

Creative Possibilities Arising from Original Music

Countless films, TV shows, and video games have been elevated by original scores, often subverting conventions. Media creators and composers will have their respective sets of references, which should be discussed to inform your

Commissioning Original Music **151**

collaboration. To flag just a few examples: Alex Garland's *Ex Machina* (2014) draws on original music in powerful ways. Composers Ben Salisbury and Geoff Barrow started working from the script, and, over ten months, accompanied the film throughout its production and post-production. The score is one of the very few film scores that "lies" to the audience because it paints the android protagonist in a sympathetic light. This is a bold choice that could only be made because the creative stakeholders aligned on their outlook for the project. Scoring *Breaking Bad* (2008–2013), Chris Porter made a compelling contribution with his music, creating the sonic fabric of his scores through experimentation, at both the expressive and the technical levels, using vintage instruments and unusual objects (e.g., mixing bowls) to record the music. Denis Villeneuve's *Sicario* (2015) has an unsettling score by Jóhann Jóhannsson. The cue <u>The Beast</u>, heard during the helicopter shot of SUVs racing down a road, relies on low-frequency pulses, mimicking the sub-bass of a helicopter rotor, nausea- and fear-inducing in the narrative context of the scene.

Among the huge number of other examples one could mention here, a few stand out for their fascinating and ambitious use of original music, at the service of an engaging narrative:

- *Arrival* (2016)—Jóhann Jóhannsson's haunting and atmospheric score greatly enhances this opaque narrative.
- *Birdman or (The Unexpected Virtue of Ignorance)* (2014)—Drums!
- *Mr. Turner* (2014)—Gary Yershon surprises with the experimental tone and quirky instrumentation of his score, both incongruous with the time period depicted in the film but motivated by the main character's exploration of an increasingly abstract painting style.
- *TRON: Legacy* (2010)—Daft Punk's sleek and impactful dance tracks meet a symphony orchestra.
- *Micmacs* (2009)—Raphaël Beau's energetic score for this zany comedy uses scrap metal and other objects, in keeping with the story set on a garbage dump.
- *Requiem for a Dream* (2000)—Clint Mansell provides an unforgiving minimalist score of synthesizers and digitally processed string quartet score for this devastating film.
- *Lola Rennt (Run Lola Run*, 1998)—Tom Tykwer's masterpiece with dance music stomping the beat to music video-style editing.
- *Witness* (1984)—Maurice Jarre's bold synthesizer score accompanies a story set in a low-tech Amish community.
- *The Draughtsman Contract* (1982)—Michael Nyman's score introduced minimalism to mainstream film scoring.

152 Commissioning Original Music

Adaptations of Existing Music for an Original Score

Occasionally, a story may require that existing music be adapted into an original score.

- *Amadeus* (1984) depicts the rivalry between Wolfgang Amadeus Mozart (Tom Hulce) and Antonio Salieri (F. Murray Abraham). Mozart's music was adapted to fit the narrative and dramatic requirements of the film.
- For *Black Swan* (2010), Clint Mansell adapted music from Tchaikovsky's "Swan Lake," deconstructing the score into a nightmarish sound world.
- Benjamin Wallfish and Hans Zimmer adapted Elgar's "Enigma Variations" for Christopher Nolan's *Dunkirk* (2017), an apt choice given the association of the music with Remembrance Sunday in the UK.

Takeaways

- Weigh up the pros and cons of newly commissioned music for the project at hand.
- Creative possibilities arise from original music and collaboratively working with a composer towards the finished score.
- Original music can be tailored flexibly to serve the project needs.
- Original music is not immediately available.
- Original music may require a substantial music budget.

6.2 Introducing Musical Themes

Characters, Situations, Objects

Newly commissioned scores can contain musical themes, also called **leitmotifs**. These often come in the form of a **recognizable melody**, but may instead be a **series of chords**, an **instrumental color**, or even a **rhythmic figure** (e.g., recurring drum patterns in the *Terminator* franchise). Having musical themes recur throughout a narrative is a tried and tested storytelling device in audiovisual media. It was first introduced by the early pioneers of film music in the Hollywood Golden Era and borrowed from European opera and concert music. In order to establish a link between a theme and a character, situation, or object, the musical theme needs first to be presented in the presence of that character, situation, or object, or while reference is being made to them / it in dialogue or voice-over. The theme may subsequently represent the character, situation, or object in their absence. Musical themes work exceedingly well as storytelling tools. They are also great for characterization: Who in the story is the hero, the villain, the wise mentor, the challenger, the love interest, the seductress with ulterior motives, the fool, etc.? The actual musical language employed to accompany different types of **characters** has changed over time. One may compare, for example, the very different musical treatment of the same character in different decades:

Robin Hood

- *The Adventures of Robin Hood* (1938), <u>Main Title</u> (Erich Wolfgang Korngold).
- <u>*Robin Hood Prince of Thieves*</u> (1991) (Michael Kamen).
- *Robin Hood* (2010), <u>Fate Has Smiled upon Us</u> (Marc Streitenfeld).

Batman

- *Batman* (1966 TV series) <u>Batman Theme</u> (Neil Hefti).
- *Batman* (1989), <u>The Batman Theme</u> (Danny Elfman).
- *The Dark Knight* (2008), <u>A Dark Knight</u> (Hans Zimmer).
- *The Lego Batman Movie* (2017), <u>Who's the Bat(Man)</u> (Patrick Stump).

Musical themes can also help identify **objects** of desire (love interest, a prize or trophy, a treasure) and objects that present a threat or challenges (weapons, potions, dangerous inventions, spaceships). What objects are the characters chasing or hoping to find, and/or what are they afraid of or fighting or trying to neutralize?

Musical themes, finally, may also come to represent **situations** (a war, an impeding battle, a planned escape, an act of liberation, a victory, a defeat), commonly picking up on the experiential aspect of how characters are feeling in the respective situation in the narrative (experiencing hope, despair, the effects of injustice, etc.).

Monothematic Scores

Some original scores are **monothematic**, with only one musical theme recurring throughout, while all other music is incidental and non-thematic. Bernard

154 Commissioning Original Music

Herrmann's score for *Citizen Kane* (1941) is a great example of a monothematic score. The Kane theme starts with a recognizable musical phrase of four notes in low woodwinds, first heard in the Prelude. It then returns throughout the film and represents the conflicted main character. John Williams's score for *Jaws* (1975) is also monothematic, forever announcing the looming threat of the toothy predator in the waters off Amity Island. With maximum economy, Williams uses just two alternating notes to build his theme (Main Title and First Victim), varying the instrumentation and dynamics to great visceral effect. In both *Citizen Kane* and *Jaws*, the sole recurring theme is introduced at the very start of the film, notably in the absence of the respective main character, and then repeated often, in different situations and sometimes in different musical arrangements. Audiences may not pay focused attention to these musical themes but they may be affected by them at the subliminal level nonetheless. The score for Garth Davis's *Lion* (2016), by Dustin O'Halloran and Hauschka, is another example of a monothematic score. The theme comprises a chord progression that recurs throughout the film in different guises. It can be quite clearly heard in the River cue early on in the film.

Monothematic scores may draw on a musical theme derived from a theme song: In Kevin Reynolds's *Robin Hood: Prince of Thieves* (1991) the musical main theme picks up from the song (Everything I Do) I Do It for You by composer Michael Kamen and singer Bryan Adams. James Horner's score for James Cameron's *Titanic* (1997) quoted material from the theme song My Heart Will Go On, which was co-written by the composer.

Polythematic Scores

In media formats where the narrative unfolds over extended periods of time, including feature films, episodic television, and video games, there is ample scope for the introduction and development of multiple musical themes. Bernard Herrmann's dramatically charged orchestral score for Hitchcock's *Vertigo* (1958) contains several musical themes:

- A binary set of unsettling chords dedicated to the titular fear of heights experienced by John "Scotty" Ferguson (James Stewart) (Prelude and Rooftop);
- a theme for Madeleine (Scotty Trails Madeleine);
- a theme for Carlotta (Carlotta's Portrait);
- a sweeping love theme (Scène d'Amour).

Not all musical themes need to be prominent, or even particularly noticeable. Some can be given less weight and importance by the way they are introduced and then used throughout the narrative. In Christopher Nolan's *The Dark Knight* (2008), composers Hans Zimmer and James Newton Howard provide six main themes that feature prominently and often throughout the film:[1]

- "Batflaps" (for Batman).
- "Batman Theme" (for Batman).
- "Joker Theme" (for the Joker, comprising a nasty buzzing tone).
- "Joker Triumphant" (for the Joker, a series of percussive stabs that celebrate the villain's successes).
- "Stranger Motif" (for the Joker, heard whenever he unveils an evil scheme).
- "Harvey Dent Theme" (a dignified theme for District Attorney Harvey Dent).

In addition, the composer provides three secondary themes that feature less heavily: "Anarchy Motif" (for the Joker), "Love Theme" (for Bruce and Rachel), and "Mourning" (for Lieutenant Gordon, seemingly, and Rachel, actually).

For HBO's *Game of Thrones* (2011–), composer Ramin Djawadi composed a main title theme as well as numerous themes for key characters, the major houses, locations, and the dragons. The musical material plays an important part in helping this epic narrative cohere. For HBO's *Westworld* (2016–), the same composer provided a recurring main title theme and leitmotifs for the Man in Black, the town of Sweetwater, and for the gradual awakening of the robots (an arrangement of Claude Debussy's "Rêverie"), among others.

Main Title Themes

... In Feature Films

In the past, feature films normally opened with an **opening main title** or **overture**, performed by a large orchestra. The film's title would be announced by use of a title card and some key credits would be listed, usually the lead creative personnel and the star actors. Main titles were effective in **building the audience's anticipation**, to emerge them in the film. The main title music, in conjunction with the visuals, helped indicate the film's genre and tone and might suggest geographic and historical placement. At the end of the main title, the audience would be suitably primed for the film. Main titles would often, though not always, contain musical material that later recurred in the

156 Commissioning Original Music

film, such as recurring musical themes. Occasionally, filmmakers would opt to precede the main title with a reel of action, notably in the *James Bond* and *Mission Impossible* franchises (the former featuring theme songs rather than a composed main title). These opening reels would throw the audience more immediately into the action.

Despite tried and tested benefits for audience bonding, the use of musical main titles or overtures has declined significantly in recent years. Only approximately one in five Hollywood films nowadays opens with a main title or overture. There may be several reasons for this trend: Firstly, purely orchestral scores in Hollywood films have declined in line with changing tastes. Music that draws on more contemporary and progressive styles of music and instrumentation may not lend itself to sustaining a prolonged opening title sequence. Secondly, memorable melodic themes have declined as well (try humming the theme of Marvel's *Avengers* franchise, as heard in the cue <u>Avengers Unite</u>), so that thematic material based on a melody—that would traditionally have been introduced in a main title—is no longer available. Thirdly, the use of a main title may feel old-fashioned. Audiences may find it far more exciting if the action starts immediately, without delay from a main title, and is then not interrupted again, à la *Mission Impossible*, by a main title.

The choice whether to have a musical opener is one of style and preference on the part of the filmmakers. Tim Burton's *Batman* (1989) opened with a rousing musical overture, which to today's audiences may feel dated and heavy-handed. By contrast, in Christopher Nolan's *The Dark Knight* (2008), the main title is replaced by a very brief visual of the Batman logo, engulfed in blue flames, and accompanied with the beginning of a music cue that carries on into the bank robbery sequence.

... In Television

Main title themes also used to be popular in television, to draw viewers' attention to the program at hand, away from domestic distractions. Besides **signaling the beginning of a program**, television main title themes also acted as "sonic logos" that **anchor viewer identification** and, alongside title cards and weekly recurring visuals, primed the audience emotionally for the program to come. Traditionally, television titles were performed by an orchestra. Over time, in line with changing tastes and stylistic trends, television music moved towards a more contemporary sound. By the early 1980s, pop-flavored scores in television often were still melodic, despite their groove-driven edge, with memorable themes played by electric guitars or synthesizers. Television shows including *Magnum, P.I.* (1980–1988), *Knight Rider* (1982–1986), and *Airwolf* (1984–1987) featured catchy main title themes. Numerous TV themes were widely familiar and entered the popular culture domain. Many viewers could readily recall the sleek neo-Americana introductions for *Dallas* (1978–1991, 2012–2014) or *Star Trek—The Next Generation* (1987–1994), and the funky and heart-warming theme for *Alf* (1986–1990). By the mid-1990s, however, many television themes had been cut down to just a few seconds, a trend countered by only a few successful theme songs: *Friends* (1994–2004, title song "I'll Be There for You" by The Rembrandts) and *Ally McBeal* (1997–2002, Vonda Shepard's "Searching' My Soul"), *That '70s Show* (1998–2006, "In the Street" by Cheap Trick), and *Big Bang Theory* (2007, "The Big Bang Theory Theme" by The Barenaked Ladies).

Elsewhere, television themes disappeared nearly altogether. The popular comedy *Scrubs* (2001–2010) used only a short out-of-context phrase from a longer song as its opening theme. *Ugly Betty* (2006–2010), otherwise plastered with wall-to-wall music, employed only a short musical signature and brief visual as a title. The successful *Glee* (2009–2015) only featured a single sung chord on a title card that shows for less than three seconds. *Modern Family* (2009–) also has a very short opening title. On the whole, extended main titles in network television are a thing of the past.

One could argue that TV main title themes used to distance the audience from the respective program, reminding them that they were watching a constructed piece of fiction. Perhaps excessively repeated previews throughout the week leading up to a show's broadcast ensured audiences needed less priming for programs they had committed to up front. For pre-invested viewers, the title theme was perhaps no longer needed to alert or hook them. Additionally, pressured broadcasting schedules required shows to cut down content duration to make time for more advertising. For its fifth season, each episode of *Mad Men* (2007–2015) was cut from 47 minutes to 45 minutes to allow more time for commercials. To maximize *plot* running time within the allocated slot, it makes sense to cut down the duration of the opening title sequence, which was traditionally accompanied by music: The themes for the network television shows *The Simpsons* (1989–) and *Desperate Housewives* (2004–2012) were shortened after the early episodes.

Shows on ad-free pay TV (such as HBO and Showtime) and streaming services (Netflix, Amazon) have held on to their main titles more successfully. This may be because, firstly, there is no revenue-driven pressure on the running time of each episode. Secondly, there may be aesthetic considerations at play. High-quality cinematic television, perhaps starting in the late 1990s, picked up many of the stylistic attributes of feature films. Shows including *The*

158 Commissioning Original Music

Sopranos (1999–2007) and *Six Feet Under* (2001–2005) held on to their opening sequences for the duration of their run (a song in the former, composed score in the latter). More recently, *Game of Thrones* (2011–) and *Westworld* (2016–) have featured appealing and quite traditional main title themes by composer Ramin Djawadi. On streaming platforms, main title sequences are as popular as ever, including Jeff Russo's 100-second theme for *Star Trek Discovery* (2017–; incidentally, recorded with a sizeable orchestra) and the opening titles for all of Marvel's *Defenders* shows on Netflix to date.

... In Video Games

Video games have always drawn on music to enhance user experience and gameplay. The role and function of music was initially **adopted from linear visual media**, notably film. Opening titles in video games serve the same functions as their cousins in linear media: To set the tone and prime the player for gameplay. Technological limitations in early video games resulted in relatively simple music. The number of chips dedicated to music production in the respective games console dictated how elaborate music could be. This did not, however stop composers from creating some highly engaging and memorable themes, including for *Pac-Man* (1980), *Donkey Kong* (1981), *Super Mario Bros.* (1985), *Castlevania* (1986) and *The Legend of Zelda* (1986), *Final Fantasy* (1987), *Sonic the Hedgehog* (Green Hill Zone) (1991), *Mortal Kombat* (1992), and *Doom* (1993). The introduction of progressively more powerful games consoles and engines gave rise to sound chips and sound cards capable of producing better-quality audio, including music. By the late 1990s, more and more computer games used music recorded in digital audio, giving composers the opportunity to record more-ambitious music. Computer game scores, especially on high-budget "AAA" titles, are commonly recorded with a live orchestra. A-list film composers have been attracted to the medium due to relatively large music budgets (in times when budgets were shrinking in film and television). Opening titles for games now rival feature film main titles in scale and musical ambition, including, among countless others, *Diablo* (1996), *Halo* (2001), *Kingdom of Hearts* (2002), *Fallout 3* (2008), *Dead Space* (2008), *Call of Duty: Modern Warfare* (2010), *Elder Scrolls V: Skyrim* (2011), and *Far Cry 3* (2012).

Studio Logos and Broadcaster Stings

Film and games studios and television stations commonly place logos at the beginning and/or end of a film, game, show, commercial break, etc., and these logos are usually accompanied by music. Music used in studio and station signature logos is designed, firstly, to **communicate brand identity** and solicit consumer loyalty and, secondly, to **prime the audience** for an enjoyable entertainment experience. The iconic **fanfares** for Twentieth Century Fox (Alfred Newman), Universal Pictures (Jerry Goldsmith and others), Walt Disney Pictures (using arrangements of "When You Wish upon a Star," written for Disney's 1940 animated feature *Pinocchio* by Leigh Harline and Ned Washington, since 2006 heard as a new arrangement by Dave Metzger and Mark Mancina), and Marvel Studios (Michael Giacchino) are just a few of the best-known studio logos. Often recorded with a symphony orchestra, these logos are an expensive indulgence. However, since they are used across a studio's portfolio of releases, and often remain unchanged for many years, the up-front investment has a lasting benefit.

Virtually all broadcasters and streaming services present their logos in short **stings** that are accompanied by music, comprising a memorable series of a few notes (ABC, NBC) or even just a single chord or tone embedded in sound effects (HBO, Netflix). Careful planning goes into these stings, and each new version that may be commissioned from time to time. The **logo sting is a calling card** that:

- needs to make the respective broadcaster or streaming service appealing and entice audience loyalty;
- represents a company ethos, target audience (age group, subset of society);
- needs to be sufficiently distinctive to help differentiate the broadcaster or streaming service from its competitors;
- needs to exude confidence and competence;
- suggests high-quality content, perhaps alludes to style and grandeur;
- reflects local culture, perhaps patriotism.

So-called sonic branding, which draws on easily memorable and recognizable short series of notes and/or a distinctive sound world, is a marketing tool that is well understood and utilized in the media industries. Sonic branding has also found broader applications in marketing and advertising (one may, for example, think of the sonic identities of T-Mobile, Intel, Audi) that are beyond the scope of this book.

Musical Themes in Franchises

Multi-movie franchises are commercially driven enterprises that can span numerous films over extended time periods, sometimes many decades.

160 Commissioning Original Music

To ensure audience appeal and retention, franchise owners must weigh repetition against innovation, familiarity with novelty. For the purpose of audience engagement and franchise continuity, maintaining consistent musical themes across installments has proven effective. For example, the long-running *James Bond* series still uses the 007 theme first composed by Monty Norman in 1962, albeit in modernized guises through the decades. Multi-movie franchises may reuse only main themes that represent the franchise as a whole, as is the case with James Bond, whereas the other musical material is different in each film. Franchises may also have multiple themes that recur in several films. For example, there are more than 45(!) musical themes in the *Star Wars* franchise (for Princess Leia, Darth Vader, The Force, Rey, etc.). Not all of these themes will be consciously noticed and decoded by the audience. Nevertheless, they are utilized repeatedly and with consistency, offering a subliminal structuring device and an added layer to help support the complex narrative. Incidentally, *Star Wars* is one of the few long-running franchises that for the longest time had only one composer attached (John Williams), until Disney decided to produce spin-off movies that reside in the same fictional universe but tell stories off the main trajectory. The first of these, *Rogue One* (2016) was scored by Michael Giacchino.

It is understandable that franchise owners periodically will update and refresh the look and feel of their material. Franchises including *Terminator* (original theme, of which later only the drum pattern survived, by Brad Fiedel), *X-Men* (John Ottman, introduced in *X-Men 2*, 2003), *Mission Impossible* (Lalo Schifrin), *Superman* (John Williams), and *Star Trek* (original TV theme by Alexander Courage) have gone through various updates and reboots, often bringing in new writers, directors, producers, and composers. *X-Men* and *Mission Impossible* have retained their respective main theme relatively intact, but with updated arrangements and instrumentation to suit evolving tastes. *Superman* and *Star Trek* have taken different approaches following repeated reboots. The original theme for *Superman* (1978) by John Williams was set to be abandoned for the re-boot *Superman Returns* in 2006. But editor and composer John Ottman faced pressure from fans to bring back the old theme, and he gave in: The main title sequence reuses the same John Williams theme. Michael Giacchino established a new theme for *Star Trek* when J.J. Abrams re-launched the franchise in 2009. The composer remembers that he struggled at first to find an appropriate theme that he felt could live up to fans' expectations.[2] Following in the footsteps of eminent composers Alexander Courage, Jerry Goldsmith (who had composed some of the previous feature film scores), and Dennis McCarthy (who had scored *The Next Generation*) must have been a daunting challenge.

In recent years, computer game franchises have exceeded the commercial success of many film franchises, sometimes with hundreds of millions of units sold. *Final Fantasy, Need for Speed, FIFA, The Sims, Grand Theft Auto, Call of Duty, Assassin's Creed* are just a few of the top-selling video game franchises. It seems logical that game franchise will endeavor to emulate films in reusing and reiterating musical themes for audience bonding. Since technological advances in video games continue to push boundaries, the field has been less settled in terms of consistency of output and creative strategies.

Takeaways

- Musical themes, aka leitmotifs, can be attached to a character, object, or situation and, once introduced, can represent or recall that character, object, or situation in their absence.

- Some original scores are monothematic, containing a single theme; others are polythematic, containing many different themes.

- Main title themes in features films are an effective way to prime and engage the audience.

- In television, main titles signal the beginning of a show and anchor viewer identification.

- Music used in studio and station signature logos is designed, firstly, to communicate brand identity and solicit consumer loyalty and, secondly, to prime the audience for an enjoyable entertainment experience.

- Musical themes can recur across multiple installments in a multi-film or video game franchise.

6.3 Original Songs

Original songs have long been used in feature films and, to a lesser degree, in TV shows. Songs specially written for a project can serve a range of purposes. A so-called **theme song** can serve as a marketable asset that attracts audiences outside the cinema. If a named star can be brought on board to record the song, their star power will be an added bonus. Music streaming and album sales can be a **lucrative revenue stream** for film studios and publishers. A theme song may play on the radio weeks before the film is released, building up anticipation for the film. Songs can also provide a powerful **emotional hook** in the narrative, providing added experiential value and facilitating audience bonding. If it reiterates a musical theme heard throughout the film, a theme song can become an effective narrative asset. Original songs may also win awards, which is a valuable marketing tool. Original songs have a key advantage over licensed existing songs in that they can be tailor-made for the project at hand. The tone of the song, style of production, and the lyrics may all be designed to suit the project. Composers working on an original score may be involved in writing original songs for the same project. There are also professional songwriters that may join a project on a non-exclusive basis to work collaboratively with the writers and the composer to provide an original song or songs. Whereas in a musical songs are commonly performed by the characters, original songs in a non-musical will usually be non-diegetic music. Here are a few different scenarios in which one may encounter original songs in a project.

Theme Song Material Used as Part of Underscore

Parts of the theme song may be incorporated in the instrumental underscore. Quoting just a snippet of the theme song is a subtle way of subliminally exposing the audience to the theme song material without having to play the actual song multiple times.

- The main theme in Pixar's *Ratatouille* (2007, score and theme by Michael Giacchino) is a lighthearted waltz (Ratatouille Main Theme). The theme is featured in the theme song Le festin performed by French singer Camille during the closing credits. The song's lyrics tie in with story.
- The theme song from *Titanic* (1997) My Heart Will Go On was written by James Horner, who also composed the orchestral underscore (lyrics by Will Jennings). The musical opening of the song forms part of the orchestral theme that is reiterated throughout the film. The song became singer Celine Dion's biggest hit, and the biggest selling single of all time.
- The love theme in Michael Kamen's score for *Robin Hood: Prince of Thieves* (1991), played on the oboe when Robin Hood first discovers his feelings with Maid Marian, draws on the melody of the film's theme song (Everything I Do) I Do It for You, performed during the closing credits by Bryan Adams.

Theme Song Heard as Background in a Key Moment

The theme song may appear in a key moment as non-diegetic accompaniment. It can be less than subtle when the actual theme song appears during the narrative. On the other hand, such a placement can feel quite rewarding if the audience is emotionally invested.

- Diane Warren's rock ballad Don't Wanna Miss a Thing for *Armageddon* (1998) is heard when Ben Affleck embraces Liv Tyler near the end of the film. Performed by Aerosmith, the song was number one in many countries and became the band's biggest commercial hit.
- The iconic training montage in *Rocky IV* (1985) is accompanied by Eye of the Tiger, performed by the band Surviver.
- The song Saturday Night Fever in *Saturday Night Fever* (1977) is one of several original songs by the Bee Gees, prominently featured during one of the character's disco outings. The soundtrack is one of the biggest-selling soundtrack albums of all time.

Theme Song Heard during the Opening or Closing Credits

Positioning the theme song outside of the narrative, either immediately before or after, gives the audience a chance to pay focused attention to the music.

- The *James Bond* franchise has consistently banked on Norman Monty's Bond theme, arranged by John Barry, who scored eleven of the films. After an opening action reel, each film features an original song during the opening credits. These theme songs, first started with From Russia with Love (1963), titular song by Lionel Bart (sung by Matt Monro), followed by the beloved Goldfinger (1964), performed by Shirley Bassey. Adele's Skyfall (2012) was the first Bond song to win an Academy award for "Best Song," followed by Sam Smith's Writing's on The Wall from *Spectre* (2015). Some of the world's biggest stars have written and recorded Bond songs over the decades (including Tom Jones, Duran Duran, A-ha, Tina Turner, Garbage, and Madonna).
- *Philadelphia* (1993) opens bleakly with Bruce Springsteen's Oscar-winning Streets of Philadelphia.
- Justin Timberlake's Can't Stop the Feeling from *Trolls* (2016) was a summer hit in its own right and probably brought the film to the attention of a much larger audience.

164 Commissioning Original Music

Original or Theme Song Performed by Characters

There are projects, including film and TV shows, that introduce musical numbers performed by characters within the diegesis but that nevertheless are not musicals. The distinction is a matter of balance: Whereby a one-off diegetic song performance does not make a project into a musical, multiple musical numbers might.

- In *The Man Who Knew Too Much* (1956), Doris Day's character is a retired professional singer. At two points in the film, she sings the Livingston and Evans song Que Sera, Sera (Whatever Will Be, Will Be), which won the 1956 Academy Award for "Best Song."
- In a poignant moment in *Magnolia* (1999), all the film's characters join together in singing Amiee Mann's understated ballad Wise up.
- Netflix's *Unbreakable Kimmy Schmidt* (2015–) uses original musical numbers to great comic effect, usually delivered by Titus Andromedon (played by Tituss Burgess).

Takeaways
- Original songs in a non-musical can provide emotional hooks for audience engagement.
- Original songs can unlock lucrative revenue streams.
- Original songs can be tailor-made for the project at hand.
- Composed underscore may draw musical material from the original theme song.
- The original theme song may be heard in the project during a key moment.
- The original theme song may be used during the opening or closing credits.
- Even in a non-musical, original and/or theme songs may be performed within the diegesis by characters.

6.4 Musicals

During Hollywood's Golden Era, musical films were a popular genre, with lavish set pieces and spectacular musical numbers appealing to large audiences. Excellent studio facilities and in-house resources ensured comfortable production conditions. The substantial logistics and costs involved in filming

Commissioning Original Music   **165**

musicals can prove problematic. Nevertheless, musicals have remained popular with filmmakers and audiences. Drawing on musical numbers to either suspend or progress the narrative, musicals usually end up as feature-length films (cinema or television release), although there have also been some musical television series over the years, including *Fame* (1982–1987), *Glee* (2009–2015), *Galavant* (2015–2016), and others.

Planning, Logistics, Pre-Records

Musicals pose special challenges for project planning and execution. Everything needs to accommodate larger numbers of stakeholders and talent, sometimes hundreds of them. The creative team must necessarily include the **songwriter(s)** and composer(s). There will also be a **musical director** (MD) who can help lead the musical performances on and off the set. The director will work closely with a **choreographer** (they may sometimes be the same person) who will work with the singers and dancers. The director of photography (DOP) and their team will need to be involved in the planning of the numbers and will need to know the choreography well in advance, so they can plan how best to capture the performances. Pre-production and production schedules must allow extra time for planning and logistics of music and choreography. Extensive **rehearsals** during pre-production will help minimize time spent on the set during production. It may also be necessary to train up talent—for example, providing vocal coaching to actors whose vocal power is not yet on a par with their star power. Musicals must naturally have a **proportionately larger music budget**, a lot of which has to be front-loaded into pre-production. To optimize the quality of the recording of the music, including the vocal performance of the singers, it is always advisable to **pre-record the music** and ask the **cast to mime to playback** during production. To facilitate synchronized choreography on set, performers must either wear in-ear headphones or have speakers placed nearby.

In the past, actors would commonly mime to voices that were not their own, casting directors perhaps thinking that good actors could not sing and good singers could not act. And so Maria (Natalie Wood) and Toni (Richard Beymer) are miming to the voices of Marni Nixon and Jimmy Bryant respectively in Jerome Robbins and Robert Wise's adaptation of Leonard Bernstein's *West Side Story* (1961). Likewise, Eliza Doolittle (Audrey Hepburn) is actually sung by the same Marni Nixon for the most part in George Cukor's musical adaptation of *My Fair Lady* (1964). Hepburn can be heard *actually* singing in Blake Edwards's *Breakfast at Tiffany's* (1961), when she performs Henry Mancini's <u>Moon River</u>. It makes good sense that the actors who are shown on screen should provide the voices the audience hears. If the actor cannot sing, why not cast decent singers who can act?

Some directors of musical film adaptations have taken matters further: They insist that their actors actually sing on set and they want to record and use that audio. This was the approach taken by Tim Burton with *Sweeney Todd—The Demon Barber of Fleet Street* (2007) and Tom Hooper with *Les Misérables* (2012). Recording singers live on set creates a lot of avoidable problems for the sound and music teams. Pre-recording offers the best opportunity to create a **pristine recording** of the singers and prevents extraneous noise on-set from spilling into the vocal track. It also prevents problems with the synchronization of singing and the accompaniment. Finally, any choreography, particularly large dance numbers, will need to be in time with the music, requiring a pre-recorded track for rehearsals and the shoot.

Adapted Musicals

Musical films sometimes adapt stage musicals that have previously succeeded on Broadway or in London's West End. With adaptations, the creative team needs to consider carefully which aspects of the popular stage version to replicate and what to change. Cinema audiences may not be interested in a straight filming of the stage production. The film version has to build upon the theatrical original and provide added spectacle as only movies can. Numerous musical film adaptations were made in Hollywood throughout the 1930s to the 1960s, as the genre was perhaps the industry's most popular at the time. *West Side Story* (1961, music by Leonard Bernstein, lyrics by Stephen Sondheim) and *My Fair Lady* (1964, music by Frederick Loewe, lyrics by Alan Jay Lerner) are just two of the best-loved film adaptations of stage musicals from the late Classical Hollywood era. Following the break-up of the Hollywood studio system, and with audience tastes changing, musical films were generally less popular in the 1970s and 1980s. Norman Jewison's award-winning *Fiddler on the Roof* (1971, music by Jerry Bock, lyrics by Sheldon Harnick), Bob Fosse's *Cabaret* (1972, music by John Kander, lyrics by Fred Ebb) and Richard Attenborough's *A Chorus Line* (1985, music by Marvin Hamlisch, lyrics by Edward Kleban) were a few adaptations of successful Broadway musicals from this period. Alan Parker's *Evita* (1996, music by Andrew Lloyd-Webber, lyrics by Tim Rice) was one of the few musical adaptations in the 1990s before several high-profile adaptations in the new millennium:

- *Chicago* (2002, music by John Kander, lyrics by Fred Ebb).
- *Sweeney Todd—The Demon Barber of Fleet Street* (2007, music and lyrics by Stephen Sondheim).

- *Les Misérables* (2012, music by Claude-Michel Schönberg, lyrics by Alain Boublil, Herbert Kretzmer, Jean-Marc Natel).
- *Into the Woods* (2014, music by Stephen Sondheim).

Potpourri Musicals

Potpourri musicals are films that collate existing songs into musical numbers. These songs may or may not be previously related or even written by the same composer. Since they cannot capitalize on the commercial success of a stage musical, potpourri musicals may pose a greater creative and financial risk to studios. Licensing existing song material can significantly drive up the music budget. Furthermore, audiences may object to the re-purposing of songs they know from different contexts.

- Baz Luhrmann's *Moulin Rouge* (2001) is a prime example of potpourri music, comprising cover versions of many hit songs. Since the songs are performed as musical numbers that relate to the narrative trajectory of the film, *Moulin Rouge* is decidedly a musical. "Come What May," by David Baerwald and Kevin Gilbert, was the only original song in the musical.
- François Ozon's *8 Femmes* (*8 Women*, 2002) is another potpourri musical, albeit of a very different tone. Bringing together some of France's most distinguished actresses, Ozon intersperses this murder-mystery with eight musical numbers (all pre-existing songs). Each song is carefully chosen to reflect on the situation at hand and to help amplify the performing characters' respective state of mind.
- The film version of *Mamma Mia!* (2008) was a pre-sold entity, banking on the popularity of the stage musical by the same title, featuring a number of hit songs by the Swedish group ABBA, and benefiting from an all-star cast. The film was a big commercial success.

Original Film Musicals

Original film musicals used to be hugely popular in the US and, by extension, Europe and other markets. Whereas adaptations of successful stage shows and potpourri musicals could benefit synergistically from pre-sold content with proven audience traction, original film musicals posed the added creative risk of new music that audiences were not yet familiar with.

168 Commissioning Original Music

Relatively expensive to make, musicals were nevertheless a risk worth taking, especially if well-known stars (such as Fred Astaire, Gene Kelly) could be attached. *Singin' in the Rain* (1952, songs by Nacio Herb Brown, lyrics by Arthur Freed, score by Lennie Hayton) is just one example of a commercially successful original film musical. Although since the 1960s original musicals have become somewhat less prominent in the portfolio of Hollywood output, some very successful films continue to be made. Until the 1970s, most of Walt Disney's animated features were musicals. They were some of the best-loved children's movies of all time and contained songs that became part of the musical canon of (Western) popular culture. Following a creative blip and an organizational reshuffle, Disney musicals had a massive resurgence starting in the late 1980s, with songs by composer Alan Menken: *Little Mermaid* (1989), *Aladdin* (1992), *Pocahontas* (1995), and *The Hunchback of Notre Dame* (1996), among others. *Beauty and the Beast* (1991) was later made into a successful stage show, before being turned into a live-action film in 2017. The original musical *The Lion King* (1994, songs by Elton John, lyrics by Tim Rice) for a long time was Disney's most commercially successful film ever. In 1999, the film was subsequently adapted as a stage musical, directed by Julie Taymor, which in turn has become the most commercially successful piece of entertainment in history. A live-action version of the same film was released in 2019, directed by John Favreau. Disney's *Frozen* (2013, songs by Kristen Anderson-Lopez and Robert Lopez, score by Christophe Beck) overtook *The Lion King* at the box office. The Broadway production of *Frozen* opened in 2018. Lars von Trier's *Dancer in the Dark* (2000, songs by Björk) was a critically acclaimed original musical, which ingeniously paid homage to the Hollywood genre in a bleak social realism setting. Damien Chazelle's *La La Land* (2016, music by Justin Hurwitz) was a popular mainstream nod to the Golden Age of Hollywood musicals.

Bollywood

To this day, there is a huge market for musicals in Indian cinema. Song-and-dance numbers with catchy songs are central to plot development in Bollywood films and audiences expect songs as part of a film. Soundtrack albums are often released prior to a film's release so audience can be familiar with the music ahead of seeing the film. Collaborative creativity and planning are an essential mode of pre-production and production in this field, with writers, lyricists, composers, directors, and choreographers working together closely. Indian cinema draws on rich cultural traditions of its own, but has also often opened up to Western influences. For example, plots may take inspiration from Western films, and song lyrics may be a combination of Hindi and English. Anyone wishing to work in this field should immerse themselves in the rich tradition of Indian cinema and align themselves with collaborators who are familiar with this sphere of cinema culture.

Some of the best-loved Bollywood musicals of all time include:

- *Mughal-e-Azam* (1960, dir. K Asif, music by Naushad Ali).
- *Guide* (1965, dir. Vijay Anand, music by Sachin Dev Burman).
- *Pakeezah* (1972, dir. Kamal Amrohi, music by Ghulam Mohammed).
- *Sholay* (1975, dir. Ramesh Sippy, music by Rahul Dev Burman).
- *Umrao Jaan* (1981, dir. Muzaffar Ali, music by Khayyam).
- *1942: A Love Story* (1994, dir. Vidhu Vinod Chopra, music by Rahul Dev Burman, Babloo Chakravorty, Manohari Singh).
- *Dilwale Dulhania Le Jayenge* (1995, dir. Aditya Chopra, music by Jatin Pandit and Lalit Pandit).
- *Kuch Kuch Hota Hai* (1998, dir. Karan Johar, music by Jatin Pandit and Lalit Pandit).
- *Kabhi Khushi Kabhie Gham...* (2001, dir. Karan Johar, music by Babloo Chakravorty, Jatin Pandit, Lalit Pandit, Sandesh Shandilya).
- *Lagaan* (2001, dir. Ashutosh Gowariker, music by A.R. Rahman).
- *Devdas* (2002, dir. Sanjay Leela Bhansali, music by Ismail Darbar, Monty Sharma).

Takeaways

- Musicals pose special challenges for project planning and execution.
- Musicals need a proportionately bigger music budget.
- Work closely with the choreographer and music director.
- Always pre-record the music and ask the cast to mime to playback during production.
- Pre-recording ensures a pristine recording of the singers and prevents extraneous noise on-set from spilling into the vocal track.
- Singers and dancers must have speakers placed nearby.
- There are different types of musicals: adaptation of stage shows, potpourri/compilation, and original musicals. The last may pose the greatest creative/financial risk.
- Bollywood is a prolific and thriving producer of original film musicals, appealing to huge audiences globally. Anyone new to the field should immerse themselves in the rich body of past works.

6.5 Costs and Budgets

Every media project requires a music budget if _any_ music is to be used. This section details typical cost factors and explains what may drive up or keep down expenditure on original music. This section will also list sample budgets and scenarios. No matter the scale and scope of their contribution, every composer should receive credit, be mentioned in promotional materials, and be invited to relevant screenings or launches so they may benefit from the success of the project. The composer will hope to retain certain music rights and share of copyright. Composers should also be paid for their work, just like any other team member deserves to be paid. The only exception to this is student collaborations, where both sides mutually benefit from the learning experience. Professional composers spend years studying and gaining experience in their craft and should be rewarded for the contribution they can make to a project. Great media music costs money to compose and produce. Depending on the scale of the music, a well-equipped studio will be required to record the music, and highly experienced session players need to be hired.

Side note: The rise of computer-based so-called virtual instruments has empowered composers to create realistic demos effectively and speedily. Composers are now able to give you a very good idea of their musical intentions by use of demos created at the computer (see also Chapter 7). However, whilst virtual instruments can go a long way towards emulating real instruments, they are no substitute for the musicianship and expressive depth that live instruments provide. Therefore, live musicians should be recorded whenever acoustic instruments are the intended endgame. Adequate funding is needed to pay for this.

Tiny Budget Project

This may be a crowd-funded project, or perhaps you are making a film without any budget or on a shoestring budget. This may be a student film or competition entry, or a no-budget mobile game without a distributor attached. If original music is needed, the composer may be a friend of yours, or someone referred by a friend. A call for composers could be put out on various networking sites. Perhaps the composer is still a student and looking for opportunities to collaborate with media creators. Working without a music budget and perhaps only a token fee, the composer will be doing you a favor, with the hope the piece is a success. Where applicable, travel and expenses should still be paid to the composer. They should not incur an actual cost at their end, such as paying for musicians or recording studio time. The musical resources that can be called upon with tiny budgets are limited. The composer will most likely use **virtual instruments** only, as live session recording is almost certainly out of the question. A meaningful conversation between the composer and the project owners might determine whether the score would benefit from a few live instruments and how these might be recorded in the most cost-effective way. In some cases, the composer may choose to record live instruments on their own initiative and at their own expense—if perhaps they feel that their score will greatly benefit and serve as a calling card for future projects. However, this cannot be expected nor taken for granted by the project owners.

Small Budget Project

This may be a project that has a small budget overall but that also has some money set aside for original music. Perhaps it is a speculative pilot or pitch, an ultra-low-budget feature, or a small but ambitious mobile game. There will be a creative team involved and possibly the prospect of some commercial success. The composer should be supported in their work and be paid a fee commensurate with the scope of the project. It is likely that the original score will be predominantly produced with virtual instruments. The music budget should cover any live recording of session players, where applicable. It will be well worth investing at least a small sum in live recording, such as a few solo instruments, as this will noticeably uplift the sound quality of the music. If there is prospect of future work (e.g., pilot commissioned to series), a relatively higher music expenditure may pay off to present the project in the best possible way. The composer may occasionally choose to invest some resources into the music themselves, such as using part of their fee to fund additional recording time or players' fees. However, you should not expect this. By prior agreements, all reasonable music expenses should be covered, and studio time paid for, if needed. The composer may accept a so-called "package deal" or deferred-pay deal. Note that package deals are all-inclusive payments so will be higher than a composer fee (see also later in the chapter). The score should preferably be mixed in a professional mixing studio, but this may not be feasible due to cost. The composer may instead mix the music on their own equipment.

Medium Budget Project

These may be TV pilots, TV episodes, medium budget games, independent feature films, and mid-budget studio features, possibly with distribution lined up and/or heading to festivals. Although the overall budget will need to be managed carefully, it is worth remembering that the higher expenditure should hopefully be recovered when the project is sold. The budget for original music should be commensurate with the overall budget. A composer with a proven track record may agree to work on the score for a negotiable fee. It is possible that a package deal is agreed, but it is equally possible that the composer fee and music production costs will be handled separately. There should be a budget for music production, live scoring sessions, and musicians. The music team will comprise a number of people working alongside the composer in supporting roles (see later in the chapter), all requiring payment. A professional music mix is preferable to meet industry standards (broadcast, cinema).

Large Budget Project

A studio feature film with guaranteed release, cinematic TV (HBO, Showtime, BBC) and AAA games will have a healthy overall budget. Whilst there is no such thing as an unlimited budget, the music budget on these large projects should be large also, commonly running into millions of dollars. A named composer with a proven track record in the respective field will likely be sought for an original score. Directors and producers will normally have existing relationships with a composer and tend to give them first refusal. A large music budget for music will allow for ambitious music solutions, high-quality music production, and live session recording. Some of the best-loved scores of the twentieth and twenty-first centuries have been film and computer game scores, often comprising huge symphonic orchestras and large choirs seldom heard on that scale in other music genres. At this level of media production, package deals for music are less likely.

Music Budget Commensurate with The Overall Budget

Since project budgets change constantly, any fixed number stated here would quickly fall out of date. It is more useful to think of the music budget as a portion of the overall project budget. There used to be a rule of thumb that one should allocate 10 percent of a production's budget to music. This rule no longer applies, for reasons too numerous to discuss here. These days, it is more likely that a production will assign **2 percent to 5 percent of the overall budget** to music. If music plays a particularly important role in the project (for example, in a musical film), the music budget must take up a larger proportion of the overall budget. In 2015, The Hollywood Reporter (THR) reported that the **feature film** musical *Annie* (2014) cost a total of $77,747,714 to make, of which $4,325,000 was spent on music, or **5.56 percent**.[3] This relatively large music budget is to be expected with a musical that requires songs, underscore between songs, many musicians and singers, etc. Sony, the producing studio, paid an <u>additional</u> $4,250,000 for the rights to the story, original songs, and lyrics (permission to use the compositions in a new recording). The music budget was entirely filed under post-production costs even though, this being a musical, there will have been music expenses during pre-production, for pre-recording of the songs for sync and miming on set. THR also reported that the **TV pilot** of *Battle Creek* (2015), at a running time of 44 minutes for a 60-minute broadcast slot, was reportedly produced for $3,564,567, with music costing a total of $86,500, a mere **2.43 percent**. For this rather small music budget, it is unlikely the composer will have been able to record any of the music with a real orchestra, opting instead to use samples and electronic instruments.

How a Music Budget Breaks Down

A comprehensive breakdown of a music budget is given in Table 6.1, indicative of cost items in the music budget of a large project such as a mid- to high-budget feature film or a AAA computer game. The line items are listed as percentages of the total music budget, as this indicates the weight of each item in the overall expenditure. On smaller projects, some, or even many, of these items may apply to a lesser degree, or not at all. Only the biggest, most expensive scores, for example, record with very large orchestras. Some small projects that require very few musicians will not call in the services of a music contractor. Some composers may choose to conduct, rending that budget line obsolete.

Composer fee ($–$$$$)

Media composers will base their fee on a wide range of factors, including:

- their standing in the industry (previous credits) and years of experience;
- the nature of the project (no budget, small budget, large budget, etc.);

174 Commissioning Original Music

- the amount of music required (how many minutes?);
- the nature of music required (for example, a large orchestral score may require more work that a small ensemble score or purely electronic score);
- the amount of time required for the project (how long will they spend on the project);
- the distribution prospects for the project (is the credit worthwhile? guaranteed release? speculative pilot? non-franchise computer game with uncertain prospect of success?).

Table 6.1 Breakdown of Percentage Share Per Line Item in a Music Budget

Assumed Feature Film Budget	*$100 m*
Music Budget	*$4 m*
Composer fee	**45.0%**
Orchestrations	**2.0%**
Music copying and printing (notated score and parts preparation)	**2.0%**
Electronic music programming and production	**6.0%**
Conductor	**0.4%**
Music contractor (aka "fixer")	**0.6%**
Musicians and singers	**15.0%**
Overtime, doublings best to budget contingencies	**$$$**
Principal chair (orchestra leader)	**2.0%**
Booth score reader/music producer	**0.4%**
Music editor(s)	**6.0%**
Recording engineer	**1.5%**
Travel, local transport, accommodation, living expenses, catering	**1.5%**
Instrument cartage (transport)	**0.2%**
Scoring stage hire	**3.0%**
Mixing studio hire	**1.0%**
Additional space and room hire	**2.0%**
Instrument tuning	**0.1%**
Instrument rentals	**0.1%**
Consumable supplies (audio tape, CDs, hard drives)	**0.4%**
Equipment hire/acquisition (computers, rigs, recording equipment, e.g., Auricle)	**0.4%**
Communication (phone, internet etc.)	**0.4%**
Fringes	**10.0%**

Commissioning Original Music **175**

Even composers with relatively fewer credits may have had years of training and experience. They are highly skilled specialists who will not only write the music but also oversee the music production process and ably interface with the production requirements of a project. Composers may charge per minute of music (from very little to $20,000+ per minute), or per day or per week. Some composers will accept different payment structures, including back-end share of sales revenue (gross/net) or so-called deferred-pay deals in which the composer only gets paid once a project has found a distributor. Even on a smaller project, the composer will incur the cost of running their equipment and providing music production facilities. Almost all media composers run their own studio facility of varying sizes, often requiring significant capital expenditure and incurring high running costs. Established composers will have a team of staff that needs paying. Approaching the composer fee flexibly but fairly, the negotiating parties need to identify cost factors and agree an acceptable fee up front. The music production budget will be paid separately, unless a package deal is agreed.

Special Case: Package Deals

Package deals offer the composer an all-inclusive lump sum, usually paid in three installments throughout their engagement that covers their composer fee as well as all expenses arising from the composition and production of the original score. The onus of keeping costs under control is thus placed on the composer. On small and mid-budget projects, package deals are fairly common. Some composers will refuse to accept a package deal, preferring that the project owners bear the cost of music creation and production, which may include increasing the music budget if such a need arises. On larger projects, package deals are less common.

Orchestrations ($$)

The orchestrator translates the composer's ideas into written scores that will be used during the scoring session. Taking the composer's recorded demos and sequencer files, the orchestrator transfers the music into notation software for typesetting and printing. Orchestrators may be retained on a per day basis or be paid per page, e.g., $80 to $100 per score page orchestrated. Orchestrators may sub-contract a small team that helps with file transfers, proofreading, etc.

176 Commissioning Original Music

Music Copying and Printing (Notated Score and Parts Preparation) ($$)

There are specialized service providers that take care of the printing and binding of scores and parts. There may be a one-off fee to hire a team of contractors for a set number of days or any other scope of project agreed in advanced. A team of copyists may be required to meet the workload of having to prepare an orchestral recording session (where dozens of cues require hundreds of printed parts), and copyists will be present during the scoring session to comply with ad hoc changes, print amended parts, etc. The sheer number of printed scores and parts required for a large-scale score is the reason why copying is such a large line item in the music budget.

Electronic Music Programming and Production ($$)

The composer may charge a package fee to cover electronic aspects of the score that are produced in their studio, to compensate for equipment hire or acquisitions, equipment maintenance and usage, as well as the composer's technical expertise in operating and programming this equipment. This budget item may also cover flat rates to hire additional help. The fee may be charged per minute of music, per day, per week, or for the duration of the project.

Conductor ($)

Scoring session conductors specialize in conducting music to picture. They usually require some preparation time to familiarize themselves with the music, and then conduct all scoring sessions. Conductors may be paid by the hour or per day. For a top-level professional, an hourly fee of $100+ is not unusual, or $700+ per day (comprising 2 × 3-hour sessions), with extra compensation for score preparation, billed as a set-up day. Less-experienced session conductors may charge lower fees, but union rules may apply and stipulate a minimum charge per hour.

Music Contractor (aka "Fixer") ($$)

The music contractor (called "fixer" in the UK) is in charge of sourcing all the musicians and singers required for the scoring sessions. They maintain an extensive roster of experienced session players and singers that they can call upon. On smaller projects, contracting services may be undertaken by the composer or one of their associates. Professional music contractors may charge a percentage of the total budget spent on hiring musicians. Alternatively, they may charge a per day or per project flat rate.

Musicians and Singers ($$$$)

Experienced scoring session players (and singers) are some of the most skilled and versatile performers in the world. They will ably sight-read a score and perform beautifully on the first take. This high level of talent and musicianship comes at a cost, as players often have dedicated their lives to improving and maintaining their skills. On smaller projects, the composer may rely on their own professional network and hire musicians they have worked with previously. These musicians should nevertheless be paid fairly. Depending on the production territory, musicians' union rules may apply and certain projects may be bound by these rules. Some musicians may also opt to decline non-union work, especially in Los Angeles, for fear of being excluded from future union work as a penalty for having worked non-union sessions. Musicians will normally record in three-hour blocks, two blocks in one day. Musicians' union rules in the US and UK stipulate how much usable music can be recorded per hour (number of minutes recorded per hour) and the number of hours musicians may work in a day. As a result, the number of minutes of music to be recorded affects the number of recording hours required. Your music contractor can advise on this. The rate of pay per player, per session, per hour, etc. depends on the nature and scale of the project, the number of musicians employed, and the specific work undertaken. Musicians' unions in the US and UK regularly publish applicable session player rates.

> UK Musicians' Union: www.musiciansunion.org.uk
> American Federation of Musicians: www.afm.org
> The Musicians Union of Los Angeles: www.afm47.org

Overtime and Doublings ($$)

If musicians are asked to work overtime, on weekends, or recording so-called doublings or overdubs, different multipliers are applied to their standard session or hourly rate. For example, a flutist may be "doubling" on flute and piccolo in the same session. "Overdubs" are multiple takes of the same music

178 Commissioning Original Music

recorded to thicken the sound of a music passage with relatively few players. Musicians' unions prescribe punitively high session rates to discourage this practice. More players should be hired instead. It is advisable to allow budget contingencies in case an unexpected need of doublings arises.

Principal Chair (Orchestra Leader) ($$)

The leader of the session orchestra (principal first violin) gets paid double the standard session or hourly rate or another multiplier.

Booth Score Reader/Music Producer ($$)

A booth score reader and/or session producer will sit in the control room during the scoring sessions and ensure all music is recorded to a sufficient standard. As an extra pair of eyes and ears, they may also spot errors in the printed score and call out requisite changes. They may get paid by the hour, per session, or per day.

Music Editor(s) ($$)

See Chapter 4. Music editors may charge different fees depending on their prior professional experience and the type of project at hand. In the US, music editors will likely be union members and standard rates may apply, per hour, per day, or per week.

Recording and Mixing Engineer ($$)

Highly specialized recording engineers record and mix media music. The recording engineer and mixing engineer may be different individuals. These specialists will command higher fees than other recording engineers. For smaller projects, cheaper alternatives are available.

Travel, Local Transport, Accommodation, Living Expenses, Catering ($$)

This budget item covers any and all travel and transport for the composer and their team, and accommodation and living expenses while they are on-site

Commissioning Original Music **179**

for creative meetings and scoring sessions. Allowances must also be made for subsistence. Catering may be required for musicians per union rules.

Instrument Cartage (Transport) ($)

Musicians are entitled to instruments transport per union rules. Especially larger instruments (heavy percussion, harp, piano) may require specialized transport.

Scoring Stage Hire ($$)

Recording studios that specialize in media music tend to be well equipped and kept to an excellent standard. These facilities are expensive to hire and may be in high demand. For smaller projects, smaller studio spaces may suffice. Large scoring stages such as the Newman Scoring Stage in Los Angeles or Abbey Road 1 in London can cost $5,000+ per day, which includes venue hire and technical support staff on-site but not the lead engineer time, catering, etc.

Mixing Studio Hire ($$)

After the scoring session, music has to be edited and then mixed. Whilst a lot of the editing may be done during the scoring session, dedicated mixing facilities will better serve the needs of a mixing engineer. These studios may cost $5,000+ per day or more, excluding the mixing engineer. The studio hire cost pays for equipment that gives the score a particular sound that can only be achieved with highly specialized hardware (amplifiers, compressors, etc.).

Additional Space and Room Hire ($$)

This item covers any expenditure arising from space requirements by the various members of the music team. Music editors may need to work in suitable rooms near ongoing post-production work. The orchestrator may need to be close to the composer. Copyists may need a space to work locally prior to the scoring sessions. The composer may require a writing room locally.

180 Commissioning Original Music

Instrument Tuning ($)

A tuner will charge for tuning of pianos, organs, harpsichords, and other instruments that are not customarily tuned by the players. An instrument may need to be tuned daily or several times in a day during intensive use and tuners may charge per hour or a daily retainer.

Instrument Rentals ($)

For certain projects, special instruments may have to be hired that are not provided by the musicians that play them, nor the recording venue. Specialist ethnic instruments, large percussion, or electronic instruments may need to be brought in for a daily or weekly fee.

Consumable Supplies (Audio Tape, CDs, Hard Drives) ($)

The cost of data storage is rapidly decreasing and online / cloud-based storage is replacing physical data storage. Nevertheless, costs may arise during the scoring process from purchasing physical hard drives (for data backup and transport) and possibly physical multi-track tape for recording, at significant cost.

Equipment Hire or Acquisition (Computers, Rigs, Recording Equipment) ($)

Additional computer equipment may need to be hired or acquired to facilitate the workflow of the music team. Specialist recording equipment (microphones, mixing desks, outboard audio processing gear) may be required, as well as amplifiers. The Auricle system is commonly used for the generation of click tracks and visual cues to ensure music and picture sync. In Los Angeles and London, the system can be hired and operated by a specialist. Large screens and projectors may also need to be hired if visual cues are to be used.

Communication and Cloud Storage (Phone, Internet, etc.) ($)

The cost of telecommunication is rapidly decreasing, although fast, reliable, and secure cloud storage solutions now eat into this budget item. Consumer options such as Dropbox may suffice to transfer files and offer a cost-effective choice for smaller projects. On bigger projects, where intellectual property

Commissioning Original Music **181**

must be carefully guarded, and leaks prevented, more costly storage may be required. International phone calls may not cost as much as they used to but the cost of international roaming calls and mobile data can add up. For some recording sessions, top-quality, zero-latency video links may be required that will incur a significant per-minute cost.

Fringes ($$$)

This covers any additional allowances and budget contingencies for costs that may arise, as well as the employer's share of payroll costs which may include Social Security, State Unemployment Insurance, and Federal Unemployment Insurance, property damage and public liability insurance, workers' compensation insurance, vacation and holiday pay, contributions to pension and welfare funds, Federal Payroll Taxes, Federal Unemployment Insurance, and State Unemployment Insurance.

Managing the Music Budget

Just as the overall production cost in media production will always be a concern, so too may the music budget require some budget discipline. Project owners should liaise with the music team in advance to agree budget line items and schedule expenditure throughout the course of the music production process. Some production companies and studios have dedicated team members to oversee the music production process from a budget and logistical perspective. Fox Studios, for example, have a Senior Vice President for Film Music Production in charge of music. This person can liaise with the project composer, matching the intended scope of the score against the available music budget, planning scoring sessions to optimize efficiency, and avoid excessive costs by planning judiciously and cautiously. For instance, few film scores need a huge orchestra for every cue, and it is quite common that the composer will agree to record with a very large orchestra for some days and then record for a further few days with a smaller ensemble.

Cost Spiraling out of Control

The cost of an original score will increase dramatically when:

- a lot of music is needed, resulting in many session dates;
- an excessive number of instruments are used;

182 Commissioning Original Music

- many changes are made to the project (picture edit, running time), requiring changes to the music also and causing costly delays;
- additional scoring sessions are needed because the project has changed;
- re-scores are needed because project owners have changed their minds about the music *after* it has already been recorded live;
- the composer is fired, and a replacement has to be hired. This risks wasting any portion of the composer fee already paid and adds a significant new cost to record all-new music to replace the previous material.

Keeping Cost under Control

The cost of an original score can be kept under control by:

- working with a less-established (= less-expensive) composer where necessary (giving a young composer a chance may unlock amazing creative talent!);
- generally judging the scale of the music (number of musicians employed) to reasonably meet the project needs;
- reserving big orchestral cues for a few key moments in the project and covering other cues with smaller ensembles;
- striking a balance of live instruments and sampled/electronic elements ("hybrid score") in small- or medium-budget projects;
- sensibly judging the amount of music required ("needs basis");
- allowing contingencies in advance (a budget buffer).

Takeaways

- Every media project requires a music budget if any music is to be used: Great media music costs money to compose and produce.
- Every composer should receive credit.
- Composers should be paid for their work.
- The music budget should be commensurate with the overall budget, usually ranging around 2 percent to 5 percent.
- Costs can include many different line items, beyond the composer fee.
- Specialist creative stakeholders can help keep the music budget under control.

6.6 The Commissioning Contract

Once the project owners feel confident they have found the right composer for the project, a **commissioning contract** must be drafted and subsequently signed. It should be clear up front what the composer is being asked to do in terms of the scope of the project, fees and budgets, timelines and deadlines. A **synchronization license** (see also Chapter 5) may also be required, allowing the project owners to use the composer's material in conjunction with the project. It is best to get agreements signed before work on the project commences and it is advisable that project owners seek qualified legal advice whenever large sums of money are at stake. The higher the project budget, and, accordingly, the music budget, the more important it will be to seek legal guidance on drafting contracts and agreements. Most importantly, legal concerns and contract negotiations should never get in the way of a fruitful collaboration between the creative stakeholders.

Laws and regulations pertaining to contracts generally, and commissioning agreements in particular, may differ from one country to another. It is always advisable to seek the input from qualified professionals when preparing these contracts, to ensure all paperwork complies with local laws and regulations and provides all parties with the rights, protections, and assurances they require. A commissioning contract may fit on a single sheet of paper or cover many pages. A film production company may have agreement templates ready to use. A composer may have a basic template that can usefully be adjusted. Some organizations (including ASCAP in the US, PRSformusic and BASCA in the UK) may offer guidance and contract templates to their members upon request.

Any commissioning contract broadly needs to answer these key questions:

- What is the scope of services expected of the composer?
- What are the timelines and deadlines?
- What are the fees and expenses payable?
- How will the composer be credited?
- Who will own the copyright to the music?
- How will royalties be handled?

Scope of the Work: Composer Services

What is the composer being asked to compose? All of the composed underscore (as per spotting)? Any original songs? What component parts of their work does the scope comprise (demos, conducting and recording with live ensemble,

184 Commissioning Original Music

mixing, mastering, final delivery)? A clause about "**reasonable changes**" can stipulate how the composer will comply with requests for changes to the music, and at what stage. For example, it is quite reasonable for a director to suggest changes to the music upon hearing a demo. It may feel unreasonable if changes are demanded after the live scoring sessions. The commissioning agreement is made between the composer and the project owners (or a production company or studio, etc.) In entering the agreement and accepting a specified scope of the work, the composer becomes responsible for the delivery of work within that scope. However, especially on larger projects, the composer may choose to **delegate select tasks** (programming, orchestration, conducting, mixing) among a team of assistants and support staff.

Will the composer be expected to work **exclusively** on the project? For the entire term of the agreement? Perhaps they are expected to work exclusively on the project covered under the agreement until the score has been recorded with live ensemble. Then, in the later stages of post-production when the music is being mixed and mastered, the composer may work on the project on a non-exclusive basis. Some agreements instead state more generally that the composer offers their services on a non-exclusive basis but will give first priority to the project covered by the agreement.

Timelines and Deadlines

The agreement needs to set clear start and completion dates for the composer to plan their workload. Whilst many composers will gladly join a project early on, their services may not start officially until the project is ready for scoring. The composer might be given the date of the spotting session as a start date, with delivery of the final, recorded, and mixed score at a fixed date after that (for example, 12 weeks later). Alternatively, the project may have tent pole deadlines, which can serve as useful dates for the composer also; or the commissioning agreement might set the start date at the date of signing and give the composer a number of weeks from that date until final delivery.

Fees and Expenses Payable

The commissioning agreement needs to state what fee the composer will receive for their composing services and when this will be paid. The agreement should set out a payment schedule—for example, total sum payable in three equal installments:

- First installment payable upon signing of the agreement.
- Second installment payable when recording sessions commence.
- Third installment payable upon final delivery of the mixed score.

The agreement may also address the music budget available to the composer and what services and expenses are admissible to be covered by this budget. The composer may incur expenses when travelling to join the other creative stakeholders locally. On larger projects, the composer may employ a team of assistants, hire musicians, require studio facilities, etc., and these costs will need to be covered by the music budget.

The exception to the above-mentioned budget types are so-called **package deals**, which offer the composer a fixed sum to cover their composer fee *and* any costs and expenses arising from score creation (including assistants, hiring musicians, recording, mixing, etc.). Package deals may be a sensible arrangement for some projects where the scope and budget are relatively small. Especially on larger projects, some composers may refuse to accept package deals, as these place a larger financial risk on them.

Composer Screen Credit

The composer should receive a screen credit, and the exact wording and positioning of this should be covered in the commissioning agreement. For example:

Original Score by John Williams

or

Music by Mickey Mouse

or

Score composed and conducted by Nicki Minaj

The composer may also be listed on any advertising materials and other publications relating to the project.

Copyright Ownership

This clause may differ significantly depending on the jurisdiction in which the agreement is made. In the US, copyright law stipulates that when composers enter a work-for-hire agreement they assign the copyright to their music to the other party. That party, then, owns the copyright to the work as though they were the composer in the first place. This grant-of-rights is not possible in some other countries (including the UK), so it is advisable to seek qualified advice when drafting this clause. The project owners require the ability to use the music they have commissioned exclusively and to publish it in conjunction with their project around the world, in all media. The commissioning agreement needs to assure the project owners of this exclusive right.

Royalties

For media composers, performance royalties are a crucial part of their income stream. The commissioning agreement should specify which royalties the composer has the right to receive, such as performance royalties, mechanical royalties, sheet music royalties, foreign royalties, and synchronization royalties. Particularly on large projects, where secondary revenue streams such as soundtrack albums may result in significant revenue, any royalty splits may be dealt with in a separate music publishing agreement. The composer will be a member of a performing rights organization (PRO), which collects royalties on their behalf.

Other Considerations

There are ancillary considerations that may be addressed in the commissioning contract, including:

- **Chain of Command**—Whom does the composer report to? Who will be their main point of contact? Do they agree to comply with reasonable requests and instructions from all parties identified in this clause (e.g., the director, the producer(s), etc.)? Who is authorized to approve recording budgets and ongoing expenditure?
- **Use of the Score**—Clarifies that the project owners have no obligation to accept the finished score or to use the finished score.

Commissioning Original Music 187

- **Warranties**—Reassures the project owners that the composer is free to enter the agreement and will do their job to the best of their abilities.
- **What Happens If It All Goes Wrong…**—Including provisions detailing what happens if the composer is unable or unwilling, for a wide range of reasons, to continue their work; what happens if progress on the project is interrupted, suspended, or cancelled.
- **Copyright Infringements**—What happens if an infringement of music copyright is alleged and claims are made against the production as a result? For example, will fees not yet paid be withheld from the composer until the dispute is resolved?

Takeaways

The commissioning contract is an important document that broadly needs to address:

- What scope of services is expected of the composer?
- What are the timelines and deadlines?
- What are the fees and expenses payable?
- How will the composer be credited?
- Who will own the copyright to the music?
- How will royalties be handled?

Further Reading

Jackson, D. M. *Sonic Branding: An Introduction. An Essential Guide to the Art and Science of Sonic Branding*. London and New York: AIAA, 2004.

Rodman, R. *Tuning In: American Narrative Television Music*. New York: Oxford University Press, 2010.

Thompson, R. J. *Television's Second Golden Age*. 1st edn. Syracuse, NY: Syracuse University Press, 1997.

Musical Themes

Cooper, D. *Bernard Herrmann's Vertigo: A Film Score Handbook. Film Score Guides*, no. 2. Westport, CT: Greenwood Press, 2001.

Halfyard, J. K. *Danny Elfman's Batman: A Film Score Guide*. Scarecrow Press, 2004.

Hexel, V. *Hans Zimmer and James Newton Howard's The Dark Knight: A Film Score Guide*. Lanham, MD: Rowman & Littlefield, 2016.

Song Written for a Film

Brabec, J. and T. Brabec. "Music, Money, Success & the Movies: Part Two." https://www.ascap.com/help/music-business-101/music-money-success-movies/movies-part2

Musicals

Bradley, E. M. *The First Hollywood Musicals: A Critical Filmography of 171 Features, 1927 through 1932.* Jefferson, N.C.: McFarland, 2004.
Cohan, S. *Hollywood Musicals, the Film Reader.* Hove: Psychology Press, 2002.
Green, S. *Hollywood Musicals Year by Year.* Milwaukee, WI: Hal Leonard Corporation, 1999.
Siefert, M. "Image/Music/Voice: Song Dubbing in Hollywood Musicals." *Journal of Communication* 45(2) (1995): 44–64.

Bollywood

Ganti, T. *Bollywood: A Guidebook to Popular Hindi Cinema.* London: Routledge, 2013.
Mishra, V. *Bollywood Cinema: Temples of Desire.* London: Routledge, 2002.

Notes

1 To find out where these themes occur in the film, see Vasco Hexel. *Hans Zimmer and James Newton Howard's The Dark Knight: A Film Score Guide.* Lanham, MD: Rowman & Littlefield, 2016.
2 Giacchino in a talk at the Royal College of Music, hosted by the Royal Albert Hall in the Elgar Room on 18 October 2017.
3 www.hollywoodreporter.com/news/budget-breakdowns-what-a-typical-827862, accessed 14 February 2018.

Collaborating with a Composer

7

7.1 Introduction

In his book *Working Together: Why Great Partnerships Succeed*, former Disney CEO Michael Eisner highlights the amazing potential that lies in a collaborative partnership. Whilst commissioning a composer technically stipulates a top-down hierarchy of employment (the composer provides "work-for-hire"), they join the project as a creative voice. They can make a contribution that is far greater than a purchasable commodity could ever be. That is the whole point of calling upon original music in the first place versus ready-made, existing music. In other words, inviting a skilled composer to contribute collaboratively to the project, in a creative two-way dialogue, fosters working conditions that can produce powerful results.

Confident media creators will oversee their project with a sense of leadership and authorship, but they will also graciously invite the contribution of their collaborators. Media composers feel passionate about their work, borne out of a love of music and years of immersion in audiovisual multimedia. Working with a composer requires all creative parties to be open to a degree of flexibility and experimentation, always communicating clearly and constructively. Making the composer a creative stakeholder will enfranchise him or her to the project, to make a meaningful contribution while pursuing a shared agenda. Given sufficient time to implement changes, media composers will respond well to reasonable feedback on works-in-progress. In a creative work environment, making changes should never be simply about complying with other people's demands. Alterations to the music should be informed by a creative dialogue.

190 Collaborating with a Composer

This chapter sets out guidelines for finding, onboarding, and working with a composer towards original music for a project. Choosing the *right* composer for a project is essential, so this chapter first gives some pointers on how you can go about finding and identifying suitable talent. The chosen composer then needs to be briefed on the project, which includes discussing creative aims and project timelines. Understanding how best to interface with the chosen individual(s) will help keep their creative progress on track. Good communication with the composer (and all other creative stakeholders) will help you maintain a rewarding creative process and satisfactory outcome. This chapter will also take a look at different modes of collaboration, taking into account the composer's creative process and workflow.

7.2 Finding and Choosing a Composer

There are different routes to finding a suitable composer. The overall music requirements, music budget, production schedules and deadlines, the project owners' standing in the industry, and the target reach of the project will all affect which composer(s) might be suitable and available for your project. Your composer search will (1) be informed by the music requirements of the project at hand. You will then (2) review composer showreels, composer bios, perhaps a number of pitches. Having (3) narrowed down the search finally to just one or two candidates, and having met with these shortlisted candidates, you (4) can hire the composer who shows the best prospect of being a good creative fit.

Step 1: Composer Search and Review of Showreels

Established industry professionals will often have existing connections with composers, from previous projects, or in their wider professional network. It is quite common for composers to work repeatedly with the same set of directors and producers. Having a go-to composer, who will work on every project with director X or production company Y, is perfectly reasonable. There are many benefits to **lasting partnerships** between composers and director (see also later in the chapter). In the absence of existing contacts, finding media composers is not intrinsically difficult. However, finding the *right* composer for the project at hand, someone who will embrace the project requirements and get along with the other creative parties involved, may require a little more effort. You may never have worked with a composer before. If, on top of that, the budget on the current project is relatively small, it may be best to put out a **call for composers** online. Collaboration hubs such as mandy.com, productionhub.com, shootingpeople.org, and talentcircle.co.uk are great places to advertise a call for composers, at low or no cost. There are also numerous groups of media creative and media composers on various social networks that can be helpful. Professional industry bodies such as the American Film Institute (AFI) and the Academy of Motion Picture Arts and Sciences (AMPAS) in the US, the British Academy of Film and Television Arts (BAFTA) and the British Film Institute (BFI) in the UK can be helpful to make new contacts but may not always be open to media creators just starting their careers. The call for composers should state concisely what the music needs of the project are, the music budget, a deadline for submissions, and the project owners' contact details. Warning: Every call for composers will probably produce a large number of responses! Many eager aspiring composers will jump at even the smallest opportunities. Your biggest challenge will be to filter responses down to those few that seem most capable of delivering suitable music for the project at hand.

Among other factors, the size of the **music budget** will determine which composers are interested and available. Music budgets for newly composed scores can range from next to nothing to several million dollars (see also Chapter 6). Although one can find anecdotes of established composers doing some film students a favor, it is unlikely that Hans Zimmer will pounce at the opportunity to score a student film. Reversely, if there is a sizeable music budget, the composer search should filter out inexperienced composers, unless of course a particular composer is known to the creative team and/or has been specifically recommended for the project by a trusted third party. It is best to use common sense when factoring the music budget into the composer search: Without an appropriate budget, a named composer and large-scale scoring solutions will be unavailable. If, on the other hand, there *is* a sizeable music budget, this need not be blown just to attract a big name. If you are new to your respective industry, you will be drawing on a relatively small professional network. It is advisable to continually grow this professional network: Friends and colleagues who have worked with composers before may be willing to share their experiences. If they had a bad experience, it is worth exploring why. Useful lessons about collaboration can be learned even from failed collaborations.

Whilst just about any generalist musician will be able to bring *something* musical to the project, it is worth keeping in mind that a **trained and/or experienced media composer** will possess a **specialist skill set**. Granted, there are countless musicians who have come to media music via different

192 Collaborating with a Composer

routes, but the technical and musico-dramatic requirements of media projects are not acquired quickly. A talented musician who has never worked on a film before may need a lot of technical support that can quickly eat into the music budget. An otherwise wonderful guitarist may hold up the production pipeline on a video game if they do not interface well with the highly technical music production process.

First-hand research by **browsing composer websites** where emerging composers post their works can bring good results. Besides composers' personal sites, free-to-use portals such as SoundCloud, YouTube, or Vimeo are useful, in addition to the common music **streaming services** that tend to cater to more established composers and musicians. An introductory message or email should helpfully explain how and where you noticed the respective composer and why you feel they may be right for the current project.

Step 2: Reviewing Showreels

When searching for a composer, you will understandably be tempted to assess each possible candidate on their prior work. Rather than reducing the composer to the specifics of previous projects, which may or may not suit your current needs, perhaps you can detect the underlying craft, skill, and quality that indicate what the composer is capable of. The composer, if chosen, will compose new music anyway. "Having done one" is a big deal in the creative industries. It is why actors get type-cast, why comedy writers get stuck with comedy, why soap directors struggle to break into more serious content, etc. You may be surprised how **versatile** some composers can be. If during a preliminary search a composer stands out as potentially interesting but their **showreel** is not quite right for the current project they will probably be able and willing to adapt to the needs of the current project. BAFTA Award-winning composer Jason Graves insists that "you want to be creative and you constantly ask yourself how you can top a previous project creatively."[1] A motivated and driven media composer will never be complacent about his musical language and will continue to explore new techniques and modes of expression.

Delegating the Search: Composer Agencies and Music Production Companies

If you are working on a bigger project and/or have some clout in the industry, you may opt for different channels to find a composer: **Composer agencies**

Collaborating with a Composer **193**

that will consider your project requirements and help identify a suitable composer. Agencies including Gorfaine/Schwartz Agency, Inc., Kraft-Engel Management, and Air-Edel look after extensive rosters of film, TV, and games composers. A huge number of **music production houses** worldwide can take care of all music needs of commercials, TV idents, etc. You can delegate much of the composer search to such companies, focusing instead on a discussion of the music itself. At a certain point in your career, you may prefer to delegate responsibility for finding a composer to a producer, and perhaps involve a music supervisor. However, as the creative owner of the project, ultimately you should always remain involved in the composer search and selection process: Whichever composer gets chosen, they will be a key member of the creative team.

Competitive Pitches

A pitch is a composer's submission of music to the project owners so that they can be considered for a job. On larger projects, there are various scenarios in which a composer may **pitch for a project**. Occasionally, composers will hear of a project and **pitch speculatively**, sending some music tracks to a producer or director in the hope of catching their attention. One may liken these speculative pitches to fabric samples that are indicative of the look and feel of a larger piece of furniture, yet to be custom-made. A number of composers may also be **invited to pitch** for a specific project, perhaps having been provided with a script or a written project brief. This is fairly common practice in television production, to gauge what a composer might bring to a project before committing to them contractually. The production team or music supervisor would normally identify a number of composers who are then asked to pitch.

Inviting composers to pitch requires preparation on your part: A written or verbal brief has to be agreed and communicated (see also later in the chapter), timelines set (for the pitch and for the actual project), and budgets confirmed (for the pitch and for the actual project). Music pitches take time, because composers will usually compose new music for the occasion. Music pitches also cost money: **Composers should receive a fee for their pitches**, because they have to put in the hours, use studio time, and employ their specialist expertise. Even though there are many occasions in current industry practice where pitches are unpaid, this does *not* make it right. The time and labor spent by each composer is incommensurate with zero prospect of compensation. Actors auditioning for a part have to spend time preparing as well (reading

194 Collaborating with a Composer

the script, etc.) but their preparation does not require costly music production equipment that must be maintained. Pitching fees may range from a few hundred dollars to several thousand and may or may not be taken by intermediary agencies (who take a cut from the successful client in the end anyway). Being realistic about the current project, one can helpfully limit the scope of the pitching process, limit the number of composers involved, the number of agencies approached, etc. It is absolutely fine, for example, to reach out to a composer agency that represents 100+ composers and ask them to put forward no more than three individuals, at the same time communicating the specific brief so the agency is able to undertake an informed internal search and pre-selection. One of the key benefits of obtaining competitive pitches is that these will be demos that are customized to the project at hand, thus giving a clearer indication as to what the respective composer might bring to the project. Pitches can helpfully inform the composer selection.

Depending on the type of project, different sets of composers may be considered. For the BBC's *Planet Earth 2* (2017), a number of composers pitched, including UK-based composers with prior television credits, but also Hollywood heavyweight Hans Zimmer, whose team eventually scored the show. Pitching is common on big-budget feature films as well. Composer Marco Beltrami remembers that he had to pitch to *World War Z* (2012), but he is reluctant to disclose how many other composers pitched for the film.[2] In advertising and commercials, the pitching process is usually devolved to advertising and/or music agencies. A Coca-Cola commercial may consider fifty or more pitches via different agencies before shortlisting a few and eventually selecting one. Different music tracks may be chosen for the same commercial to play in different territories. The whole music selection process in this case can be time-consuming and labor-intensive.

Step 3: Selecting a Composer

Whether the project owners opt for a pitching process, identify possible composers based on past projects, or consider personal recommendations, there should always also be an initial **meeting with a shortlist of prospective composers**, in person or by video call. In this digitally connected age, there is no good reason why a production based in London or New York or Sydney requires the composer to be based nearby. Having the composer in a different time zone can actually be an asset when it comes to 24-hour working during post-production! But a meeting, if only via Skype or FaceTime, is important: Regardless of what you may already know about the composer and their

Collaborating with a Composer **195**

music, you also need to *like* working with that composer. Can you get along with him or her? Does a constructive dialogue seem possible with this individual? Is there a sense of mutual understanding? Do they make the team feel confident that the project would be in good hands with them? Some of the most successful film composers possess a wonderful interpersonal skill: They always put directors and producers at ease. Time and time again, you will find that successful creative people who are also skilled collaborators exude an air of competence and calm. Besides the great music these composers will hopefully write for the project, it is this initial sense of core competence and levelheaded approach to their craft that should transpire in a call or meeting before the composer is hired. In this first conversation, there is no need to get too far into the specifics of the project (that happens with the brief; see later in the chapter), unless questions arise in conversation. This is a getting-to-know-each-other call, not yet a creative or business meeting, and key pointers (creative aims and objectives, key dates, scope of the work) should suffice.

Composer Availability

The more successful a media composer, the more in demand they will be. It is good professional practice if a composer is honest and upfront about being unable to take on new projects. No one wants to get stuck with a creative partner who is spreading himself or herself too thinly, is distracted by other commitments, or is overworked. It is not uncommon for composer A (unavailable on this occasion) to recommend composer B, who they think will do a good job for the project in their stead. This is a gesture of helpful professionalism. Composers A's recommendation of composer B, whom they are happy to endorse, coincidentally, is a useful seal of approval, possibly saving the project owners the time and hassle of a continued search for a different composer. Composer peer-to-peer recommendations are fairly common in the industry: John Woo wanted to work with Hans Zimmer in 1997 when he was making the action-thriller *Face/Off*. Owing to other commitments, Zimmer was unavailable, and he instead recommended his then-protégé John Powell (who later scored *Shrek* and the *Bourne* movies). Powell was accepted onto the project with a "Zimmer-guarantee" attached, meaning that Zimmer assured Woo he would be happy with Powell's work or he would otherwise step in. Zimmer has offered this kind of a guarantee to many filmmakers and for quite a number of composers in his company, Remote Control. Asked whether he felt pressured to write in Zimmer style rather than being his "own man" in this creative setting, Powell admits without cynicism that he indeed emulated

196 Collaborating with a Composer

Zimmer's style and that in this case "being your own man would be stupid."[3] When Steven Spielberg was working on *Bridge of Spies* (2015), his usual composer John Williams was unavailable, working on *Star Wars: Episode VII—The Force Awakens* (2015). Williams recommended Thomas Newman, also an industry veteran, and Spielberg gladly went ahead with Newman. Spielberg had of course worked with Newman before, when he produced *American Beauty* for Dreamworks in 1999.

Composer Collaborations

A different, somewhat peculiar scenario arises from hiring two composers to collaborate. Asking two composers to work together is similar to asking two directors to collaborate: The result might be fantastic, or a complete disaster. It all comes down to the individuals involved. Asking two composers to collaborate should be a carefully reasoned choice that needs to be explained to the composers so that they can understand why you think their collaboration might be useful to the project. The composers must also be allowed to discuss and agree to the collaboration: They will end up spending a lot of time working together, and they need to feel they are creatively compatible. Working with multiple composers *can* work very well, drawing on the respective partner's musical intuition and artistic strengths. There are several examples of creatively successful composer teams: Hans Zimmer asked James Newton Howard to join him for *Batman Begins* (2005) and *The Dark Knight* (2008), seeking help with the "lovey dovey stuff."[4] Trent Reznor and Atticus Ross created mesmerizing synth scores for *The Social Network* (2010) and *The Girl with the Dragon Tattoo* (2011). The pop duo Daft Punk took their established collaborative ways to an impressive film score with *TRON: Legacy* (2010). Dustin O'Halloran and Hauschka were personal friends before director Garth Davis asked them to collaborate on the music for *Lion* (2016). The score ended up being nominated for numbers of awards, including an Oscar. Then there are less-inspired collaborative pairings. Composers John Powell and Harry Gregson-Williams worked concurrently on *Shrek* (2001) and were basically both scoring the same scenes with Hans Zimmer walking the film's producer Jeffery Katzenberg from one room to the next to see which version worked better (in Katzenberg's view). This mode kind of working is redundant and hardly collaborative. Instead, it is pressured and competitive, and the two composers, then less well established, now admit they really only pulled through because they "were hungry" for the work.[5]

Step 4: Hiring the Composer

Once you feel confident that you have found the right composer for the project, a **commissioning contract** (see also Chapter 7) must be drafted and signed. It should be very clear up front what the composer is being asked to do in terms of scope of the project, fees and budgets, timelines and deadlines. A **synchronization license** (see also Chapter 5) may also be required, allowing the project owners to use the composer's material in conjunction with the project, and this may be finalized retrospectively when the original score is completed. For smaller projects, these contracts can be very brief. For larger projects they may run into many pages. It is advisable to seek specialist legal advice whenever large sums of money are at stake. The higher the project budget, and, accordingly, the music budget, the more important it will be to seek legal counsel in drafting contracts and agreements. Most importantly, legal concerns and contract negotiations should never get in the way of a fruitful collaboration between the creative stakeholders. It is best to get agreements sorted and signed before work on the project commences, and qualified legal advice should be sought when drafting any paperwork.

> **Takeaways**
>
> - You may find a composer from your own professional network or following a recommendation from a trusted third party.
> - You may find a composer by putting out a "call for composers" (passive) or by browsing composer websites and social media profiles (active).
> - For bigger projects that have a larger music budget, you may find a composer with the help of a composer agency.
> - Competitive pitches can be a useful way to see what different composers may choose to bring to a project. Pitches should be paid.
> - The project owners should meet shortlisted composer candidates before deciding whom to hire.
> - Some composers may not be available for a project.
> - Collaborations between two composers are somewhat unusual and should only be instigated for specific reasons.

7.3 Onboarding the Composer

The most important thing is to take a lot of time to think and talk to the director before you write a single note. It's really important to come up

198 Collaborating with a Composer

with a concept. Watch the film, talk to the director, and try to understand the underlying themes, or what is required by the film, and also what the director is trying to say so that you can help through music.[6]

Mychael Danna, composer

Once a composer has been chosen, the **onboarding process** should get him or her fully involved in your project. Agree the **scope of the project** and **key deliverables**. Devising **a project plan** may be useful, spelling out the music budget, indicative schedules, deadlines, and goal posts. Who are the key stakeholders with whom the composer should liaise? By what date does the creative team hope to receive **demos**? What are the intended **deadlines** for final delivery of music? Dubbing dates? Perhaps there is an original song that will be needed by a specific date in the production **schedule**, so that a character can sing it in a scene? Or maybe there are a few key segments the composer should prioritize? For example, for a video game, there may be important gameplay segments that require attention first, whereas linear narrative vignettes can be scored later. Perhaps the composer needs to undertake some research such as traveling to shooting locations, or meeting other key creatives? All of this should be agreed and confirmed so everyone is on the same page. It may be necessary to establish project-specific **criteria and benchmarks** for the key deliverables (scope, quality, timeline for revisions, if required). Agreeing **modes of communication and collaboration** going forward will ensure everyone can actively stay involved with the composer's progress throughout the project.

Finally, **all creative stakeholders** directly involved in or affected by music (music supervisor, composer, editor, sound designer, etc.) **should meet** and know each other so that they can collaborate and problem-solve without always having to involve the project owners (director, producers, etc.). An active exchange of ideas between the **composer and the editor** can greatly benefit both parties. In linear audiovisual media, the composer should be in contact with the editor so that any work-in-progress edits can be shared and reviewed. Moment-by-moment scoring choices can be affected by a single frame shifting one way or the other. Reversely, the editor will appreciate hearing demos for a particular scene or segment, perhaps using these in the edit-in-progress to better gauge the effectiveness of the mood or flow or structure. A two-way dialogue between the editor and composer can be hugely beneficial in order to achieve the best results. An active dialogue should also take place between the **composer and the sound design team**. It can be very helpful if both sides choose to align on all aspects of the soundtrack: Will there be sonic competition between music and sound effects? Where should sound effects take priority? Are there any passages where music might come to the foreground? Joint planning with regards to frequency ranges, timbre, sound color, etc. can inform an aligned approach to the soundtrack and prevent conflicts later on (see also Chapter 8).

Onboarding During Pre-Production

If onboarding takes place during scripting or storyboarding, the composer will benefit from having access to these materials. If mood boards or test footage are available, these should also be shared with the composer, so their musical ideas can be inspired by these materials. If there is any uncertainty over music requirements for the project, pre-production is the perfect time to discuss this before the pressures of production take a toll on the project owners' resources. Oscar nominee Gary Yershon has composed music for several Mike Leigh films, and he gets involved in projects early on. Leigh famously only writes one-page treatments and does not use scripts. Recalling his collaboration with Leigh on *Mr. Turner* (2014), Yershon says,

> We'll talk about terms of color or emotion or instrumental colors that might be interesting to explore. "Cause Mike is musically very literate; that's something he can talk about with confidence." Leigh says of his composer, "We're on the same wavelength. He has a complete, total, and impeccable sense of theater, cinema, storytelling, to his bones. You know, he is a natural." Leigh says that when the two men first met to discuss the music for *Mr. Turner*, he insisted it would not be a period score. "I said to him, 'Look, certainly we don't want to have faux or pastiche period music,'" Leigh says. "I mean, we've been very meticulous in the look and the detail of the film in its period accuracy, but the music, the score, should somehow be a voice that comes from a different place. It should somehow be an expression of the essence of Turner's painting in some way."[7]

Having had an instructive discussion about *Mr. Turner* during pre-production, Yershon could start experimenting with musical ideas.

Onboarding for Post-Production: Spotting Sessions

Traditionally in linear media, onboarding and briefing the composer would take place at the start of post-production and involve a so-called **spotting**

200 Collaborating with a Composer

session. The director and the composer would meet, watch the film, and agree on music requirements scene-by-scene. A music editor would be on hand to take notes and record all start and end points, the duration of each music entry (or "cue"), as well as any comments on what music should achieve. Spotting notes in the past were so detailed that a composer might not need to see the film again until the scoring session. These days, digital media production and post-production are more flexible, meaning that music requirements are often less precisely determinable. Composer Michael Giacchino says he will start writing music and, at some stage, fix all his music timings on a specific version of the film, to have some certainty for music timings during the scoring session. Any changes required after that version—because the film has been re-cut yet again—may or may not involve Giacchino. The music editor may instead conform recorded music to the latest picture cut.

Since the locked picture is a thing of the past, some directors choose not to have a spotting session at all. This is not ideal: Even though the picture cut may change, it is still important to discuss with the composer what the role and function of music in the project should be and to relate this discussion to a picture edit. For every scene or segment, the key question is whether there should be music at all? And if so, where and how much? Are there places where music will certainly have a place? Are there places where music will certainly be omitted? Having determined whether and where music should occur, any pointers on desired tone, style, instrumentation, and possible functions ascribed to music in the project (see Chapter 1) should be discussed and tentatively agreed during spotting.

The Importance of Honesty

The creative dialogue between the project owners and the composer must be open and honest. The composer must have **full access** to the project. You cannot keep secrets from the composer if they are to make a meaningful contribution to the project. Any problematic aspects of the project, perhaps under-developed characters, less than perfect actor performances, a slow-moving scene that needs speeding up, can be helpfully discussed with honesty. Composers will do their utmost to provide the best musical solutions to help tell the story, but they must be party to any and all there is to know about a project, including perceived shortcomings or creative risks. If the project owners are worried about information slipping into the public domain, **non-disclosure agreements** may be required.

Collaborating with a Composer **201**

Likewise, if and when concerns arise over the music, project owners should raise this with the composer immediately and openly. It is best to try to articulate and share concerns if and when they arise rather than letting the composer continue down a creative path that does not feel right. The composer can easily make changes, especially if concerns are raised early on. A music supervisor can facilitate this dialogue.

Changing Your Mind and Going off Brief

When it comes to music, nothing needs to be set in stone early on. The onboarding and briefing process are merely the starting point. Some exciting possibilities arise when the composers go off brief, probing outside set perimeters, pushing boundaries, and heading in unexpected directions. Alfred Hitchcock was adamant that the now-famous shower scene in *Psycho* (1960) be left un-scored, and he briefed composer Bernard Herrmann accordingly. Herrmann had a different idea and persuaded Hitchcock with his piercing violin stabs. Similarly, M. Night Shyamalan did not feel he needed music in *The Sixth Sense* (1999) until composer James Newton Howard convinced him otherwise (with score demos). Many directors, especially when they are as yet unsure about their project and/or their music requirements, will be tempted to minimize the amount of music. Composer Marco Beltrami recalls working on the low-budget independent *The Hurt Locker* (2009) working with director Kathryn Bigelow. She initially only wanted *one* cue for the film, but Beltrami "had some other ideas" and played different demos to Bigelow. She liked the ideas and then asked him to write far more music than she had wanted initially. Beltrami feels that because there was no studio attached to the film there was perhaps more creative flexibility, and an opportunity for him to work more freely with the director.[8] There will not always be time or creative scope for experimental deviation from the brief, but, where schedules permit, it can be inspiring to allow the composer to go off brief here and there. Demos (see later in the chapter) are a useful way for the composer to share their ideas with the project owners and can usefully be drawn upon to gauge whether an off-brief alternative to what was previously agreed feels right.

It is also quite common, and perfectly understandable, that project owners change their mind about the music, just as their outlook on the project as a whole may be changing. Perhaps there has been input from other stakeholders, from the marketing team, or test audiences. Any and all considerations that affect the project as a whole may have repercussions for the role

202   Collaborating with a Composer

and placement of music. It is important to discuss these changes with the composer as and when they arise. Most composers are excellent problem-solvers and they will do their very best to adjust their approach to changing requirements.

> ### Takeaways
>
> - The onboarding process should set out timelines and deliverables and also establish key stakeholders and lines of communication.
>
> - Active dialogue between the composer and the editor and between the composer and the sound design team should be encouraged.
>
> - Onboarding the composer during pre-production enables them to get involved early on and start experimenting with music ideas.
>
> - For linear media, **always have a spotting session** in which the composer gets to meet with the director to agree on music requirements scene-by-scene.
>
> - The creative dialogue must be open and honest.
>
> - Going off brief can be exciting.
>
> - It's okay to change your mind about music requirements, but communicate clearly when you change your mind.

7.4 The Media Composer's Workflow

Every media composer will follow a technologically enabled workflow that leads from the early conceptual stages to the final score, recorded and embedded within the final audiovisual product. The exact steps taken will vary depending on the nature, scope, and scale of the project, which also affect the scoring medium (what instruments, what size ensemble, etc.?), target output format (linear or interactive?), timelines, and budgets. The following provides a general overview of the most common steps a composer will take. On some projects, some of these steps may be skipped. For example, not every project warrants so-called suites (see later in the chapter). And not every music budget allows for live scoring sessions. The order of the steps may change as well. For example, a short recording session may take place early on, if pre-recorded tracks are needed during a shoot. More established media composers employ a **team of assistants** to facilitate their workflow. These helpers may contribute to any aspect of the composer's work and even undertake ancillary creative tasks, under the composer's supervision.

Allowing Enough Time

Remember that **composers need time** to do their work. Most media composers flag lack of time as a big hindrance to their creativity. There are anecdotes of composers who have to score an entire feature film in four weeks. TV composers commonly score an episode per week. Music for commercials sometimes gets turned around overnight. Whilst an experienced media composer can certainly push himself or herself to work fast, nothing suggests that speed leads to *good* results. A composer may be able to compose between **one and three minutes of usable music per day**. Some composers work more quickly, others more slowly. If one hour of music is required for a project, and if one assumes five working days per week, that's at least 20 days, or four weeks, of composing. If that music is designated to end up in an important scene or segment (for example, a main title theme), the composer may prefer to work much more slowly to get the best result. There must also be room for trial and error and to make revisions or change course along the way. Recording sessions, editing, mixing, and mastering of the music takes place after composing and must be added onto the total. For a feature film score, scoring sessions alone can take five days or more plus mixing. The composing and recording of a feature film score really should not be squeezed into fewer than six weeks after the composer has been briefed. Eight to ten weeks are more comfortable for all involved. This requires deliberate **proactive scheduling**, firmly factoring music composition and production into the post-production schedule, thus making sure the composer is given sufficient time to do their job. Everyone understands that schedules shift. But there is a systematic problem in media production when music almost always gets squeezed for lack of planning. **Onboarding composers early on** is an excellent way of facilitating their creative process. **Safeguarding realistic timelines** nearer the end of post-production is the best way to help the composer complete their work in conditions that are conducive to constructive creative working (Figure 7.1).

Step 1: Onboarding: Agreeing the Project R31equirements

As part of the hiring and onboarding process the composer will need to be put in a position to fully understand the requirements of the project at hand (see also 7.3). Depending on where in the creative process they join the project, composers may be invited to read a treatment or script, have detailed discussions with the project owners, or align on narrative and emotional requirements of the

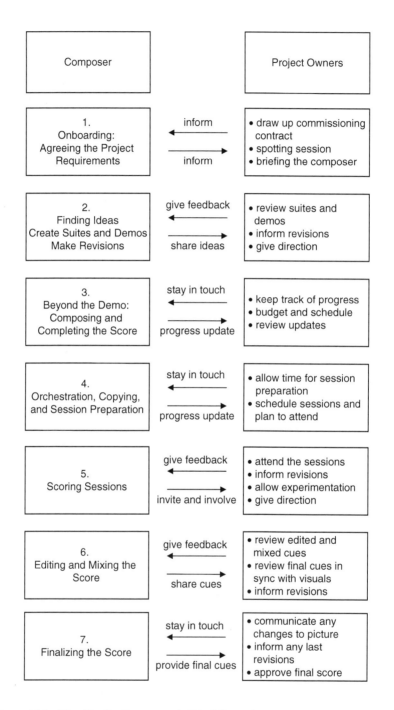

Figure 7.1 The Media Composer's Workflow: Overview.

project. It is really never too early to bring a composer on board. Composers will happily read scripts, which can inform the early development of music ideas. By the time final picture edits are produced, or footage rendered, or game levels compiled, the composer can and should be well underway with their scoring process. Composer Gary Yershon (*Mr. Turner* (2014)) highlights how useful it can be for the composer to be involved early on:

> I start sketching as soon as possible, without asking too many questions. If there's a script, I read it. If there's a read-through, I attend. Visual ideas from the designers are always helpful in finding out what the world of the project is going to be. But the important thing is just letting my imagination roam and follow where it leads. I sketch onto manuscript paper, which is fine for most projects, although it has its limitations: it can lock you into certain ways of thinking, as can improvising on a piano or a guitar, so I'm pretty ruthless when it comes to critiquing what I've put down.[9]

Step 2: Finding Ideas, Establishing the Language

This second stage is crucial in the composer's creative process. It can be exciting or utterly terrifying for the composer to start from scratch and, based on materials shared and conversations had, to start searching for **suitable musical ideas**, "establishing the language" for a project, as Hans Zimmer calls it. It is important to give the composer some time to think and breathe at this important stage. Some composers start by **improvising** on their instrument of choice. Ramin Djawadi (*Game of Thrones* (2011–)) prefers to improvise on guitar. Michael Giacchino always starts at the piano. He tries to distill the emotional needs of a scene, a character, the whole film, into musical ideas. This might be a single chord (he says that *Star Trek* to him was initially just a D-minor chord), a short melodic phrase, a rhythmic pattern. Once this initial grain of a musical idea is found, the whole score germinates and then grows from there. Giacchino then inputs ideas found on the piano into his sequencing software on the computer, developing and arranging material along the way. Composer Rachel Portman (*Never Let Me Go*, *Chocolat*) also improvises at the piano first but then records her improvisations. Her music tech assistant later translates these recordings into a software sequencer and the resulting score is arranged and orchestrated around the initial recording. The composer may undertake some **research**, into a specific geographic setting, time period, or ethnic influences. Some composers like to review the project materials

206 Collaborating with a Composer

over and over, thoroughly immersing themselves in the project and allowing musical ideas to "percolate," as composer Richard Bellis calls it.

The composer may or may not choose to involve the other creative stakeholders in the process of finding initial ideas. Michael Giacchino acknowledges that much of the communication early on in the scoring process, when the musical language for the project is as yet unsettled, is about "putting the director at ease." It is understandable that non-musicians may feel nervous or apprehensive about music before they *know* the composer is working on something that will work for the project. Trying to find the musical theme for the Joker in *The Dark Knight* (2008), Hans Zimmer made director Christopher Nolan listen to 3,000 bars of continuous music, comprising different versions of what would end up becoming the Joker Theme: A long distorted drone comprising synthesized elements, electric guitars, and electric cello. Nolan remembers that he "dutifully listened" to the recording. His feedback to Zimmer was that although he was not sure where exactly the Joker Theme was in those 3,000 bars it was certainly "in there."[10] It was then left up to Zimmer to extract something from the long recording for the final score.

Many composers nowadays immediately tend to **compose at the computer**, using softwares that are virtual production and recording studios. These can record digital audio, incorporate so-called virtual instruments and synthesizers, as well as software samplers that can mimic real (orchestral) instruments convincingly. Layering any number of sounds and instruments, a composer can explore colors and timbres, develop and revise ideas, and build whole music cues. The resulting recording is a sketch that gives a good impression of the intended final outcome, and can conveniently be shared with the other creative stakeholders for review.

Creating and Reviewing Suites and Demos

Suites

Suites and demos can quickly and unequivocally convey the composer's intentions. So-called suites are potpourri compilations of musical themes, moods, instrumentation giving the project owners a flavor of the score the composer intends to write. Suites have become increasingly popular with the emergence of ever more convincing orchestral samples at the composer's disposal. Informed by the brief and creative discussions held up-front—but away from any moving image or precise picture-sync—the composer may create one or several longer-form compositions that comprise all the musical ideas the composer wishes to bring to the project. For the first J.J. Abrams *Star Trek* (2009), Michael Giacchino composed one suite, inspired by the idea that the film was about two best friends who go on an amazing space adventure and face their respective personal struggles. Hans Zimmer composed four suites for *The Dark Knight Rises* (2012): *Selina Kyle Suite, Wayne Manor Suite, Bane Suite,* and *Orphan Suite.* These four suites range in length from five to 22 minutes and feature examples of pretty much all the musical material Zimmer envisaged for the film. It can be reassuring for the project owners to have suites as the basis for further discussion, before the composer then goes ahead and composes the actual score, whose structure, development, and internal timings are determined by the moment-to-moment architecture of the final project.

If the composer chooses to provide one or several suites, it is important that you review this music and give timely feedback. Open lines of communication ensure that the composer can revise their approach or proceed in the direction of the suite(s). Not every composer will be able or willing to compose comprehensive suites up-front. Perhaps their individual workflow does not lend itself to this approach. Or they may lack the technical skills or studio set-up to create convincing suites at the computer. And, in some circumstances, notably on projects with tight schedules or quick turnaround times, suites may be impractical because they take too long to create.

Demos

Demos are commonly used in the media scoring process and every composer understands the need to demo. In the past, composers would sit at the piano and play their musical ideas to the director, expecting them to imagine what the music would sound like when played by a full orchestra. These days, no one gets away with that sort of demo anymore: Media creators cannot be expected to be able to imagine an orchestra when all they hear is piano. And, in any case, sophisticated computer software has made it exceedingly easy to mock-up the sound of an orchestra on the computer (or any other ensemble, for that matter). The composer may ask their assistants to help with the programming of demos, especially when deadlines are tight and the composer has to work quickly. Project owners commonly expect comprehensive demos, especially on larger projects, to gain a good overview of the composer's intentions. Costly scoring sessions (see later in the chapter) cannot go ahead unless all project owners are satisfied with the composer's ideas.

208 Collaborating with a Composer

How to Listen to Suites and Demos

How *much* the composer needs to demo depends on the particular project at hand. Demos are created at the computer, much like suites, and they are a draft of the composer's intentions for a specific scene or segment. When **listening to suites and demos**, bear in mind that they are <u>not</u> the final music. This is perhaps like having a fitting with a tailor, where a suit may have to be measured and then tried on several times before it is finished. No one would take issue with chalk marks or loose threads during the first fitting: It is understood that things will need to be tidied up and finalized before the suit is ready to wear. The same goes for music demos: Some instruments may sound less than realistic, simply due to the nature of digital sampling. Some aspects of the overall score may sound a little synthetic or lack depth or warmth. The composer will readily identify these shortcomings and they should not be held against the music: It is simply one of the limitations of demos programmed at the computer. Depending on the style and nature of the music, it may be necessary to replace parts or all of the demo with real instruments. For example, strings programmed at the computer will often sound quite convincing, certainly good enough to give everyone an idea of the composer's intentions. However, real strings will have vastly improved expressive scope, completely transforming the sound of the music. It is a difference as big as a black and white versus a color image. So, when reviewing the demo, ignoring minor deficiencies, you should instead **focus on the bigger picture**: Is the music striking the right tone? Does it have the requisite energy and emotional charge? Does it feel to be in line with the conversations held during onboarding? The composer can take on board any feedback and criticism and make revisions as needed before moving on to the next step.

Giving Feedback on Suites and Demos

On bigger productions, where big budgets are riding on every aspect of the project, it has become common for composers to provide demos of **every single cue** prior to recording. The project owners will review these demos and commonly ask for changes. Composers may offer alternative versions of the same cue or compose more than one demo for the same scene. Everyone should feel comfortable and confident to form and express an opinion about the demos they hear. If there is any uncertainty over any aspect of the demo (for example, a director may be unsure about the sound of a specific instrument), then an open and constructive conversation should ensue: "I'm not sure about..." or "I don't know the name of the instrument I'm hearing, but..." are perfectly reasonable starting points. When it comes to choosing one demo over another, trying to address similarities and differences may be a useful way to determine the preferable option. Anecdotes of directors expressing preference for one demo over the other when they have in fact been played the same demo twice (an in-joke amongst composers) serve as evidence for filmmakers' hidden insecurities when it comes to music. If two demos seem quite similar, it is reasonable for a director to say so, or to ask, "What's the difference between demo A and demo B? I'm not hearing it." How many times a composer has to re-draft a demo depends entirely on the project owners involved.

One important consideration is how many stakeholders should review and comment on the demo? On smaller projects, it is likely that demos are only reviewed by the director and then directly discussed between the director and the composer. On larger projects, more and more stakeholders may try to wrestle in on the review process. Composer Joe Kraemer recalls that he had to re-score the opening of *Jack Reacher* (2012) multiple times, providing demos each time, because the director and various producers were not in agreement over the music. Although it happens quite frequently that stakeholders are in disagreement, it is detrimental to the composer's creative process when it is left to him or her to try to reconcile those differences. Ideally, only one set of feedback should be given to the composer. This approach saves time and effort on the part of the composer and is more likely to produce usable music more swiftly.

Case Study: No Demos for Dead Space

The blockbuster computer game *Dead Space* (2008) is an interesting case because the composer was freed from some commercial constraints, which enabled him to take a musically more experimental route. Asked by audio director Don Veca to compose "the scariest music you can possibly write," composer Jason Graves decided that an aleatoric approach with full orchestra would be most appropriate ("aleatory" is a compositional technique that involves elements of random choice— for example, asking players to perform a random series of notes, often resulting in a lot of noise).[11] Graves drew inspiration from techniques employed in Penderecki's <u>Threnody for the Victims of Hiroshima</u>. In 2006, when Graves started working on *Dead Space*, commercially available sample libraries did not yet provide many aleatoric patches (that

210 Collaborating with a Composer

void has since been filled). Graves asked other composer colleagues if they had any aleatoric bits of orchestral playing in their personal libraries, but was unable to find suitable material. Therefore, the dilemma he faced was that the aleatoric score he envisioned could not be demoed. Expecting that without a demo he would never be given a budget for scoring sessions, Graves consulted the audio director. He explained that in order to compose truly terrifying music he would have to work with a live orchestra *before* a single note was written. He would then need three months to catalogue and splice the audio recordings and build customized sampler instruments with them. Then he would require a further two months to actually compose his score, using these new samples. Much to Graves's surprise, the audio director gave him the go-ahead and signed off on the budget for six hours of orchestral recording sessions. Graves went on to craft the musical palette for *Dead Space* from multiple layers of aleatoric performances, recorded separately across the full range of the orchestra. Demos would have been completely impractical on this occasion. The high level of trust invested in Graves by Don Veca temporarily liberated the composer from financial and logistical restraints that would have obstructed, if not prevented, this creative achievement. The score for *Dead Space* is an example for improved musical creativity and a compelling outcome that was made possible by a high degree of creative trust vested in the composers and lowered up-front fiscal pressures. The score is considered a remarkable achievement in delivering truly terrifying gameplay and won Graves two BAFTA awards, for "Best Original Score" and "Best Use of Audio."

Step 3: Beyond the Demo: Composing and Completing the Score

Once a demo has been approved, the composer can work towards the final recording. This may involve re-recording parts or all the instruments with real musicians. Whatever the demo may lack in terms of realism, dynamic range, visceral impact, and expressive depth will be brought out in the final recording, probably involving live instruments. The composer may choose to retain some samples, perhaps to bolster the sound of the recorded ensemble or for other aesthetic reasons. There are many ways in which real and synthetic instruments may be combined, and the composer will decide how best to proceed, taking into account budgets, timelines, etc.

Collaborating with a Composer **211**

This step may go hand in hand with the demoing process, depending on whether every single music entry has to be demoed or not. If every cue is demoed, then the composer effectively has to compose all the music in the process. If some cues are demoed but others are not, then these are the cues that need completing before any scoring sessions can take place. Once demos have been approved, the composer may also choose to tweak and finesse cues that have been demoed, ensuring there is a sense of unity and cohesion across the whole score. The composing process often takes place at the computer, in the same softwares used for demoing. Some media composers prefer composing with notation software such as Sibelius or Finale, but this is becoming increasingly rare. The composer will take into account the timescales and resources available for the project, as this informs their further planning: On smaller budget projects, including most television content and commercials, it has become customary to rely solely on virtual instruments and samples for original music. Budget restraints preclude expensive live sessions, and quick turnaround times often make real recordings impossible. If the composer's sequenced tracks will *be* the final score, then music composition may seamlessly segue into music production. Where applicable, assistants may help adapt, edit, and conform cues to fit a chaining picture edit and generally ensure the entire score comes together. They will also check that all relevant audio files are of the correct format and collated in one place in preparation for final delivery.

Step 4: Orchestration, Copying, and Session Preparation

If live instruments are to be recorded, the scale of the score and available budget will determine the number of instruments to be used, which, in turn, has implications for a suitable recording studio. An **orchestrator** or **arranger** will take the composer's sequencer files and create notated scores and parts for the performers (see also Chapter 6). The orchestrator will also listen to the approved demos so they can effectively translate the composer's intentions to be brought to life by real musicians. **Copyists** look after the physical printing of scores and parts that will be used during the session. This requires an eye for detail, as even small errors during collating and sorting can result in costly delays during the scoring session. **Click tracks** are normally used during the sessions to ensure that the synchronization between the music and the image works out as planned by the composer. The click track is played to the conductor and the performers via headphones. **Music editor(s)** look after

212 Collaborating with a Composer

the creation of the click track (see Chapter 4). Occasionally, other methods are used for synchronization—for example, visual cues that are superimposed over the image, projected on the scoring stage during recording. These are also prepared by the music editor(s) and discussed with the **conductor** ahead of the first session. There are benefits and drawbacks to the various synchronization methods used on the scoring stage, and it is best left up to the composer and their team to determine which method suits each respective cue. **Backing tracks** are existing parts of music that will be complemented by live parts but retained in the final recording. They usually need to be available during the scoring session, so they can be played to the performers on headphones to support the timing and intonation of the performance. Once again, the music editor(s) are in charge of preparing these backing tracks and ensuring that they correspond with any click tracks that might be used.

Step 5: Scoring Sessions

Nothing can as yet replace the expressive scope of a real string quartet or brass section or full symphony orchestra. This is why projects that place importance on the quality of the accompanying music will find the requisite money for scoring sessions. For the composer, these few days of intensive live recording are the culmination of several weeks of composing. For all creative stakeholders, scoring sessions are an exciting opportunity to hear the score come to life. The scale of scoring sessions can be impressive: For a large-budget feature film and AAA games, the session orchestra can comprise 100+ players. Sometimes soloists and a choir are added on top. The sight and sound of such a large number of musicians performing an original score is very powerful. The composer will actively work with the project owners to help keep **recording costs** to a minimum. Depending on the project, studios may have in-house counsel or executives who get involved in the planning and budgeting of recording sessions as well. Schedules may be arranged so that the largest group of instruments is used only for a short time, and then preference given to smaller groups and soloists for the rest of the time. The composer can also advise whether and how best to combine real instruments with synthetic elements, a technique that can be cost-effective and nevertheless produce results that sound convincing. Recording in different cities or even countries can have significant implications for the recording cost, which includes travel expenses, venue hire, hourly rates for players, and union rules. Availability of studios, ensembles, and soloist must also be taken into account.

Collaborating with a Composer **213**

A **music contractor** (called "fixer" in the UK) is in charge of finding and hiring qualified players for the score. Contractors have an extensive list of contacts and know performers local to the recording venue. A **music supervisor** and a **score producer** may be present throughout the scoring sessions to ensure all music lined up for recording is actually recorded. They will write notes and keep a track of every recorded take to help with editing and mixing of the music later on. In order to prepare for the sessions, they must be briefed by the composer as to the session requirements, schedules, a breakdown of music cues, etc. The **orchestrator/arranger** and **copyists** tend to be on hand throughout the scoring sessions to help implement changes and print revised parts as necessary.

The project owners normally attend the scoring sessions. Some like just to sit back and enjoy the occasion, perhaps having completed many months of production. Others like to observe closely and gauge whether the music turns out the way they had hoped. Inevitably, nerves sometimes run high in these late stages of post-production and there are many egos in the room. Everyone will have an opinion of the music and some of the stakeholders may choose to comment, even demand **changes** to the music. Rather than conducting their score, many media composers prefer to be in the control room with the project owners so they can observe their response to each cue and possibly suggest changes where needed. It is common for changes to be made to the score during the scoring session, which can range from minor adjustments to substantial revisions. This is understandable because the recording session is the first time the creative stakeholders actually hear the score in its full orchestral glory. As sophisticated as sequenced demos have become, they still do not truly capture the orchestral palette in all its nuances and expressive range. Sometimes instrumental balances shift when played live. Sometimes a melodic line, or a rhythm or a single instrumental color, feels different than in the demo. Orchestrator Jeff Atmajian remembers how director Angelina Jolie was taken aback by the sound of the orchestra when she attended the scoring session for her *In the Land of Blood and Honey* (2011). No matter how elaborate the score demos may have been, they had not made Jolie aware of the full range of depth and subtlety she then encountered—in this case to her delight—at the recording session.

Whenever the project owners feel a change needs to be made, it is important to be as clear and constructive as possible. Knowing that everyone has worked very hard to get this far in the scoring process, and understanding that making changes is possible and not a problem, everyone can calmly voice what concerns them. There is always room for some **experimentation on the scoring stage**, and composers will happily try something different from what

214 Collaborating with a Composer

they had originally planned. Making changes on the scoring stage can take time. And session time is expensive when 100+ players are sitting around awaiting further instructions. Sometimes it only requires the composer or the orchestrator to call out a few adjustments to the players (e.g., "horns, please don't play bars 15–20 on the next take," or "flutes, please play bars 5–13 up an octave"). Other times, the copyists will quickly go back to the notation software to print revised parts for the players. Anticipating that changes may be required, some composers and their orchestrators may have alternative versions of each cue already prepared. For example, they may have printed the orchestral parts in such a way that a melody can be reassigned from one instrument to another and it has already been printed in their parts as an optional line.

Some composers agree to record larger ensembles in separate sections— for example, strings, percussion, brass, and woodwinds. When the ensemble is playing to click, recording so-called **stems** (or **stripes**) is possible. In film music jargon, stems are mix-downs of groups of instruments into separate tracks, usually in preparation for the dub. The recorded orchestral film score is customarily delivered in stems of woodwinds, brass, percussion, strings, and additional instruments such as synthesizers, guitars, etc. Using a click track ensures that even sections recorded separately will line up when combined later in the mix. There are some **advantages of using stems**: Firstly, they give the mixing engineer clear separation between sections, or reduced "bleed." On a large scoring stage, when an ensemble plays *tutti* (i.e., all the instruments together), different microphones will pick up noise from other sections. Secondly, stems provide added flexibility on the dubbing stage, when music meets sound effects and dialogue. Being able to reduce the volume on some parts of the orchestra but not others provides different balance options. Thirdly, stems may provide more options for music editing after the session, if the picture edit changes or the creative stakeholders require changes to be made to music for any reason. A **potential drawback of using stems** is that the orchestra does not play together, preventing a higher degree of musical interpretation, inner balance, natural performance. Recording stems can also feel tedious or boring for the performers during the scoring session. Although recording stems has become increasingly common in the industry, some composers still record *tutti* only, notably John Williams and Michael Giacchino.

Step 6: Editing and Mixing the Score

After the scoring session, the music editor and a team of studio engineers collate and edit a huge number of takes into **final versions of each cue**, which are then mixed in preparation for the dub. The composer and their team will be involved in this labor-intensive process, which can take many days. If there is to be a soundtrack album, then this will usually require a separate music mix. Especially if pre-dub music has been kept in separate stems, the soundtrack album mix may be very different from the music mix heard in the film or video game. *The Dark Knight* (2008) is a good example of a film score whose soundtrack album contains completely different music edits and mixes from the actual film.

Step 7: Finalizing the Score

The composer and their team will continue to handle the recorded and mixed score until the dubbing session. Changing picture edits or other alterations may require creative music editing, so-called **conforming**, to ensure the recordings still fit the revised picture cut. Different media require different formats of music delivery, and the implementation of music into the final project will also vary. For video games, the recorded score will need to be integrated in the game by use of middleware such as FMOD, Unity, or Wwise. In linear audiovisual media, a final dubbing session will implement music in the overall soundtrack mix. The composer and some members of their team may be present for the dub (see later in the chapter).

Takeaways

- Composers need time to do their work.
- Good music is worth waiting for.
- Proactive scheduling of post-production must allow and safeguard enough time for music composition and production.
- Music suites are potpourri compilations of musical material the composer envisions for your project.
- Demos are draft compositions to give you an impression of the composer's intentions for a particular cue.
- Feedback on suites and demos should be prompt and articulate.
- Making changes on the scoring stage can take time and cost money, but it is possible.
- The composer and their team will handle score editing and mixing until the final dub.

216 Collaborating with a Composer

7.5 Different Modes of Collaboration

Different Communication Methods

Creative people have different communication styles. Some are very good in a face-to-face meeting but tend to write emails and music notes that can come across as rude and aggressive. Others prefer email because it is more convenient for them than scheduling more meetings. Some people like to know the aims and objectives of a meeting before it takes place, so they feel less anxious about what the meeting might bring. When we are comfortable with the chosen mode of communication, we communicate at our best. Establishing how the creative stakeholders on a project, including the composer, *prefer* to communicate, can remove potential barriers to creative thinking and working. Meetings in person will always work best so that all parties can get a clear sense of each other's feelings and intentions. Sitting with the composer in their studio can actually be fun: It is often a quiet and calm place, entirely different from an editing suite or sound stage. It is also the ideal place for the composer to discuss and demonstrate their ideas in the setting in which they develop them. Therefore, it is advisable that you make yourself available for **meetings** at the composer's place of work. Sufficient time should be allowed for the composer to prepare, revise, and/or finish music ideas in between meetings. Composers tend not to work very well with a filmmaker breathing down their back. If any changes are agreed during a meeting, it is worth keeping in mind that composers are not only skilled technicians (who will work as swiftly as possible to implement agreed changes), they are also creative stakeholders who may want to take a reasonable amount of time to make changes. This cannot always be rushed. **Phone calls and video conferencing** are useful when, for example, changes to a picture edit are to be discussed or feedback given on materials previously shared. Perhaps the composer has sent over some revised demos and now they need to get feedback and/or the final sign-off. **Emails** can be useful if the parties involved are not able to meet or speak at a specific time. For example, the composer may be working in a different time zone, or the director is shooting on a remote location. Emails may, however, be the communication tool least suited to a fruitful discussion. So much can get lost in translation, and many inflections of both parties' meanings that would be instantly understood in person are lost in written message. Emails also notoriously give their author a false sense of distance and safety, possibly encouraging them to employ less than thoughtful and constructive language. The rule should be not to use email if a meeting or phone/video call is possible instead.

Different Communication Styles

It is useful to understand of ourselves what type of leader, communicator, and collaborator we are. Most creative people tend to be somewhere on a spectrum between loud, extroverted, egotistical, and assertive at one end to anxiety-ridden, introverted, and easily hurt at the other. Add a budget and a schedule and it is a miracle anything ever gets done. But remembering that everyone should work together to make the project at hand the best it can possibly be, open and constructive communication can bind together a diverse set of personalities. Starting with ourselves, it is worth trying to recognize the type of collaborator we are, can be, and want to be—and this may change from one project to the next. Understanding our preferred style of leadership, style of communication, and mode of collaboration can be an empowering starting point for clear and open communication with our team.

- **Confidence**—How sure are you of yourself and your ideas for this project? A confident project owner will graciously allow their collaborators to work flexibly around an idea, to push boundaries and perhaps take ideas in unexpected directions.
- **Who's the Boss?**—Who are the other stakeholders on the project and what are their responsibilities? Will they have an active creative role? How assertive do you want to be with your ideas (on this project)?
- **Delegation**—Are you a happy delegator? How much autonomy do you think you can give the composer? Identifying overlaps in collaborators' creative spheres, and seeing that everyone is working toward a shared goal, you may discover possibilities for delegation and distribution of creative workload. Just like a costume designer or DOP will get on with their work once the scope and aims have been agreed, so too can the composer proceed independently once briefed. You will, of course, be expected to check in at agreed points, which is part and parcel of a collaborative effort.
- **Shared Responsibility**—How much creative control are you prepared to give up, allowing other creative shareholders to contribute?
- **Top-Down or Flat?**—What are the managerial hierarchies on this project? Some project owners are most comfortable with a top-down hierarchical approach to management, whereas most creative collaborators perform best in a collaboration of equals. It is the difference between a "demand economy," which treats original music as a purchasable commodity, and a joint effort, which is far more conducive to creative working.

218 Collaborating with a Composer

- **Creative Freedom and Experimentation**—Are you happy for the composer to take a speculative approach and are you willing to allow some room for experimentation? Or does the project at hand require a tried and tested approach? There will inevitably be creative and commercial pressures that can affect all areas of media production. Sometimes, you may be able to protect some artistic decisions from commercial pressures. Other times, certain aspects will have to be revised, perhaps including music. So long as a constructive and reasonable working environment can be retained, composers will readily comply with demands for changes. There is never an extreme polarity of the project owners having total control versus giving total freedom.

Giving the Composer a Degree of Creative Freedom

The composer thrives when they are given some creative space, time, and flexibility with which to work. Some composers are very happy sticking closely to a very detailed brief, ticking all the right boxes, and delivering on time. As a result, their music may not be particularly original or memorable, but they will have done the job asked of them. Then there are less compliant composers who push boundaries, may go off brief, and occasionally may be perceived as difficult to work with. Bernard Herrmann, for example, was notorious for his bad temper and frequent disagreements with directors and studio bosses. He may have found more work throughout his career if he had been an easier collaborator. However, his film music was undoubtedly brilliant and some of his scores unquestionably elevated Hitchcock's films to unexpected heights, sometimes precisely because Herrmann chose to disagree with Hitchcock and went against the director's instructions. Famous film composers such as Henry Mancini (*Pink Panther* (1963), *Breakfast at Tiffany's* (1961)) and Erich W. Korngold (*The Sea Hawk* (1940), *King's Row* (1942)) had nothing to do with film when they first started out but they had a voice as a composer and were given space to express that voice to great effect in the films they worked on. There are some directors and producers who give their composers a lot of creative freedom—for example, Peter Lord and Nick Park, who worked with composers John Powell and Harry Gregson-Williams on *Chicken Run* (2000). During production, the composers installed themselves in the Aardman Studios in Bristol for three weeks, where the stop-motion animation was being shot on 23(!) sound stages. They spent three weeks writing themes and coming up with general music ideas for the film. Later, back in Los Angeles, they then adapted those musical ideas to the finished edit, sharing their thoughts with the directors along the way.[12] This approach would not have been possible had the filmmakers insisted on controlling every aspect the music.

Project Owners Trying to Control Music

Producer Jerry Bruckheimer likes to give hands-on feedback on music and make detailed suggestions, including motivic development and even melodic phrasing.[13] Producer Jeffrey Katzenberg is known for being closely involved in all aspects of the films he oversees, including music.[14] In one anecdote, Katzenberg and Dreamworks co-founder David Geffen directly interfered with the score to *Mousehunt* (1997) in less than constructive terms, demanding that director Gore Verbinski should reconsider what they called "crazy oompah music."[15] Having opinions and giving feedback on music is the project owners' prerogative, of course. In fact, it is required of them. However, it should be kept in mind that composers are authors of their own scores. They are highly trained and often have years of experience. That does not entitle them to be precious about their music. But if project owners get too closely involved in the minute details of the score, this can crowd the composer creatively. There is no problem with producers taking an active interest in the score for their film, but too often comments on the music are made without the composer present or without commentators knowing what previous discussions and decisions may have informed the composer's creative process. Problems arise when project owners start trying actively to contribute to or dictate music development, composition, and production without inviting a dialogue with all creative stakeholders. With an active and constructive dialogue, interesting developments are possible. Sometimes what may at first strike the project owners as an odd musical choice may turn out to be a good solution: When Steven Spielberg was co-producing Ridley Scott's *Gladiator* (2000), he initially weighed in heavily against Lisa Gerrard's vocals being incorporated into the score, an idea that composer Hans Zimmer had brought to the table. A highly musical filmmaker, Spielberg then let himself be convinced that Zimmer's intuition was right on this occasion. The score famously became one of the most celebrated aspects of the film.

A director who has a clear creative vision for their film, and a steady hand at managing their production partners, may be able to shield their composer from distractions and potentially detrimental influences from other stakeholders: Director Garth Davis approached German composer and prepared piano musician Hauschka at the merchandise table after a concert in Australia. He wanted him to compose the score for his next film *Lion* (2016), together

220 Collaborating with a Composer

with the American pianist and composer Dustin O'Halloran. As it happened, the two composers were actually good friends, and the collaboration was a happy one. The film was released to critical acclaim, and was nominated for six Oscars and four Golden Globes, including for "Best Original Score." Only much later did Hauschka learn that Davis had had to fight hard for him: his producers had strong reservations against a relatively unknown and inexperienced film composer.[16]

Trusting the Composer

Exciting possibilities arise when the project owners occasionally trust the composer. Their creative ideas and input should be considered and discussed with an open mind. Director David Fincher enjoyed a respectful and fruitful collaboration with Trent Reznor and Atticus Ross on *The Social Network* (2010). Fincher had temp-tracked parts of the film with pieces from *Ghost* (1990), an instrumental concept album by Reznor's industrial rock project Nine Inch Nails.[17] Reznor's account of the experimental nature of the team's collaboration gives rare insight into a process in which the composers helped shape the final score and were given creative space to augment and alter the director's vision:

> We did quite a bit of talking. When I officially took this on, late winter, [David Fincher] had shot the film and was in the process of putting together a rough edit. I'd read the script a couple of times and then saw the first 40 minutes to get a rough idea of the look and the pacing [...] to get a sense of the vibe. We talked at length, to try to get inside his head to find out what he wanted from me, why did he want me on this project. David isn't the kind of guy who just wings it. He can tell you a very clear idea of what he thinks you should be like. So, he suggested let's avoid an orchestra, let's keep things somewhat synthetic. He threw out names like Tangerine Dream and Vangelis. He set-up some parameters, and gave me a phase one of spending two weeks generating [...] sketches, and then said if anything resonates, I'll go down that path. In my mind it wasn't so much scene specific things but tones and tonal ranges. [...] With that 40 minutes of material [Fincher] had created, he used the *Ghosts* material. From that I thought I could tell what he wanted us to do. I could also see that for a movie that is primarily people talking in a room, how important the emotion and tempo of the music could drive the film. After the very first break up scene, those opening shots were so powerful with [Mark Zuckerberg

(Jesse Eisenberg)] running across campus and the credits coming up but the first cut I saw had some college-rock, I can't remember what it was [...] I just remember some jangly college rock, a sort of "everything's alright, let's all have a beer" sort of track. The film then sort of became some sort of John Hughes-esque, kids at college, light life. Which is not what the film should be. [...] The jangly guitars didn't work and it really made the film feel different off the bat, with this afternoon movie vibe. I think we all felt that. We generated these things and David responded very positively and respectfully. I went to a screening a few days later at Sony. We showed up to a room full of people and that scene I was mentioning earlier with him running across the street, felt so much different. It felt like a much darker and more brooding movie. It was great for all of us to get over that first hurdle and realize we had gotten the tone and emotion of the film right.[18]

Too Many Cooks...

On some projects, especially large-budget feature films, there can be too many stakeholders trying to interfere with the music. If the creative hierarchies are not clearly established from the start, and if different project owners disagree on key creative decisions, problems can ensue that eventually affect music also. Sometimes a film is in trouble (perhaps test screenings have not gone well) and everyone goes into damage control mode. Music may be one of the last things that can be changed, piling more pressure onto this aspect of post-production. It is not helpful if a composer receives conflicting input from different stakeholders and cannot be sure whom to follow. Marco Beltrami encountered this when working on *World War Z* (2012), which had ongoing problems throughout its development and production. Working with two producers who disagreed on the approach to the music, Beltrami eventually had to write two complete scores for the film: One large-scale orchestral score and another for a small chamber orchestra. It is highly unusual for a composer to have to compose two complete scores of contrasting style and instrumentation for the same film. The project owners were so conflicted that they could not agree on the final score. Finally, decisions as to which music cues to use where were not made until the dub. Frustrated by the process, Beltrami chose to leave the decision-making to the producers and dubbing engineer, saying, "You figure it out."[19] Having too many proverbial cooks involved in the scoring process can lead to a frustrating, creatively wasteful, and very expensive experience. It is better to clarify roles and responsibilities from the start and ensure only a single set of feedback is given to the composer.

222 Collaborating with a Composer

Case Study: Four Scenarios

Four contrasting scenarios from five-time Academy Award nominee and three-time BAFTA winner George Fenton's (*Gandhi* (1982), *Planet Earth* (2006)) career can usefully illustrate different modes of collaboration between filmmakers and a composer.[20]

Vague Input, Open-Ended Challenge

Shadowlands (1993) tells the true story of renowned Christian theologian, writer, and professor C.S. Lewis, who leads a passionless life until he meets a spirited poet from the US. Director Richard Attenborough had given Fenton, who had previously gained ample experience writing music for theatre and television, his first break as a film composer with *Gandhi* (1982). During pre-production for *Shadowlands*, the director informed Fenton that he wanted to open the film in a chapel, saying, "I want to start with an anthem." Fenton wondered what kind of anthem, as Attenborough was not being specific: In the style of Orlando Gibbons (1583–1625), Charles Villiers Stanford (1852–1924), or Victorian era à la "God Save the Queen"? Attenborough furthermore asked Fenton to start with a man's voice and with a boy's voice. Unable to find an existing piece, he wanted Fenton to compose something new, in just three weeks. The musical ideas set out in the anthem should also contain music that then ties in with the musical main theme for the film. Fenton felt the (self-imposed) pressure of treating 500 years of choral music with integrity, but he eventually arrived at a solution.

The composer had to balance a relatively high level of creative freedom with uncertainty over what the director was expecting. Clearer instructions from the director as to suitable style, placement, and form of the music would have helped the composer in terms of finding ideas.

Too Much Pressure

Amidst a pressured post-production schedule for *The Long Walk Home* (1990), director Richard Pearce apparently did not believe Fenton would be able to deliver the finished score on time. To make matters worse, Pearce did not give Fenton a detailed brief for the film, leaving the composer with a good deal of uncertainty. Just to see that there was enough music, Pearce made the composer pull two all-nighters and then had him play the entire score on piano at a hotel in Los Angeles. By the early 1990s, it was increasingly uncommon for a composer to have to demo a full score on the piano. Fenton was made to feel nervous over his piano skills, whether he could convey an orchestral score on the piano, and trying to impress the director and keep his job.

The director could have allowed more time for music composition by briefing Fenton sooner and in more detail. He could also have avoided adding pressure on the composer having him play the full score on the piano. Instead, it might have been more useful (and less stressful for Fenton!) just to play through key ideas, themes, perhaps a few scenes, to inform a creative dialogue.

You're Fired!

Fenton got fired from *Interview with the Vampire: The Vampire Chronicles* (1994). Producer David Geffen had wanted a high level of control over the music and did not think that the director Neil Jordan's composer of choice would deliver a satisfactory score. Geffen was basing this assumption purely on Fenton's past scores. Jordan and Fenton wanted the score to be dark, as this is what they felt the film was. But test screenings without music placed the film in the 90 percents and Geffen had a different idea for music. Fenton feels he got fired for "what Geffen thought [he] would have recorded." Elliot Goldenthal's score for the final film undoubtedly is excellent, but we will never know what Fenton might have brought to the film. Excessive control exercised by the producer interfered with the collaboration between director and composer. To add injury to insult, Geffen allegedly never spoke with Fenton in person, leaving Fenton to lament, "They have no shame in Hollywood, nor guts (they don't even tell you to your face that you're fired)."

The producer should have trusted Fenton and allowed a creative dialogue to take place, rather than dismissing the composer preemptively for music as yet unwritten.

Less Is More

For his Palme d'Or-winning socio-realism piece *I, Daniel Blake* (2016), director Ken Loach insisted that there be no music until 70 minutes into film. Having understood the director's intentions, and having seen the work-in-progress edit, Fenton agreed: He felt that the absence of music made the "tension almost unbearable" when watching. Appreciating that sometimes "silence is golden," Fenton and Loach were able carefully to control the effect of music where it *was* used: What little music there is comprises understated, subdued, low-frequency sound beds, some solo cello and piano notes. For Fenton, who can just as easily write large-scale symphonic scores, this was a most positive collaborative experience.

Deciding on the sparse placement of music together, the composer and director found ways of incorporating music to maximum effect (often by its absence).

Takeaways

- Establishing the creative stakeholders' preferred mode of communication removes potential barriers to creativity.
- You should try to meet the composer in their studio.
- Recognize that there are different communication styles and attitudes towards collaboration.
- Understanding your preferred style of leadership, communication, and collaboration can be an empowering starting point for clear and open communication with your team.
- The composer should be allowed to have a voice.
- Don't micro-manage music. Manage the big picture.
- Trust the composer and give them some creative freedom.

7.6 Change the Music, Not the Composer

Too many projects, particularly Hollywood feature films, have gone through several composers and different original scores. A constructive collaborative partnership *cannot* result in the composer getting fired. Something has to go very wrong in order for this to happen. Did all channels of communication fail? Did the scoring process trip over irreconcilable differences? Anecdotes of composers being kicked off projects abound, and film composers themselves candidly acknowledge that everyone gets "let go" once in a while. Composer Gabriel Yared has openly spoken about his traumatizing experience of being fired from *Troy* (2004).[21] His score was deemed too historically authentic and lacking impact for a film that aimed for blockbuster appeal. Recounting his experience on *Wrath of the Titans* (2012), composer Javier Navarrete reveals that he felt his position was most at risk when the film was deemed not to be "working."[22] Test screenings in mid-January 2012 were "disastrous" but, pushed against a release date of late March 2012, it was too late for yet another round of additional photography. Director and producers grew increasingly unhappy with the score. Navarrete feels music became a scapegoat because there was nothing else they could "be angry with," and that nothing else could be changed. This then placed more pressure on the music, which, in Navarrete's view, is "when many composers get fired."

Some project owners seem to think that if a score is not working for the film they must not only change the score but also the composer. This is not the right approach. Although it may be fairly common in Hollywood for collaborative partnerships to fall apart, it certainly is not desirable practice. With remarkable consistency, composers are replaced for *perceived* shortcomings or failings in the score when they themselves would surely be capable of making the desired changes. Lack of communication is a consistent problem. Director Doug Liman fired Carter Burwell from *The Bourne Identity* (2002) when his score had already been recorded.[23] Composer John Powell was brought in to replace Burwell even though a creative dialogue may quite possibly have enabled Burwell to deliver the score Liman was hoping for. Creative differences naturally arise in the course of a collaborative process. But these can be articulated and resolved. Firing a composer is a destructive measure that is highly disruptive to the post-production process and really does not do anything in the short-term to produce a "better" score. It just means betting on the hope that maybe a different composer will do a "better" job, only with much less time available.

Sometimes, composers quit, either to preempt getting fired and/or because they feel they no longer can sustain unending demands for changes to their music. When *Rogue One: A Star Wars Story* (2016) underwent extensive re-shoots, and director Gareth Edwards was reportedly pushed aside by other stakeholders, composer Alexandre Desplat left the project.[24] Officially, this was due to scheduling conflicts (he would have had to compose new music to fit the altered film). In the end, however, Michael Giacchino composed a completely new score, replacing all of Desplat's music. It is unclear whether the late Jóhann Jóhannsson, a long-time collaborator of director Denis Villeneuve, resigned from or was squeezed out of *Blade Runner 2049* (2017), with Hans Zimmer and Benjamin Wallfisch replacing all of his music.[25]

In the interest of the project, it is always better to try to work with the composer to resolve conflicts and creative differences amicably. This is also the cheaper option, because replacing a composer late in the post-production project is often costly. Who is to say the next composer will do better?! There is

226 Collaborating with a Composer

hardly any time for a period of reflection that might help the creative stakeholders see where the scoring process got derailed. Instead, whoever is in the unfortunate position to inherit a project from which another composer has been fired will likely work in a pressured, top-down hierarchy, serving the demands of project owners who are, by now, stressed and nervous about the music.

> **Takeaways**
> - A collaborative partnership cannot result in the composer getting fired unilaterally.
> - Replacing a composer is never the best option, except if they prove incompetent (in which case they should never have been hired).
> - When unhappy with the music, ask the composer to change the music.
> - Change the music, not the composer.

7.7 Lasting Partnerships

> The greatest award in Hollywood is to be asked back again.[26]
>
> *Anonymous Hollywood film composer*

Once channels and means of communication have been tried and tested, it is comforting for stakeholders to work with the same composer again and again. There is something reassuring about knowing each other's idiosyncratic ways of working. Oftentimes, composers have accompanied media creators throughout their careers. Many established media composers got their first big break when their director friend got to make their first TV show or feature film or AAA game. Marco Beltrami points out that music is an abstract language and that it takes time to develop an effective dialogue and comfort level between directors and composers. He gives the examples of the successive projects with director James Mangold on *3:10 to Yuma* (2007) and *Logan* (2017).[27] Teddy Castellucci finds reassurance in having a reliable rapport with filmmakers: "A great relationship with a filmmaker seems to be very productive, because it allows the composer to free up the 'what ifs.'"[28] Having worked together repeatedly removes a great deal of uncertainty for all parties. Asked to identify his favorite working relationship, Carter Burwell answers, "My work with [writers and directors] Joel and Ethan Coen has been strikingly enjoyable, partly because they're entertaining, but mostly because

Collaborating with a Composer **227**

they don't presuppose what music can accomplish in their films. Also, they never seem to be put off by my not knowing what I'm doing."[29] For composer Michael Giacchino, discussing the score-in-progress normally "feels like working with friends." He has worked with a number of directors repeatedly, notably Brad Bird and J.J. Abrams. Having built up trust and friendship, some composer–director pairs confess to knowing each other "like an old couple."[30]

A director may sometimes need to shield their trusted composer from the detrimental input of other stakeholders. Standing up for the composer can, in turn, strengthen the bond between composer and director. The most prolific and artistically successful lasting partnerships between directors and composers or producers and composers are those based on trust, mutual understanding, respect, perhaps even friendship. There are numerous lasting director–composer partnerships whose remarkable output is worth exploring. Only a small selection is listed here.

Noteworthy Lasting Director–Composer Partnerships (A Selection)

- Director Paul Thomas Anderson and composer Jonny Greenwood.
- J.J. Abrams and composer Michael Giacchino.
- Darren Aronofsky and composer Clint Mansell.
- Wes Anderson and composer Mark Mothersbaugh.
- Richard Attenborough and composer George Fenton.
- German director Wolfgang Petersen and Klaus Doldinger.
- James Mangold and Marco Beltrami.
- Tim Burton and Danny Elfman.
- Sam Mendes and Thomas Newman.
- Brad Bird and Michael Giacchino (five films).
- Mike Leigh and Gary Yershon (five films).
- Polish director Krzysztof Kieślowski and Zbigniew Preisner (seven films).
- German director Werner Herzog and Popol Vuh (eight films).
- Alfred Hitchcock and Bernard Herrmann (eight films).
- Japanese director Hayao Miyazaki and Joe Hisaishi (10 films).
- Swedish director Ingmar Bergman and Erik Nordgren (11 films).
- Kenneth Branagh and Patrick Doyle (12 films).
- Indian director Mani Ratnam and A.R. Rahman (14 films).
- French director Luc Besson and Éric Serra (14 films).
- The Coen Brothers and Carter Burwell (16 films).
- David Cronenberg and Howard Shore (16 films).

228 Collaborating with a Composer

- Robert Zemeckis and Alan Silvestri (17 films).
- Italian director Federico Fellini and Nino Rota (17 films).
- Japanese filmmaker Ishirō Honda and Akira Ifukube (19 films).
- German director Rainer Werner Fassbinder and Peer Raaben (27 films).
- Steven Spielberg and John Williams (30+ films).
- Chilean filmmaker Raúl Ruiz and Jorge Arriagada (45+ films).

Further Reading

Eisner, M., and A.R. Cohen. *Working Together: Why Great Partnerships Succeed.* New York: Collins Business, 2010.

Faulkner, R.R. *Music on Demand: Composers and Careers in the Hollywood Film Industry.* New Brunswick, N.J. and London: Transaction Publishers, 1983.

Friedman, L.D., and B. Notbohm, eds. *Steven Spielberg: Interviews.* Jackson: University of Mississippi Press, 2000.

Laporte, N. *The Men Who Would Be King: An Almost Epic Tale of Moguls, Movies, and a Company Called DreamWorks.* Reprint. Boston and New York: Mariner Books, 2011.

Morgan, D. *Knowing the Score: Conversations with Film Composers about the Art, Craft, Blood, Sweat, and Tears of Writing Music for Cinema.* New York: HarperCollins, 2000.

Smith, S.C. *A Heart at Fire's Center: The Life and Music of Bernard Herrmann.* Berkeley and Los Angeles: University of California Press, 2002.

Notes

1 Graves speaking at SoundTrack_Cologne 10 on 21 November 2013.

2 Beltrami in a talk at the Transatlantyk International Film Festival on 8 August 2013.

3 John Powell in conversation with Tommy Pearson at the Royal Albert Hall's Elgar Room on 10 July 2017.

4 www.empireonline.com/interviews/interview.asp?IID=1532, accessed 14 February 2018.

5 Powell, op. cit.

6 Quoted in Christian DesJardins. *Inside Film Music: Composers Speak.* Los Angeles: Silman-James Press, 2006, p. 55.

7 www.npr.org/2015/02/22/387239255/to-set-the-mood-in-period-drama-a-composer-paints-around-the-emotions, accessed 28 March 2017.

8 Beltrami, op.cit.

9 www.m-magazine.co.uk/genres/soundtrack-genres/interview-gary-yershon/, accessed 15 February 2018.

Collaborating with a Composer **229**

10 Jon Burlingame, "20 Billion-Dollar Composer: For Hans Zimmer, 'The Real Risk Is Playing It Safe,'" *Variety*, http://variety.com/2014/music/features/ 20-billion-dollar-composer-for-hans-zimmer-the-real-risk-is-playing-it-safe-1201173698/, accessed 15 February 2018.

11 Graves, op. cit.

12 Powell, op. cit.

13 Laura M. Holson, "Will Jerry Bruckheimer Change His Ways in a More Austere Hollywood?" *New York Times*, 13 November 2006, sec. Media. https://www.nytimes.com/2006/11/13/business/media/13bruckheimer.html, accessed 15 February 2018.

14 N. Laporte. *The Men Who Would Be King: An Almost Epic Tale of Moguls, Movies, and a Company Called DreamWorks*. Reprint. Boston and New York: Mariner Books, 2011, p. 49.

15 Ibid., p.137.

16 Anecdote shared by Hauschka in personal conversation in August 2017.

17 http://ghosts.nin.com/main/home, accessed 15 February 2018.

18 Trent Reznor, in "Trent Reznor Discusses *The Social Network* Soundtrack," interview by S. Adams, online forum post, 11 October 2010, http://drownedinsound.com/in_depth/4141283-interview--trent-reznor-discusses-the-social-network-soundtrack, accessed 15 February 2018.

19 Beltrami, op.cit.

20 Fenton shared the four scenarios in this chapter in a talk at the Royal College of Music in London on 2 November 2016.

21 Yared in a talk at SoundTrack_Cologne 4 on 30 November 2007.

22 Navarrete in a talk at the Royal College of Music in London on 7 February 2012, one day after scoring sessions had finished.

23 www.independent.co.uk/arts-entertainment/classical/news/john-powell-interview-i-sold-myself-to-the-devil-just-a-bit-9466955.html, accessed 20 March 2018.

24 www.hollywoodreporter.com/heat-vision/star-wars-rogue-one-replaces-929387, accessed 20 March 2018.

25 "Jóhann Jóhannsson Has Been Totally Removed from the Blade Runner 2049 Soundtrack." *FACT Magazine: Music News, New Music* (blog), 15 September 2017. www.factmag.com/2017/09/15/johann-johannsson-removed-blade-runner-2049-produc-tion-team/, accessed 20 March 2018.

26 R.R. Faulkner. *Music on Demand: Composers and Careers in the Hollywood Film Industry*. New Brunswick, N.J. and London: Transaction Publishers, 1983, p. 50.

27 Beltrami, op.cit.

28 Quoted in DesJardins, op.cit., p. 40

29 Carter Burwell interviewed by Dan Goldwasser in "Being Carter Burwell," published December 1999, www.soundtrack.net/content/article/?id=48, accessed 16 February 2018.

30 Giacchino in a talk at the Royal College of Music, hosted by the Royal Albert Hall in the Elgar Room on 18 October 2017.

Finalizing Your Project   **8**

8.1 Introduction

This chapter takes a closer look at the last stages of your project, when all visual and sound elements, including music, need to be finalized and fixed. Who is invited to participate in creative decisions at this point? Who is in control of the project and who gives final approval to the music? This chapter highlights how developments in digital filming and editing technology, moving away from linear workflows to **non-linear and flexible processes**, can affect music planning and the placement of music in films and other linear media. Evolving **digital technology** has transformed the way in which you can continually revise your material, and music may need to adapt flexibly along the way. Besides digital filming and editing, this chapter also addresses **digital sound** recording, editing, and dubbing, where music meets dialogue and sound effects.

This chapter focuses on film and TV production and post-production. Reflecting on opportunities and pitfalls in these areas will also be of value to creators of non-linear media such as video games. Video games have always challenged composers to provide malleable interactive music that can accompany open-ended gameplay. As a result, video game composers had to devise innovative composing techniques and music solutions from the get-go. These were different from traditional approaches to music composition, alien to traditional film composers, and not immediately accessible or musically appealing to them. This is one of the reasons why many game composers tend to be specialists who only work in that field. Over the last few decades, however, more and more film composers have turned to video game scoring, and vice versa: Both media have a lot in common in terms of aesthetic and stylistic demands on music, narrative and dramatic requirements, and the roles and functions music performs. As compositional tools and techniques have evolved, they have gradually been shared between both camps.[1]

Put simply, a non-linear media production workflow that leads to a linear target output (film or TV show) poses challenges for composers whose creative process (i.e., composing and producing) and product (i.e., the final score recording) have traditionally been linear. If a project undergoes **changes and revisions during post-production**—including changing picture edits and sound design choices—some accommodation should be made in order, firstly, to help composers cope with digital post-production demands, and, secondly, for original music to continue to serve the project as effectively as intended. Active **communication and collaboration** during post-production can help composers better interface with and navigate non-linear workflows. These concerns affect composers of original music first and foremost, who are involved in the creative process as it unfolds, including any revisions that are required. Therefore, this chapter places less emphasis on licensed music. The picture editor or a music editor can make changes to existing licensed music since the composer of licensed music is not normally involved in the project directly.

> **Takeaways**
>
> - Digitally enabled non-linear media production that leads to a linear product poses creative challenges for composers whose process and product have traditionally been linear.
> - Active communication and collaboration can help the composer better interface with and navigate non-linear workflows.

8.2 Digital Film Technology and Its Impact on Music

Past Practice: Analog Filming and Editing

In the days of analog technology, film production was a **linear process**. Original music was not composed until after a film had been edited and locked. In a so-called **spotting session**, the director and composer would agree the music requirements for the film and the composer could then start composing. Long before video files or even videotape existed, composers might not actually *see* the film again until the scoring session. And they did

232 Finalizing Your Project

not need to: Having taken notes about the music requirements of each scene, the composer could rely on **unchanging edits**. In recent decades, however, progressive developments in camera technology, digital non-linear editing, and CGI have totally transformed post-production processes. As a knock-on effect, new ways and possibilities in which to plan and implement music in audiovisual media must be explored. Media composers have had to adapt their methods and workflows to cope with changing demands of the industry.

Unlocking the Picture: Digital Filming and Editing

> You've made a masterpiece. Don't change a single frame of it.[2]
>
> *Producer Steven Spielberg to director Sam Mendes*
> *during post-production of* American Beauty

Spielberg's comment gave Sam Mendes a much-needed boost of confidence in his debut feature film. The instruction not to change a single frame was doubly poignant: Mendes by this point had already re-cut the film several times, departing dramatically from the shooting script, most notably by changing the beginning and ending. And, by 1999, repeated editing and re-editing or a film was so commonplace that the instruction to *stop* changing the film may have felt necessary.

Digital editing has made the cutting and re-cutting of a film quick and cheap, so everyone is doing it. Digital camera and editing technologies have revolutionized the way footage is shot and edited, giving project owners and editors an unprecedented degree of creative freedom and flexibility. When in the past filmmakers had to economize with costly footage, and plan every scene and shot carefully, over-shooting for coverage now costs almost nothing. In 2018, director Stephen Soderbergh shot the horror thriller *Unsane* using just three iPhones! Filmmaking and video game design have, of course, always been at the pioneering edge of technology and have probably been a key driving force behind most technological innovation in the area of digital production tools. Changing industry needs (for production and delivery), product differentiation (for example, new spectacular visual effects), economics (cost-cutting), and audience expectations (spectacular visuals) have all been factors.

Digital data storage costs a tiny fraction of traditional film stock. While editing magnetic tape had already increased the speed at which editors could work, virtual editing pushed the envelope further. The editor's workflow is facilitated by computer workstations that offer instant access to every frame.

These workstations also allow the instant replay of a scene or segment without having to rewind. Director John McTiernan (*Die Hard* (1988), *The Hunt for Red October* (1990)) acknowledges that Avid software "eliminated the last vestige of reluctance to cut, the cost of cutting."[3]

The ability to edit in a non-destructive and non-linear fashion has drastically altered production and post-production practices in that project owners and editors now spend proportionately more time *editing* their material. On the one hand, media creators' ability to repeatedly revise and refine their material offers them the benefit of greater creative freedom with little added expense. On the other hand, digital editing can undermine the need for filmmakers to have creative vision and forethought. Editors lose the tactile experience and once painstaking process of handling physical film. Picture cuts now often change faster and more frequently than music can be revised.

Helping Composers Cope with Changing Edits

Music is affected by digital editing because traditional scoring methods were relatively inflexible. The **planning of music** now has to take into account that any audiovisual material may not yet be in its final version. Where in the past composers sat down to spot a film and could then sculpt their scores to fit a locked picture, these days, the picture may not be finalized until very shortly before the dub. For some composers, having repeatedly to revise their music can be a challenge: Unlike visual editing—where a few frames can easily be dropped here and there—music, particularly once recorded, cannot be chopped up as easily or quickly. Hollywood composer and orchestrator Patrick Russ once joked that "scoring a changing picture edit is like trying to dress a runner—while he's running." Why is changing music tricky? Because every musical expression has a beginning, a duration, and ending. If we think of a musical phrase as a sentence, cutting into the phrase is like omitting words from the sentence. We risk altering or obscuring the meaning of what was said. Composers will of course compose their music to fit a given scene, but they will also try to maintain some sense of musical integrity and coherence within their composition. One may also think of a custom-built cabinet that has been crafted to fit on a wall: If the measurements of the wall subsequently change, or if the customer decides to put the cabinet on a different wall, the cabinet will no longer fit the way it was designed to. Project owners and composers can take steps to ensure the composers' workflow and output remain compatible and serve digitally enabled productions successfully.

234 Finalizing Your Project

What You Can Do

- Whilst you and your editor will undoubtedly benefit from greater freedom and flexibility during editing, you should make an effort to communicate actively and frequently with the composer.
- Acknowledging that the edit may change, creative stakeholders can nevertheless align on the intended overarching *relationship* between music and visuals in any given scene. Will music be present in a given scene or not? Limiting the scope of the score up front (i.e., agreeing what scenes to leave un-scored) can reduce waste in the creative process. Some extended chase scenes have no music, such as, for example, the first half of the motorcycle chase in *Mission Impossible—Rogue Nation* (2015).
- What is the intended effect and impact of music + visuals at any given moment, and how can this best be achieved? Even if the moment-by-moment architecture of a scene is still being developed, you can discuss your intentions and goals.
- What role should music play? Is it a key element in a given scene or just filler? Is it helping with the rhythmic drive, and/or the emotional charge? Arguably, there are many moments in film when music is assigned a lesser role. For example, when the Avengers are fending off aliens and demolishing Manhattan in the process, music is clearly not the most important part of the spectacle.
- Are there moments when music can be given time and space to conclude in a "musical" manner? Allowing enough time in the edit to let a musical phrase conclude, as is the case in the aforementioned moment in *The Jungle Book* (2016) when strings play the second-half chorus of "Bare Necessities" after Mowgli has saved the baby elephant.
- Are there opportunities to edit visuals *to* music? Reversing the workflow can lead to compelling solutions—for example, in *Baby Driver* (2017) and *Lola Rennt* (*Run Lola Run*, 1998).

What the Composer Can Do

Composers find different coping mechanisms to serve a changing edit. Virtually all media composers work with computers these days so that making changes to their music at the technical level is not much of a problem, certainly not at demo stage when everything is usually still based on virtual instruments. Composers can make changes to a computer-based composition relatively easily, so long as they are informed of changes to the edit and given some time to make the required changes. This simply means that the editor should send over new cuts at regular intervals. It is also helpful if the editor can share a log of changes so that the composer or one of their assistants can identify the moments that need addressing.

There are also some compositional strategies a composer may pursue to accommodate frequent editing changes. Hans Zimmer describes a modular approach to composition, devising what he calls a "Lego set" of musical snippets that can flexibly be adjusted to fit a changing scene. He explains that, for him:

> picture changes aren't a problem. On *Batman Begins*, for instance, which James [Newton Howard] and I did together, I knew we were going to have a car chase, but I knew it wasn't going to be the stereotypical car chase, absolutely no way. But Chris [Nolan] hadn't really attacked that scene yet, and hadn't really figured it out. So I wrote the car chase music as a kind of Lego set, since I knew he was going to move the picture around like crazy. And it's a car chase, so we're not really concerned with the integrity of a beautiful melody here! In fact, if there's anything more boring to write than a car chase, I can't think of it right now. So it just became this Lego set, and as Chris was moving chunks of car chase around, it was very easy to adjust.[4]

A modular approach to music composition and production and a flexible variation technique produces flexible scoring solutions. Nevertheless, all changes to the picture edit should be logged and passed on to the music team so that the timings of score-in-progress can be adjusted. Composer Javier Navarrete took a modular approach to changing picture edits when scoring *Wrath of the Titans* (2012): "Every week, we were conforming to a new cut. I couldn't even look at the orchestrations," Navarrete recalls.[5] To keep up with changing edits, Navarrete created musical snippets and made a collection of vertical and horizontal structures he could later place wherever suitable. Working with a live orchestra, he recorded not only sections but also numerous rhythmic parts that ended up in the hands of the music editor, a total of 48 variations that could be freely placed throughout the film. Asked who was ultimately in charge of scoring decisions or quality assurance, Navarrete admits that he feels he had very little control over the final score.

Some composers are not willing to forego musical integrity of phrases and internal balance in favor of a modular approach. They prefer to take a more traditional scoring approach, maintaining a higher degree of structural unity and coherence. Composer Michael Giacchino is one of these composers. He composes his scores at the computer and makes adjustments during the composing phase as and when changes to the edit are communicated to

236 Finalizing Your Project

him. At some stage, however, he then settles on *a* version of the picture, to which he plans the music sync, and then he proceeds to the scoring sessions with live orchestra.[6] If further changes are subsequently made to the film, Giacchino's music editor will have to make adjustments to the recorded audio. Occasionally, the composer himself will come in for a "fix day," to supervise re-editing of the recorded audio to the changed picture cut.

Takeaways

- Communicate actively and frequently with the composer about changing edits and give them time to make changes to their music.
- Consider limiting the scope of the score if and when the picture cut changes frequently.
- Don't lose sight of the intended effect and impact of music + visuals.
- Remember what role music should play.
- Are there moments when music can be given time and space?
- Are there opportunities to edit visuals *to* music?
- Composers may choose to adjust their compositional methods to cope with changing edits. This may result in music that is structurally different from traditional music (modular approach).

Helping Composers Cope with Increased Editing Speeds

The visual pace of digitally edited films has increased as a direct result of digital technology being used. The film scholar David Bordwell has analyzed a large number of Hollywood films, determining the average shot length (ASL) in each film: From an ASL of five to seven seconds in the early 1980s (for example, *Raiders of the Lost Ark* (1981)) to as low as two seconds in the late 1990s (*Dark City* (1998)). This results in "hyperactive action sequences verging on visual chaos: [for example] *Matrix Revolutions* (2003)."[7] But this trend is not limited to action films. Even family-friendly animated films such as *Finding Nemo* (2003) feature remarkably shorts ASLs. Bordwell notes that "rapid editing obliges the viewer to assemble many discrete pieces of information, and it sets a commanding pace: look away, and you might miss a key point."[8] Believing that a movie can be made in the cutting room, directors overshoot, further fuelling the temptation to shape the film during post-production. Shorter ASLs have a profound impact on the interrelation of sound, music, and visuals, especially sync points. As the visual pace of films increases, more and more information is compressed and conflated in ever-shorter segments.

Finalizing Your Project **237**

Faster editing speeds can be problematic for the fitting of music to picture. Musical close-scoring, whereby events in the score coincide with events on screen, can be rendered impossible by prevalent fast editing.

What You Can Do

Faster cutting need not mean that music must frantically try to keep up (that may feel redundant!). Working with the composer, you should take a view on the intended structural relationship between music and image: If a segment is cut rapidly (short ASL), what and how much should music try to "hit?" Is it important that music coincides with on-screen events? Perhaps music can instead work in broader brushstrokes, proceeding at a slower rhythm than the visuals? There are many different ways musical beats and events can interrelate with visual cuts: the speed may match (conformance), contrast (counterpoint), or engage flexibly (complement). You may choose to experiment with different approaches—for example, pairing a relatively slow and/or sustained underscore with rapidly cut images. Other times, it may feel appropriate to pair fast cutting with busy music. The possibilities are endless.

What the Composer Can Do

Where close-sync with fast cutting *is* desired, composers may rely on fast rhythmic textures, with short subdivisions, which ensure that the music is more likely to hit cuts by coincidence. Composer Harry Gregson-Williams took this approach to the cue "The Stanton Curve" in Tony Scott's *Unstoppable* (2010): In an action-driven segment late in the film, a runaway train threatens to derail from an elevated rail track.[9] The visual language of the scene comprises helicopter shots, dynamic camera swerves, and the intercutting of long shots and close-ups of the speeding train. A busy sound effects track contributes to a visceral viewing experience. Asked to help escalate the segment's impact further, Gregson-Williams resorted to a collection of mutually compatible musical loops that could be freely re-combined: Fast percussion patterns, harsh and scratchy string figurations, and a synthesizer bass groove. Superimposed hits were used to accentuate selected cuts for emphasis. With its busy rhythmic texture, the resulting score is remarkably static and expressionless, when heard on its own. And yet, in combination with the visuals and sound effects track, the music undoubtedly adds to *Unstoppable*'s break-neck pace and sonic overload.

Other times, composers may prefer to take a broader approach. Composer Gabriel Yared disassociates himself from the picture edit. He explains that he

238 Finalizing Your Project

"cannot stand being in front of a video all the time."[10] He feels that it is futile trying to fit music to images that may be edited at much faster speeds than in the past. Yared says that music "should capture the spirit of the image rather than trying to hit every little detail." Agreeing with your composer as to what the relationship between music and visuals should be in terms of structure and tempo can inform their preferred approach on each occasion.

Takeaways

- Take a view on the intended structure relationship between music and rapidly cut visuals: conformance, counterpoint, or complement?
- Discuss the desired approach and resulting effect with the composer.
- The composer can take different approaches to match their music with the image either closely or loosely.

Helping Composers Cope with Computer-Generated Imagery

The use of photo-realistic computer-generated imagery (CGI) has a longstanding tradition in filmmaking and is, of course, a key selling point for video games. CGI can visualize even the most fantastic settings and characters, adding to a project's spectacular mass appeal. In linear media, special effects such as painted backdrops, rigged sets, and explosions are usually filmed on set, but CGI is added in post-production. Therefore, these visuals are not available to the composer when they first start composing. The same goes for video games, where, early on, composers usually have little more than still shots or perhaps an animatic to work with. This affects the relationship between music and picture, as the composer has to imagine what the final visuals will look like. Working on *Harry Potter and the Goblet of Fire* (2005), Patrick Doyle composed his score to work prints with visual placeholders where CGI was later used to create the Triwizard Tournament.[11]

What You Can Do

Budgets permitting, CGI can be a powerful tool at your disposal. Some projects will rely on it heavily, others less so. To allow the composer to anticipate the effect and impact of final CGI sequences, you may share early artwork, storyboards, and animatics with them: Anything that can help convey as complete a sense of what the final sequence may look like and feel like. Perhaps the composer can be put in touch with the visual effects (VFX) team so they can liaise directly. Informing the composer of any details about CGI-heavy sequences will help avoid redundancies and wasted efforts. For example, your script may call for a chase scene in a post-apocalyptic world. But in the edit-in-progress the composer only sees actors in zombie make-up and green screen. Without further input, the composer may be tempted to ramp up their music to create a sense of horror and dread. When the CGI is finished it turns out the visuals quite effectively convey a sense of devastation and the music need not work so hard. You can also help prevent a mismatch in tone or emotions between music and image by communicating aim and intentions in advance.

What the Composer Can Do

Composers will find different ways of tackling CGI-heavy scenes, where they may be working only to visual placeholders while composing. Sometimes composers will anticipate the contribution and impact of CGI and judge their musical approach accordingly. Their approach will be informed by conversations with the project owners, other creative stakeholders (including, potentially, the VFX team), and by professional experience. Alternatively, composers may sometimes choose to compose music away from the image and leave it to others later to match music to CGI segments. The timing of a finished CGI sequence can differ significantly from what the composer may originally have been told, meaning that completed music cues may need to be edited (for example time-stretched) in the dubbing theater to fit the scene (sync points, start and end points). Composer Steve Jablonsky provided music up-front for some passages in the highly CGI-reliant *Transformers: Dark of the Moon* (2011). Relinquishing some creative control over his music, Jablonsky allowed the editor and director to cut and adapt his music later to fit the assembled picture.

Takeaways
- When using CGI, discuss aims and intentions with the composer.
- The composer may helpfully liaise directly with the VFX team to anticipate the tone, impact, and timings of a CGI-heavy sequence.
- Composers can try to anticipate the effect of CGI in a scene and adjust their musical approach accordingly.
- Composers may, alternatively, choose to compose music away from the image and leave it to other creative stakeholders to adapt the score to the image.

240 Finalizing Your Project

8.3 Digital Soundtrack Creation and Its Impact on Music

Digital technology has revolutionized audio recording, editing, mixing, and playback. Sound processing during media post-production has changed drastically, affecting the way sound effects and dialogue are recorded, processed, and reproduced. Since music exists on the same soundtrack, side by side with and in amongst other soundtrack elements, the implementation of music in the finished medium has changed also. The creative possibilities arising from digitally enabled soundtracks are a powerful storytelling tool at your disposal. However, now more than ever, it is important that during soundtrack creation you keep your composer in mind: as the project owner, you can encourage joint creative thinking and help maintain efficient workflows.

It is worth remembering that the advent of high-quality audio in the cinema is relatively recent: Mono sound was common in cinemas until well into the 1960s. On the one hand, cinema owners were worried about the cost of installing new equipment. On the other hand, operators and the film studios had to keep appealing to audiences by differentiating their output from competing formats, notably television. Ever-increasing sound clarity and dynamic range was one way of setting the cinema experience apart from watching television at home. Stereo sound became widespread in the 1970s. The Dolby A system was introduced in 1977, THX in 1983, SDDS in 1992, DTS with *Jurassic Park* in 1993. Early on, 5.1 or 7.1 surround sound was by no means common in cinemas, with only multiplex cinemas adopting these expensive innovations. Contrarily, the 128-track Dolby Atmos sound system was launched in 2012 and adopted by the industry and by cinemas relatively quickly. With each digital soundtrack innovation, the **range of frequencies** that could be reproduced, as well as the **dynamic range** from quietest to the loudest sound, increased. Digital recording, editing, and mixing also meant that soundtracks could contain more separate channels, or "tracks," whereas analog tape had previously offered only a relatively small and finite number of channels. Finally, digital sound editing, just like digital film editing, offered the advantages of increased editing speeds, non-linear workflows, and multiple undo/redo capability. This encouraged sound designers to become ever more ambitious, adding layer upon layer of sophisticated sound effects.

With digital soundtracks, there is increased risk of **sonic competition** between music and other soundtrack elements. Digital soundtracks put music under threat of being either **drowned out (volume levels)** or **crowded out (soundtrack too busy)**. Creative stakeholders involved in sound design and

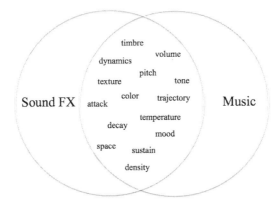

Figure 8.1 Conceptual Overlaps between Music and Sound Effects.

music creation should collaboratively approach the shared sonic territory and conceptual overlaps between music and sound effects (Figure 8.1).

You should introduce your composer to your sound design team early on so they can exchange ideas and liaise freely without your constant involvement, if you choose. Acknowledging conceptual overlaps between music and sound effects, creative stakeholders may then determine how best to work toward the overall soundtrack:

- What sound effects elements will be present in a given scene or segment?—The composer can benefit from knowing the intended soundscape of a given scene (is it cold, metallic, hot, windy?) and potentially adjust their musical approach accordingly.
- Are there key sound design elements that will be foregrounded and that music should leave space for? For example, the audience should be able to hear the sound of Darth Vader's breathing.
- Are there times when sound effects are likely to be prioritized (for example, during a battle scene)? In these scenes music may take a back seat. Composers in the past often complained about their music drowning under sound effects. With advance planning, the composer can anticipate clashes and perhaps choose to focus their creative energy on other scenes. (Why exert oneself in a scene where music won't be heard anyway?)
- What role should music play (prominent or in the background)? Knowing the intended status of music in a given scene can help the composer plan their music better.

242 Finalizing Your Project

- Is it important that music is audible in a given segment? Perhaps there are segments in which music should be heard—for example, to state a character's theme or to introduce an emotional marker that is important for the narrative. Knowing this, the sound design team may leave room for music to become clearly audible at a specific moment.
- Are there times when music can come to the foreground and other elements recede? Reversely, for scenes where music can shine and take center stage, the composer may wish to pull out all the proverbial stops.
- What is the intended effect and impact of the overall soundtrack at any given moment, and how can this best be achieved? This is an open-ended question that should jointly be addressed by the project owners, the sound design team, and the composer.

These are just a few of many considerations that can be discussed. Since they are likely to use the same software (such as Pro Tools), music and sound design teams can exchange ideas quickly and easily. You may prefer to leave these detailed discussions to the sound specialists, taking only a broad view of these matters. Or you may prefer to be very actively involved in shaping the sonic qualities of your project. There are different ways in which creative teams can jointly navigate towards a shared goal, identifying creative soundtrack opportunities along the way. Ultimately, creative control remains with you, as one of the project owners, so you should be prepared to express your views on a work-in-progress, and to give the final approval when the time comes.

Takeaways

- With digital soundtracks, there is increased risk of sonic competition between music and other soundtrack elements.
- Digital soundtracks put music under threat of being either drowned out (volume levels) or crowded out (soundtrack too busy).
- You should introduce your composer to the sound design team early on so they can exchange ideas.
- Creative stakeholders should collaborate toward the overall soundtrack, jointly determining the status and placement of music and sound design during planning and implementation.
- You may choose to lead this collaborative effort or just to inform the process, leaving the details to the respective specialists.
- You, as one of the project owners, remain in charge of your project. This includes having to give your opinion on work-in-progress soundtrack solutions and giving final approval.

Helping Composers Cope with Digital Soundtrack Creation

Faced with evolving digital technology, composers have developed coping mechanisms that help them navigate digitally enabled soundtrack creation. The underlying problem is twofold: Firstly, new digital technologies have enabled project owners and other creative stakeholders to make changes to any aspect of the soundtrack, often to the detriment of music late in the game. Secondly, lack of communication in the late post-production stages—for which both sides are to blame, to be sure—has resulted in misunderstandings and damaged creative relationships. This is unfortunate and preventable. Several strategies can prove useful in avoiding conflict and wasteful processes.

Coping Mechanism 1: Get in Early, Leave Early

The composer may choose to join a project early in the creative process, during pre-production, to improve their chances at planning their music with an awareness of the other soundtrack elements. If onboarded early on, the composer can communicate with the sound design team during the conceptual stages of the project. Beginning with some preliminary music ideas, the composer can then share their work-in-progress with the sound design team. In turn, the sound design team can share some of their early efforts with the composer. This exchange of ideas enables both sides to adjust their approach, to give each other sonic space, and/or to align on priorities and preferences for music versus sound design in selected areas. The composer stays involved in the project until there is a useable edit, based upon which the music is finalized. Where applicable, scoring sessions take place. The composer edits their music, delivers complete recordings, and then relinquishes control over how these tracks are used in the project (laid in during the dubbing session; see later in this chapter). Effectively, they leave before the project is finished. In the past, composers have rarely attended the dubbing session, either because they had already moved on to the next project and/or because they dreaded what damage might be done to their music.

PRO

One advantage of this approach is that the composer has a chance to collaborate with the creative team early on, giving them a good chance to plan their musical approach with foresight and with more time to do so than if they were

244 Finalizing Your Project

to join when post-production starts. With the composer relinquishing control over their music, the project owners are free to make music-placement, mixing, and editing choices without having to discuss these with the composer.

CON

Effectively losing the collaborative contribution of the composer during the dub also means losing the potentially beneficial input from a trusted creative voice. It might be preferable to have the composer present during the dub, in case changes to the music are needed or if music edits might helpfully be addressed by the composer. For example, during the dub a particular instrument in the score may suddenly be clashing with a sound effect in the same scene. If the composer were still involved, they could potentially revise the cue in question and omit the problematic instrument.

Coping Mechanism 2: The "Goodie Bag" Approach

The composer provides a selection of pieces inspired by the project, based on the script, storyboards, and early discussions with the project owners. These tracks are not necessarily synchronized to picture. The composer labels their tracks according to mood, tone, ambience, situation, or theme. They cede control over the placement of the music to the project owners, the editor(s), and the dubbing engineer(s). This approach tends to work well on projects where the edit may change frequently. For example, a documentary may have to be re-cut repeatedly depending on target outlet (public broadcaster, commercial broadcasters, online streaming). With a "goodie bag" of music, the picture editor can choose from a selection of pieces for each new edit, without having to wait for the composer. This approach can also work well in video games that require linear audio vignettes placed flexibly throughout gameplay. With music provided up-front, the sound design team can make some informed choices about their contribution. Leaving decisions over the positioning and mix of these music tracks in the final film to others, the composer is not involved in the dubbing session.

PRO

This approach gives the composer greater freedom in terms of planning their score because they do not have to engage with the detailed architecture of a scene or segment. The project owners also have greater freedom in that they can choose music from a range of options (the composer will likely provide more tracks than are required for the project). This can be helpful in trying out different alternatives for the same scene or when a format keeps changing.

CON

Handling complete music tracks can pose challenges for the sound design team, who may at times find that their work-in-progress has to be revised to adjust to a fixed music track. Losing the collaborative contribution of the composer during the dub also means losing the beneficial input from a trusted creative voice.

Coping Mechanism 3: Get in Early, Leave Late

The composer is onboarded early but *stays involved* in the project until and including the dubbing session. This approach may be the most demanding on the composer's creative resources and requires the composer to adjust their compositional method, both musically and technically. The creative stakeholders begin collaborating during the early conceptual stages. The composer may choose to create some musical elements that can be flexibly recombined (stems, loops, alternative versions). Ideas are exchanged with the sound design team to prevent the creation of redundant or clashing soundtrack elements. The composer delivers open tracks, such as stems of audio, to the dub. The malleable score, delivered in musical layers, is finalized during the dub alongside the other soundtrack elements. The composer stays involved, and attends the dub to help shape the use and placement of music in the final mix. This approach provides the most flexible scoring possibilities with the involvement of the composer, and ensures that musical elements can harmoniously coexist with other soundtrack elements.

PRO

The composer has a chance to collaborate with the creative team early on, giving them a good chance to plan their musical approach with foresight and with more time to do so. Since the composer *stays involved* until and including during the dubbing session, they can support the project owners during these final stages. In case changes to the music are required, the composer can address this.

246 Finalizing Your Project

CON

There really is no downside to having the composer involved in the dub. The project owners remain squarely in control of their dubbing session but having one of their key allies present means that changes to music can be made expertly and flexibly. Of course, some discussion may (need to) take place if you are asking the composer to change a cue that you previously said you approved of. But composers understand that the nature of media post-production sometimes requires changes that could not be foreseen earlier.

If creative stakeholders choose to try out different sound and music options during the dub, this may take some extra time and money. Dubbing sessions can be expensive because they require specialist facilities and staff. The more time spent experimenting, the higher the cost. If a budget dictates that cost must be kept down, perhaps some experimentation can take place pre-dub, in a less pressured and less costly environment.

Takeaways

- Digital sound technology is a tool, not a creative solution. It unlocks a wider expressive palette than ever before, but only human interaction and creative thinking can put the tool to good use.
- Different creative strategies help composers engage with digitally enabled soundtrack creation.
- The composer may get involved early and communicate with the sound design team during the conceptual stages of the project. They deliver their music and then leave early, relinquishing control over how their music is used in the project.
- The composer may provide a goodie bag of tracks labeled according to mood, tone, ambience, situation, or theme. Leaving decisions over the positioning and mix of these music tracks in the final film to others, the composer is not involved in the dubbing session.
- The composer may get involved early and stays involved (leaves late), delivering a malleable score in layers, which is finalized during the dub alongside the other soundtrack elements.

Total Soundtrack Composition

Perhaps the best approach to collaborative soundtrack creation is one that takes an holistic view on all soundtrack elements (dialogue, sound effects, and music) as contributing to one expressive entity. Inviting all stakeholders

Finalizing Your Project **247**

to collaborate in an inspired and constructive environment, Total Soundtrack Composition is:

- a soundtrack design process that embraces technology and involves the composer as part of the storytelling team;
- a speculative and experimental approach to the composite soundtrack elements with a shared goal that is articulated between the creative stakeholders;
- an approach to soundtrack planning that allows music to be a complementary and integral part of the narrative tool set;
- a mode of working in which all parties keep an open mind and agree to explore and further the potential of music as an expressive storytelling tool.

Case Study: Total Soundtrack Composition for Gravity (2013)

Alfonso Cuarón's *Gravity* is a fascinating example of a film whose soundtrack is the result of Total Soundtrack Composition. Award-winning sound editor Skip Lievsay is known for his work on the *Hunger Games* series, *No Country for Old Men* (2007), *The Big Lebowski* (1998), *Fargo* (1996).[12] *Gravity* was an unusual film, firstly, because all exterior shots were 100 percent CGI, except for face shots of Sandra Bullock and George Clooney. Secondly, the stunning visuals of the film were complemented by a sophisticated soundtrack to match. Lievsay recalls having to establish rules for the soundtrack early on: Seeking input from NASA on sound effects and the lack of sound in space, the aim was to create as realistic a soundtrack as possible whilst still delivering a gripping narrative. There are notable idiosyncrasies such as the sound of a drill operated by Bullock's character, the muffled sound being what the character might actually hear inside her suit (indicative of a particular POV). Music was called upon to complement the nuanced sound effects track. The team was looking for music that was less identifiable as orchestral sounds but instead a blend of ambient textures, synthesizer sounds, and processed instrumental sounds. Composer Steven Price, who won the Academy Award for "Best Original Score" for *Gravity*, had previously worked as music editor. This may explain why he so ably crafted musical layers that could flexibly be edited and recombined to serve the film. His approach to music was digitally enabled: Every musical layer was kept separate, later to be consolidated during editing and mixing. Price provided material

248 Finalizing Your Project

along the way, which the sound design team could consider whilst working toward the preferred balance of music and sound design and which changed fluidly in the final mix. The music is moving all the time, the sound mixer having determined the placement of all sound and music. There is a sense of constant forward momentum and directionality in the score. Picture editor Mark Sanger and Lievsay liaised by phone concerning the positioning of sound and music over three weeks of preparation and temp mixes. Director Alfonso Cuarón himself only got involved for ten days during the very final mix, having previously reviewed the temps. On a project that spent $1m per minute of film on CGI alone, it seems reasonable that the sound and music mix should have taken up a lot of time and money also. A team of four mixing engineers first mixed a 7.1 surround mix and then up-scaled to Dolby Atmos.

Takeaways

- Total Soundtrack Composition is desirable best practice, a speculative and experimental approach to the composite soundtrack with a joint goal that is articulated between all creative stakeholders.

8.4 The Dubbing Session

The dubbing session is the final step in the audio post-production process in which all soundtrack elements are mixed together to create the finished soundtrack. Depending on the scope of the project, the dubbing session may take place in a small mixing studio or on a large mixing stage that replicates the acoustic characteristics of a cinema space. The final format of the project audio (stereo, 5.1 surround, Dolby Atmos, etc.) is determined by the target distribution channels. On projects with a larger budget, including video games and some TV and streaming content, it is quite common to have multiple final mixes deriving from the same dubbing session—for example, mixing in 5.1 surround during the dub and then mixing down to stereo as an alternative format. In preparation for the dub, the sound and music editors edit and collate all audio tracks (dialogue, sound effects, and music) in a master Pro Tools session. Some dubbing stages have very large mixing desks that require several engineers to operate. The dubbing mixer(s) balance all the soundtrack elements and then record the finished soundtrack. You and your fellow project owners should be **present throughout the dub** to lead on the creative decisions that take place at this final stage. Alongside

Finalizing Your Project **249**

the other soundtrack elements, the placement and relative volume levels of music are fixed at the dub.

Composer Henry Mancini laments that "many a composer's heart has been broken" at the dub,[13] when their music gets drowned out by other sounds, is chopped up and displaced, or omitted altogether. We have already seen that, traditionally, many media composers have preferred not to attend the dub because they find being there too frustrating. Media composers fully understand that they cannot be protective of their work. During the dub, you should **remain mindful of the priorities and narrative aims of the music**. These will have been discussed with the composer long before the dub. The role and place of music, among other soundtrack elements, will have been considered in advance, including what balance to strike where these elements coexist.

In the absence of guidance from the project owners, the dubbing engineer(s) can take the reins and get the job done. But they may spend only a few days with each project whereas you and the composer have spent many weeks or months. If you do not **show creative leadership at the dub**, mixing and editing decisions made by dubbing engineers(s) will receive less creative thought and scrutiny than was available during the scoring process. In such instances, it is not uncommon for musical cues to disappear in the mix or even be moved to a different point in the project. Inviting a creative dialogue during the dub where feasible, creative control and ownership should remain with you. You should lead the dubbing process, perhaps not technically but creatively, to achieve an appropriate balance in the film soundtrack that reflects the aims and objectives discussed between the creative stakeholders (music/sound effects) during the creative process.

Composers at the Dubbing Session

Over the years, media composers have devised creative strategies that allow them to navigate the challenges of the dub. Any project is served better by music that accommodates the realities of the dubbing session, and a composer who is able and willing to offer creative choices during the dub will be a more successful collaborator.

Anticipate Clashes and Compose around Them

You don't want them to call you from the dub stage and say, "We're dropping this whole three-minute cue because that triangle note interferes with the bird-chirp sound effect that you didn't know was going to be put in there."[14]

Marc Shaiman, composer

Composers can try to anticipate moments where music and sound effects might clash. For example, if they know that there will be a big explosion somewhere in a scene they may choose to score up to that explosion but leave the actual moment un-scored to leave room for sound effects. Composer Thomas Newman acknowledges that,

> in some sequences you have an obligation. If a bus explodes there's an obligation for the sound to follow. So if a composer puts a big musical moment on an explosion, well he's not thinking really about what is probably going to happen—unless you're dealing in a much more subjective filmic realm where you're not going to hear the explosion. And that's where it really boils down to the director [to make creative choices].[15]

Newman also flags that directors may sometimes have unrealistic expectations:

> I think the cause of sound effects and music sparring and fighting is a director who may be wanting to hear it all. It's a big issue of subtraction—the best dub you can have is always subtractive—meaning that if you want to hear sound effects, take out the music. If you want to hear music, subdue some of the sound effects. Find the balance, but don't say, "Well I love the music and I love the sound effects and therefore I want them both in." If music sometimes is written to be big, with big bass drums and low contra-basses, and suddenly it's subdued, it loses the very essence of its design. And you think, "Well, why is it there at all?"[16]

The director should have an holistic vision for the place of music among other soundtrack elements. A nice example can be found in *Star Wars: Episode VIII—The Last Jedi* (2017) when the *Supremacy*, the ship of Supreme Leader Snoke, gets hit by a rebel spaceship: Director Rian Johnson chose to show the explosion in momentary complete silence, to great effect, before a cacophony of noise breaks loose. No need for music there.

Keeping Music Flexible

During recording sessions, many media composers choose to record so-called stems (or stripes) rather than recording the whole orchestra together.

Stems keep separate the different sections of the orchestra into woodwinds, brass, percussion, and strings. Using stems offers added flexibility for music editing later on—for example, being able to single out percussion or to drop brass at given moments. In a given scene that is scored with woodwinds, brass, and percussion, when it comes to the dub, the woodwinds may suddenly be clashing with the sound effects. With a complete orchestral mix, the dubbing engineer may have no other option than to lower the volume of the music altogether until it no longer clashes. With stems, the dubbing engineer can instead retain the brass and percussion at a higher volume, lowering only the woodwinds in the mix. The added flexibility provided by stems gives music a better chance to survive in the dub. However, when the volume balance between stems is altered, the resulting music mix may no longer have a realistic orchestral balance in the instrumental sections. Some composers refuse to record stems, opting instead to work with the full orchestra and get the most musically rewarding performance and inner balance of the ensemble. When preparing for the dub, you should have a conversation with your composer as to whether stems might be useful during your dub.

Attending the Dub

You should invite your composer to the dub. Communicating with the composer and their team during the dub offers key benefits: They can help inform mixing choices and advise on music-editing decisions if and when music is affected. They can also facilitate the placement of music in the project and prevent haphazard decisions or un-musical editing choices. Where composers choose to provide stems for the dub, they can, furthermore, help with the re-balancing of stems in a given scene. Being involved at this final stage allows the composer to fully explore the expressive possibilities of their score and ensure it is better integrated in the overall soundtrack. Ultimately, this may serve the film more effectively as this approach to scoring can result in music that is structurally better suited to the narrative requirements of the project.

Case Study: Dubbing The Dark Knight Rises (2012)

Mel Wesson was ambient music designer on *The Dark Knight Rises* and as one of composer Hans Zimmer's closest collaborators attended the

252 Finalizing Your Project

dubbing sessions for the film. As a member of the music team, Wesson was deeply familiar with all the music Zimmer had composed and recorded. Wesson contributed ambient textures, which were musically conceived sonic layers for the film. Furthermore, he had maintained close contact with sound editor Richard King. In the lead-up to the dub, the music and sound teams were mutually aware of each other's works-in-progress. The final dub then evolved collaboratively over several weeks (an unusually long time!), with screenings taking place at the end of each week. Director Christopher Nolan led the process and pushed for the extra time and large budget required for this expensive dub. Given that *The Dark Knight Rises* was the third of a highly lucrative trilogy, the post-production budget was clearly generous, unlocking scope for experimental working during the final mix. Mel Wesson recalls:

> When you're on the dub stage, it's your last chance to really change what you've done or to make absolutely sure that your idea is what you really intended. I can't understand why a composer wouldn't go. Things get changed constantly there. I think it's important to consider the dub part of the creative process, not just the mix. It's more than that. It's the opportunity to experiment, if you've got time. And when we were mixing [with Chris Nolan], we were mixing on the dub stage and we had seven days a week for six weeks. It was an open-ended day, so if Chris wants to keep people there 14 hours on a Sunday and he's paying them triple rate, he doesn't care. And it's just Warner's problem. In an environment like this, it's all about experiment. Try things out. But it's a very expensive way [in] a very expensive place.[17]

Some project owners are keen to **experiment during the dub**, not only with music but all soundtrack elements. Embracing the rich expressive possibilities that arise from the final sound mix, the project can be transformed at this point. However, free experimentation at the dub may drive up costs, because creative decisions made on an expensive dubbing stage take time.

Takeaways

- Everyone accepts that music may need to be changed during dubbing or may need to be adapted to the technical specifications of the dub (e.g., surround versus stereo).
- You should lead the dub.

- You should have an holistic vision for the place of music among other soundtrack elements.

- When preparing for the dub, you should have a conversation with your composer as to whether stems might be useful during your dub.

- Composers should be invited to the dub.

- Composers can offer flexible music solutions to accommodate changes made at the dub.

- Creative experimentation with music during the dub can produce fascinating results but will drive up post-production costs.

8.5 The Importance of Cue Sheets

The music cue sheet is a document that lists all the music, be it newly commissioned or licensed, used within a project alongside the associated composer and publisher. Performing rights organizations (PROs) use cue sheets to track the use of music in radio, TV, feature films, and web streaming to ensure composers and publishers are compensated for the broadcasting of their work. **It is the responsibility of the project owners to file a cue sheet** with the respective PRO, depending on which PRO the composer and publisher(s) are members of. Once the project has been finalized, the music editor, music supervisor, or a producer will prepare the music cue sheet. Publishers and PROs can provide a template for this. The cue sheet contains:

- All of the music used in the project: Listing the title of every licensed track, itemizing each cue of original music.
- How the music was used: The usage type may affect how much the composer gets paid in royalties (e.g., Background Instrumental, Background Vocal, Visual Instrumental, Visual Vocal, Main Title Theme, End Title Theme, Logo).
- Music duration in minutes and seconds from start time to end time.
- The name of the composer(s) and music publisher(s).
- Composers' and publishers' performing rights affiliation (e.g., ASCAP, BMI, PRS, SACEM, etc.).

The cue sheet is the cornerstone of all royalty payments for a project, so timely completion and filing of the cue sheet is important. Broadcasters may have strict rules about submission deadlines. It is essential that cue sheets are complete

254 Finalizing Your Project

and accurate. Since some projects use a lot of music, mistakes can easily be made on the cue sheets. It is advisable that the composer(s) and publisher(s) get a chance to review a copy of the cue sheet, so they can correct any inaccuracies before the project owners send the cue sheet to the respective PROs.

Cue Sheet Guidance and Templates

Film

https://www.ascap.com/help/music-business-101/music-money-success-movies/movies-part4#cuesheets

TV Episode

https://www.bmi.com/creators/detail/what_is_a_cue_sheet

8.6 Takeaways

Once the project is completed, the team will likely disband and everyone will go their separate ways. Since media production is a freelancers' world, it is possible that the same people may not work together again for some time. Nevertheless, it is useful to pause for a moment of reflection, to cherish the creative achievement, and to evaluate lessons learned. Audience ratings, box office returns, sales figures, reviews, and awards are common measures of success. But they do not represent the full picture: How the public is responding to the project. This is important, obviously, especially since critical acclaim and profitability are likely to lead to future opportunities for everyone involved. However, the public can only ever see the product, not the creative *process* that led to it. Only the creative stakeholders and project owners are in a position to reflect on the process.

You could contemplate:

- What has worked well on the project?
- Were there any creative stakeholders who were particularly great allies?
- Was there someone really inspired or inspiring?
- What work environments and processes should be replicated in future projects?

- Focusing on music, how did the collaboration go with the music supervisor?
- If original music was commissioned, was there a good collaboration with the composer?
- Would the team choose to work with the same composer again?
- What value did music add to the project?

If a collaboration has felt enjoyable and rewarding, hopefully the team will work together again. Lasting collaborative partnerships have resulted in some of the most compelling projects (see also Chapter 7). There are some amazing individuals working in the industry, who arguably do not write or use the best music but whose excellent communication and team working skills, paired with reliable and workable results, make them very successful.

Everyone can learn from mistakes, or, to quote Yoda, "The best teacher, failure is."

- What was problematic?
- Were there any creatives who struggled on the project?
- Why was that?
- What might have enabled them to do better?
- What processes could be improved next time?

There are some extremely gifted composers, whose music is absolutely wonderful, but who have poor interpersonal skills. When a collaboration has been less than great, it is always worth de-briefing the composer, as you would do with other stakeholders. No one gets it 100 percent right on every project. Focusing instead on the project-specific concerns, mutual feedback may reveal some valuable opportunities for learning and growth. This is particularly helpful for students and emerging media creators who are still in the process of finding their creative voice.

8.7 Looking Ahead

Composers, music supervisors, music researchers, and music editors are creative allies that can join you on your journey. Working on your next project, then, you may choose to involve a composer and/or music supervisor early on, to start a creative dialogue about music, be it licensed or original. Sometimes you may opt for obvious music choices, other times going in exactly the opposite direction. Acknowledging failed experiments, and taking setbacks in your stride, you will nourish collaborative working conditions in which an inspired and respectful creative dialogue can take place. Where these conditions exist, amazing possibilities arise from the use of music.

Pursuing your next endeavor, you will always look for new opportunities and challenges. When it comes to working with music, you will naturally have different requirements from one project to the next. Brave media creators are not afraid of music. You will feed their curiosity by continually listening to new music, by opening your eyes and ears to a range of eclectic forms of musical expression. Over time, your appreciation and understanding of music as a powerful asset and tool can evolve. Recognizing that *every* piece of music has expressive potential, it is up to you to channel this potential, finding the right context, pushing boundaries, making bold choices, and never settling for "good enough."

Further Reading

Allen, M. "From Bwana Devil to Batman Forever: Technology in Contemporary Hollywood Cinema." In *Contemporary Hollywood Cinema*, edited by S. Neale and M. Smith. London: Routledge, 1998, pp. 109–129.

Bordwell, D. *The Way Hollywood Tells It: Story and Style in Modern Movies*. Berkeley and Los Angeles: University of California Press, 2006.

Murch, W. *In the Blink of an Eye: A Perspective on Film Editing*. 2nd edn. Los Angeles: Silman-James Press, 2001.

Saltzman, S. *Music Editing for Film and Television: The Art and the Process*. London: CRC Press, 2014.

Notes

1 Just one example is the fact that Steinberg's long-established music production software Nuendo now features "Game Audio Connect," a toolset that enables a direct connection to Audiokinetic's Wwise game audio middleware. https://www.steinberg.net/en/products/nuendo/game_audio.html, accessed 21 March 2018.

2 N. Laporte. *The Men Who Would Be King: An Almost Epic Tale of Moguls, Movies, and a Company Called DreamWorks*. Reprint. Boston and New York: Mariner Books, 2011, p. 221.

3 McTiernan quoted in T. Taylor. *The Big Deal: Hollywood's Million-Dollar Spec Script Market*. William Morrow, 1999, p. 288.

4 'Breaking the Rules with Hanz Zimmer.' Interview by Dan Goldwasser published September 2006, www.soundtrack.net/content/article/?id=205, accessed 16 February 2018.

5 Navarrete in a talk at the Royal College of Music in London on 7 February 2012.

6 Giacchino in a talk at the Royal College of Music, hosted by the Royal Albert Hall in the Elgar Room on 18 October 2017.

7 D. Bordwell. "Intensified Continuity Visual Style in Contemporary American Film." *Film Quarterly* 55(3) (2002), p. 17.

8 D. Bordwell. *The Way Hollywood Tells It: Story and Style in Modern Movies.* Berkeley and Los Angeles: University of California Press, 2006, pp. 181–182.

9 Gregson-Williams in a talk at the "Sundance in London" Festival on 29 April 2012.

10 Gabriel Yared at a "BAFTA Masterclass: Composing for Film" at the BFI Southbank on 26 June 2013.

11 Observed at the scoring sessions at Air Lyndhurst in 2005.

12 Lievsay gave a talk about *Gravity* at the Music and the Moving Image Conference, New York University on 26 May 2017.

13 Henry Mancini. *Did They Mention the Music?: The Autobiography of Henry Mancini.* New York: Cooper Square Press, 2001, p. 185.

14 M. Schelle. *The Score: Interviews with Film Composers.* Los Angeles: Silman-James Press, 2000, p. 306

15 The Motion Picture Editors Guild Newsletter. "Color, Melody and ... Perfume – An Interview with Composer Thomas Newman." *The Motion Picture Editors Guild Newsletter* 17(1) (February 1996).

16 Ibid.

17 Wesson in a talk at the Royal College of Music on 13 November 2013.

Further Listening

Listening Companion to This Book

- **Apple Music** companion playlist (Apple Music subscription required, student discount available): https://tinyurl.com/yb2c3yax
- **Spotify** companion playlist (Spotify Premium recommended, student discount available): https://tinyurl.com/y7bmfae8

10 Films to Watch/Hear for Their Use of Music

- *North by Northwest* (1956), music by Bernard Herrmann
- *Psycho* (1960), music by Bernard Herrmann
- *Once Upon a Time in the West* (1968), music by Ennio Morricone
- *Lola Rennt* (*Run Lola Run*, 1998), music by Reinhold Heil, Johnny Klimek, Tom Tykwer
- *American Beauty* (1999), music by Thomas Newman
- *Requiem for a Dream* (2000), music by Clint Mansell
- *The Dark Knight* (2008), music by Hans Zimmer and James Newton Howard
- *Birdman or (The Unexpected Virtue of Ignorance)* (2014), music by Antonio Sanchez
- *Ex Machina* (2014), music by Ben Salisbury and Geoff Barrow
- *Arrival* (2016), music by Jóhann Jóhannsson

Bonus film: *The Birds* (1963), no composed underscore
Guilty pleasure: *Airplane!* (1980), score by Elmer Bernstein

10 TV Shows to Watch/Hear for Their Use of Music

- *Twin Peaks* (1990–1991, ABC/Showtime), music by Angelo Badalamenti
- *Band of Brothers* (2001, HBO), music by Michael Kamen
- *Lost* (2004–2010, ABC), music by Michael Giacchino
- *Planet Earth* (2006, BBC), music by George Fenton
- *Stranger Things* (2016–, Netflix), music by Kyle Dixon and Michael Stein
- *Black Mirror* (2011–, Netflix), music by various
- *Handmaid's Tale* (2017–, Hulu), music by Adam Taylor plus song compilation
- *Fargo* (2014–, Netflix), music by Jeff Russo
- *Westworld* (2016–, HBO), music composed and adapted by Ramin Diawadi
- *Luke Cage* (2016–, Netflix), music by Adrian Younge and Ali Shaheed Muhammad plus song compilation

Bonus show: *Empire* (2015–, FOX), music by various
Guilty pleasure: *Family Guy* (1998–, FOX), music by Walter Murphy and Ron Jones

10 Games to Play/Hear for Their Use of Music

- *Final Fantasy* franchise (since 1987), music by Nobuo Uematsu and others
- *Metal Gear Solid* series (since 1998), music by various composers, recent installments by Harry Gregson-Williams
- *Rez* (since 2001), music by various
- *Grand Theft Auto: Vice City* (2002), compilation score
- *Assassin's Creed* (since 2007), music by Lorne Balfe, Jesper Kyd, Brian Tyler, and others
- *Dead Space* (2008), music by Jason Graves
- *L.A. Noir* (2011), original music by Andrew Hale and Simon Hale plus jazz song compilation
- *Journey* (2012), music by Austin Wintory
- *Doom* (2016), music by Mick Gordon
- *Star Wars Battlefront* (since 2015), music by Gordy Haah and adapted from John Williams

Bonus game: *Monument Valley* (2014), music by Stafford Bawler, Obfusc and Grigori
Guilty pleasure: *Tetris* (1984), Music A: Russian traditional "Korobeiniki," Music B: Hirokazu Tanaka, Music C: Johann Sebastian Bach (French Suite No. 3 in B minor, minuet and trio)

Further Reading: Film Composer Biographies

Burton, Humphrey. *Leonard Bernstein*. London: Humphrey Burton, 2001.

Danly, Linda. *Hugo Friedhofer: The Best Years of His Life. A Hollywood Master of Music for the Movies*. Lanham, MD: Scarecrow Press, 2002.

Duchen, J. *Erich Wolfgang Korngold*. London: Phaidon Press, 1996.

Dyer, Richard *Nino Rota: Music, Film and Feeling*. New York: British Film Institute, 2010.

Gardner, Pearl Bernstein, and Gerald Gardner. *The Magnificent Elmer: My Life with Elmer Bernstein*. New York: RosettaBooks, 2014.

Glass, Philip. *Words without Music*. New York: Liveright Publishing Corporation, 2015.

Leonard, Geoff, Pete Walker, and Gareth Bramley *John Barry: The Man with the Midas Touch*. Bristol: Redcliffe Press, 2008.

Mancini, Henry. *Did They Mention the Music?: The Autobiography of Henry Mancini*. New York: Cooper Square Press, 2001.

Previn, A. *No Minor Chords: My Days in Hollywood*. London and New York: Bantam Books, 1993.

Rózsa, M. *Double Life: The Autobiography of Miklós Rózsa*. New edition. Tunbridge Wells, UK: Baton Press, 1984.

Smith, S.C. *A Heart at Fire's Center: The Life and Music of Bernard Herrmann*. Berkeley and Los Angeles, CA: University of California Press, 2002.

Stafford, D. and C. Stafford. *Maybe I'm Doing It Wrong: The Life and Times of Randy Newman*. London: Omnibus Press, 2016.

Wegele, P. Max Steiner: Composing, Casablanca, and the Golden Age of Film Music. Lanham, MD: Rowman & Littlefield, 2014.

About the Author

Vasco Hexel leads the Masters Programme in Composition for Screen at the Royal College of Music, London, and is visiting lecturer at the Faculty of Music, University of Cambridge. He is consultant at the Film and Television Music Research Center, Beijing Normal University, and he was Head of Music at the London Film School, 2010–2013. Vasco earned his Bachelor of Music degree in Film Scoring and Vocal Performance at the Berklee College of Music, Boston. He earned his Master's degree in Composition for Screen at the Royal College of Music where he also wrote his doctoral thesis, "Understanding Contextual Agents and their Impact on Recent Hollywood Film Music Practice." Vasco has composed music for award-winning animations, documentaries, commercials, and feature films. His music has featured in numerous broadcasts internationally. Vasco's music was used exclusively for the 2012 Christmas branding of S4/C (Wales) and he created the new sonic identity of Kanal D (Romania) in 2009. Past and current clients include RSA Films, Music Sales, SohoMusic as well as fashion brands Gucci and Boden. Vasco's music is published by Universal Music and EMI.

As an educator and scholar Vasco is passionate about coaching aspiring screen composers and filmmakers, devising and delivering relevant, industry-facing, hands-on training on the creation and function of music in screen media. Vasco's academic writing and international speaking engagements continue to nourish the appreciation of film music and explore the creative practice of film music creation and collaborative soundtrack composition.

Vasco is the author of "Hans Zimmer and James Newton Howard's *The Dark Knight*: A Film Score Guide" (Lanham, MD: Rowman & Littlefield,

2016). He is a Senior Fellow of the Higher Education Academy and a member of the Royal Television Society (RTS) and the British Academy for Film and Television Arts (BAFTA).

www.vascohexel.com

Glossary

AAA game   A video game with a very high development and marketing budget (pronounced "triple A").

ADR   Abbreviation for Automated Dialogue Replacement, a process to synchronize dialogue with footage whose audio was poorly recorded on location.

Aesthetic   Referring to a set of guiding principles underlying the project at hand, including music choices, regarding tone, feel, style, effect, etc.

Animatic   A preliminary version of a scene or sequence produced by shooting successive sections of a storyboard and adding a sound effects track.

Arranging   Here, arranging musical parts for a specific instrumental group, e.g., for jazz band, string quartet, orchestra, etc.

ASL   Abbreviation for Average Shot Length.

Atonal music   Music in which pitches do not relate to each other in a major, minor, or modal key.

Avid   (1) Avid Technology is an American technology and multimedia company. (2) "Avid/1" was the first digital editing software produced by Avid Technology, launched in 1988. It was succeeded in 1989 by Avid Media Composer, an off-line non-linear editing system for film and video.

Bed   In the context of film music, this term refers to a cue's underlying, steady texture formed of drones, held string chords, etc.

Glossary **265**

CGI Abbreviation for computer-generated imagery.

Chords Three or more musical notes sounding simultaneously. In tonal music, a chord's function is dependent on its relationship with the tonal centre.

Chromatic A chromatic scale may include up to 12 pitches within an octave. The term originates from the Greek word *khrōmatikós* = "coloured"

Classical Hollywood film A distinctive cinematic style evident in Hollywood films of 1920–1960. Comprehensively defined and analysed in D. Bordwell, J. Staiger, and K. Thompson. *The Classical Hollywood Cinema: Film Style and Mode of Production to 1960*. London and New York: Routledge, 1985.

Classical music Umbrella term commonly used for all orchestral/ Western traditional music. Strictly speaking, the "classical period" only lasted ca.1750–1820.

Close-scoring A compositional strategy whereby the film composer structures their music to closely match visual events in the film.

Commission Asking a composer to compose original music for a project, usually for a fee.

Commissioning contract Contract drawn up to commission a composer to compose an original score for a project, setting out the scope of services expected of the composer, the timelines and deadlines, the fees and expenses payable, how the composer will be credited, who will own the copyright to the music, and how royalties will be handled?

Commissioning editor Working for a broadcaster or music production company, commissioning editors commission new projects and buy new content.

Composer agent A representative for the composer's interests. Agents might reach out to project owners on behalf of their client. Conversely, project owners may reach out to agents to seek recommendations for a suitable composer. Agents will negotiate contracts on behalf of the composer.

Conductor Directs the performance of a large ensemble on the scoring stage, usually in sync with a click track (to ensure picture sync).

266 Glossary

Copyist	The person or persons in charge of printing scores and parts for a scoring session.
Creative stakeholder	All creative personnel involved in the project, including the director, producer, sound designers, composer, editor, set designer, etc. They have a shared vested interest in the success of the project.
Cubase	A popular music production software (see DAW).
Cue	A term widely used in film scoring jargon to refer to a piece of media music.
Cue sheet	The music cue sheet is a document that lists all the music, be it newly commissioned and/or licensed, used within a project alongside the associated composer and publisher. Cue sheets are filed with the relevant performing rights organization and used for the purpose of performance/ broadcast tracking and royalty calculation.
DAW	Abbreviation for Digital Audio Workstation. Umbrella term for music production and recording software used by media composers.
Demo	A music recording produced by the composer to demonstrate to the project owners what their ideas are for a specific scene or segment. Usually created with virtual instruments, later to be complemented or replaced by real instruments once the demo is approved.
Diatonic scale	A scale that includes five whole tone steps and two half steps in each octave, in which the two half steps are separated from each other by either two or three whole steps, depending on their position in the scale.
Diegesis	From the Greek word *diēgēsis*. Diegetic elements are part of the fictional world (or "part of the story"), whereas non-diegetic elements are stylistic elements of storytelling.
Digital performer	A popular music production software.
Dolby A	A noise reduction system developed by Dolby Laboratories.
Dolby Atmos	A sound reproduction system that allows up to 128 separate audio tracks to be handled and distributed in a cinema. Speakers are placed all around and above the audience. The system is gradually being adopted in television and video games.

Glossary **267**

DOP	Abbreviation for director of photography, who leads the camera and light crews working on a film, television production, or other live action piece. They are responsible for making artistic and technical decisions related to the image.
DTS	A multi-channel audio technology developed by DTS, Inc.
Dubbing session (aka the dub)	A mixing session at the end of audio post-production in which all audio tracks (dialogue, sound effects, and music) are mixed and synchronized with the image.
Dubbing stage	Large mixing facility where the final film soundtrack is assembled and mixed.
Dynamics	In music, refers to the intensity of a sound (loud/quiet). In written music, referred to by Italian names, such as *forte* for loud and *piano* for quiet.
Edit (footage)	In film terminology, editing is the process of selecting and assembling footage. "Edit" refers to either the point at which footage shot with one camera is cut against footage from another (also called "cut") or an assembled version of the entire film (also "rough cut" or "cut").
Edit (music)	Whereas footage can be cut and joined in countless different ways, music audio edits can only be made in ways that do not disturb the sonic or musical continuity of a track. Specialist music editors normally undertake this job—for example, conforming audio to changed film edits in musical ways.
Fade	In acoustic terms, the process of increasing or decreasing an audio signal's playback volume. In visual terms, the process of reducing or increasing brightness in the image to create the impression of a "fade to black" or "fade from black."
Film (music) score	Non-diegetic music accompanying a film, often newly composed.
FMod	An audio authoring tool and a cross-platform sound engine for interactive media and video games. This type of software, collectively called middleware, acts as a bridge between sound and music and video game engines.
Foley	Named after sound-effects artist Jack Foley. The reproduction of sound effects that are added to film, video, and other media in post-production to improve audio quality.

268 Glossary

Harmony	Chords accompanying a melody with sympathetic pitches.
Hit point (hit/sync point)	Jargon for the audio-visual coincidence of film and music whereby an event in the music (a downbeat, a particular note, etc. coincides with an on-screen visual or sonic event (e.g., a cut, a gesture, a spoken word).
Instrumentation	The instruments performing in a given ensemble or used in a musical composition.
Intensified continuity	A term coined by Bordwell to describe prevalent aesthetics and production techniques in recent Hollywood film. Includes the stylistic tactics of rapid editing, bipolar extremes of lens lengths, close-framing of dialogue scenes, and a free-ranging camera. See D. Bordwell, *The Way Hollywood Tells It: Story and Style in Modern Movies*. Berkeley and Los Angeles, CA: University of California Press, 2006. Also D. Bordwell, "Intensified Continuity Visual Style in Contemporary American Film." *Film Quarterly* 55(3) (2002): 16–28.
Leitmotif (aka theme)	A term borrowed from opera that is frequently used in film music jargon to refer to a musical idea (melodic or otherwise) that comes to accompany and later represent (or refer to) characters, objects, events, etc.
Library music	See "Production music."
Licensing (music)	Obtaining permission from the copyright owners to use a piece of music in a multimedia project, usually for a fee.
Licensing fee/cost	The fees paid for licensing existing music for a project. Fees may or may not be negotiable, depending on the music in question.
Locked picture	The old-fashioned concept of a picture edit that will no longer be altered.
Logic Pro	A popular music production software.
Logo fanfare	Here, refers to a short and recognizable musical piece that is used to accompany a studio logo at the start of a film, TV programme, or video game.
Master	The original of a music recording, on tape or in a digital format.
Master use license	Permission to make a copy of a master in a project, in synchronization with the visuals.

Glossary **269**

Media creators   Any project owners in film, television, audio-visual media installations, media web content, and video games.

Melody   "The most familiar strategy for organizing notes horizontally is melody, which can be defined as an extended series of notes played in an order, which is memorable and recognizable as a discrete unit (hummable, if you will). One of the most distinguishing characteristics of tonal music since about the middle of the eighteenth century is the extent to which melody is privileged as a form of organization. Its presence prioritizes our listening, subordinating some elements to others and giving us a focal points in the musical texture." (K. Kalinak, *Settling the Score: Music and the Classical Hollywood Film.* Madison, WI: University of Wisconsin Press, 1992, p. 5.)

Modal music   Music in which a series of pitches adheres to the pitch relationships of a mode, including—but not limited to—Ionian, Dorian, Phrygian, Lydian, Mixolydian, Aeolian, and Locrian.

Music brief   A set of instructions shared with the music supervisor and/or composer for existing or original music. The brief may be presented in writing but can also be agreed verbally during a meeting.

Music contractor (called "fixer" in the UK)   The person in charge of sourcing and hiring musicians for the scoring session.

Music editor   An assistant to the film composer who assists with a wide range of tasks including the creation of timing notes, cue sheets, score layouts. Also responsible for ensuring cues once recorded are correctly synchronized with the image (during the dub). Sometimes asked to create temp tracks beforehand or to alter recorded cues to fit—e.g., a revised film edit.

Music supervisor   The music supervisor helps with all music-related aspects of film, television, advertising, video games, and any other multimedia formats. They will find suitable music, secure the rights and permissions required to use that music, and oversee the production and implementation of music in the project.

270 Glossary

Musico-dramatic ...	Here, refers to music that accompanies multimedia and has a synergistic dramatic effect.
NDA	Abbreviation for Non-Disclosure Agreement, a contract by which one or more parties agree not to disclose certain information relating to a person, a process, a project, or a product.
Nuendo	A popular music production software (see DAW).
Onboarding	The process of integrating a new employee into an organization. Here, refers to the process of hiring and briefing of a music supervisor and/or composer.
Orchestrator	A specialist working with the composer to translate sequenced or notated cues into full orchestral scores for scoring session purposes.
Original music	Music specially composed for a project.
Over-dubbing	In the realm of film scoring, the process of adding layers of tracks and performances on top of previously recorded tracks. Over-dubbing is a popular method in studio recording to bolster the sound of, for example, a string section or allow a few percussionists to perform the tasks of many. Over-dubbing also occurs when actors synchronize their voices with lip movements previously filmed (see ADR).
Package deal	Package deals offer the composer an all-inclusive lump sum, usually paid in three installments throughout their engagement that covers their composer fee as well as all expenses arising from the composition and production of the original score.
Performing Rights Organization (PRO)	Also known as a "performing rights society": An intermediary for royalty collection between copyright holders and parties who wish to use copyrighted works publicly, in broadcasts, etc.
Picture sync	Describes how edited visuals and recorded audio align.
Pitch	(1) The quality of a sound as resulting from the frequencies producing it (high/low). (2) A composer's submission of music to the project owners (see below) to be considered for a job. Competitive pitching is fairly common in commercial media production.
Pro Tools	A popular music production software.

Glossary **271**

Production music   Also called "stock music" or "library music," production music is recorded music produced and owned by production music companies, available for licensing to customers for use in film, television, radio, advertising, and any other recorded media.

Project owner   The creative stakeholders in charge of the project, usually the director, producers, and studio executives, commissioning editors (in broadcasting), and audio directors (in video games). The term refers to creative ownership but also reflects the fact that project owners have authority over the other creative stakeholders and their work.

Recording engineer   Also called "audio engineer:" a specialist who records, edits, and mixes audio recordings.

Rendering   Here, the use of sounds to convey the feelings or effects associated with the situation on screen rather than insisting on the faithful reproduction of sounds that might be heard in the situation in reality. See also M. Chion, *Audio-Vision: Sound on Screen*. Translated by C. Gorbman. New York: Columbia University Press, 1994. Also in the glossary of M. Chion, *Film, A Sound Art*. Translated by C. Gorbman. New York: Columbia University Press, 2009, p. 487.

Re-recording (dubbing) mixers   Re-recording mixers, also known as "dubbing mixers," work with all of the sound elements (dialogue, automated dialogue replacement, Foley, sound effects, atmospheres, and music), mixing them together to create the final soundtrack for a film or television production.

Royalties   Also called residuals, due when music is placed in a film or TV show and then distributed, screened, or broadcast. Besides performance royalties, composers may also earn so-called mechanical royalties, due as a percentage share of the sales revenue of physical or digital copies of a composition or song, including in a broadcast

Score   (1) Umbrella term to refer to all newly composed music for a project, usually recorded in scoring sessions with live musicians. (2) A printed set of notation that summarizes all instrumental parts in a cue.

272 Glossary

Score producer
A specialist in charge of overseeing the score recording, editing, and mixing process. A close ally of the composer, the score producer is another set of eyes and ears in the recording booth to help with quality control.

Scoring session
The studio recording session in which original music is recorded, usually with the aid of click tracks to ensure picture sync.

SDDS
Abbreviation for Sony Digital Dynamic Sound, a sound processing and reproduction system by Sony.

Sequencer
A device or software that allows the composer to record, store, edit, and play back musical performance information.

Sonic branding
The strategic use of music and sound design to brand a product with a unique and recognizable identity.

Sound design
Sound design is the process of specifying, acquiring, manipulating, and/or generating audio elements in filmmaking, TV production, sound art, video game development, and other media.

Sound effects
Sounds that accompany objects or actions on screen or help convey the diegetic sonic environment whose sounds may or may not have their source off-screen.

Soundscape
A term borrowed from the geographical term "landscape," used to describe the sonic landscape of a film, which may include sound effects, dialogue, and music.

Soundtrack
(1) The component on the physical filmstrip carrying the audio signal. (2) An album that contains music from a film, TV show, or video game.

Source score
Music that emanates diegetically from a source within the narrative, visible or not.

Spotting session
A meeting between the composer and the project owners in which the musical requirements of a project are discussed and agreed.

Stems (or "stripes")
In film music jargon, mix-downs of groups of instruments into pre-mixed tracks, usually in preparation for the dub. The recorded orchestral film score is customarily delivered in stems of woodwinds, brass, percussion, strings, and additional instruments such as synthesizers, guitars, etc.

Glossary **273**

Suites	Potpourri compilations of musical themes, moods, instrumentation, giving the project owners a flavor of the score the composer intends to write.
Supervising sound editor	Also called "sound supervisor," oversees the entire post-production sound crew, including the sound editor, Foley artist, and ADR editor. Ultimately responsible for the completion and quality of all sound editing, and answers to the producer and director. May also supervise the music editor unless that person is part of the composer's team.
Sync	(1) Synchronizing music and sound effects with moving image. Sound and picture can be in sync or out of sync. (2) Agreeing with a composer or songwriter and their publisher to use a composition or song in connection with a project. A sync needs to be agreed with all rights holders and a negotiable fee paid.
Synchronization license	Permission to use a piece of music in synchronization with moving image, for a negotiable fee.
Temp track	Temporary music tracks that are placed in the film for the purposes of test screenings, to give filmmakers and the composer an impression of intended mood and pace for a scene, or to help the editor find a suitable visual and rhythmic cadence for the film during editing.
Theme (aka leitmotif)	Among filmmakers and composers, usually refers to a recognizable musical idea that is associated with a character, object, or situation. For marketing purposes may also refer to an overarching recognizable piece of music—e.g., "Theme from Superman."
THX	An audio reproduction standard for movie theaters distributed by THX Ltd.
Timbre	The sound character or quality of a musical sound or voice as other than its pitch (high/low) and intensity (loud/quiet).
Timing notes	A verbal or written breakdown of events in a chosen scene with coinciding SMPTE (Society of Motion Picture and Television Engineers) time code. Traditionally created by the music editor to facilitate the composer's workflow.
Tonal music	Music of a western tradition in which seven diatonic notes relate to each other in a major or minor key.

274 Glossary

Track
(1) A piece of music (e.g., "there are twelve tracks on this CD"). (2) A track in a music production software that holds digital audio or MIDI (Musical Instrument Digital Interface) information.

Underscore
Here, refers to all composed non-diegetic music that accompanies the project.

Unity
A game engine used for computer simulations and video game development, with sound and music implementation capabilities.

VFX
Abbreviation for visual effects.

Virtual instruments
Software emulations of real instruments such as orchestral instruments, synthesizers, etc.

Wwise
An audio authoring tool and a cross-platform sound engine for interactive media and video games. This type of software, collectively called middleware, acts as a bridge between sound and music and video game engines.

Index

A Chorus Line 166
AAA games 158, 172–173, 212
Abrams, J. J. 19, 160, 227
absence of music 10–12, 18, 224–225
absolute volume 79–81
accelerando 77
Adams, Bryan 154, 162
adapted musicals 166–167
adapting music 23, 31, 34, 50–51, 109, **127**, 130, 133, 139–140, 142–144, 152
added value, and music roles **20**, 21
Ade, Maren 11, 44
adventure movies 35–36
Air Supply 134
Airplane! 46
Alabama 3 22
aleatory music 209–210
allegro 77
Ally McBeal 45–46, 107, 133
"Also Sprach Zarathustra" 99, 100, 136
Altered States 27, 32
Amadeus 47–48, 139, 152
Amélie 30, 101
American Beauty 22, 32, 64, 196, 232
American Graffiti 34, 43, 121–122
American Psycho 42
Amiel, John 98
analog technology 231–232
andante 77
Anderson, P. T. 48
Andrews, Michael 38
Annie 173
anthems 36
Antz 98
Apocalypse Now 36, 101
appropriation 144

Aristocats 142
Armageddon 163
Arnold, David 29
Aronofsky, Darren 18
Arrival 151
Atmajian, Jeff 213
atmosphere **20**, 21–22
atonal music 66
Austin Powers: International Man of Mystery 29
Avatar 23
Avengers franchise 156
average shot lengths (ASL) 236
awe 37

Babel 145
Baby Driver 78, 234
Bach, Johann Sebastian 67
Back to the Future 129
backing tracks 212
Badelt, Klaus 88
Bang, Jun-Seok 145
Barrow, Geoff 18, 87–88, 151
Barry, John 163
Basic Instinct 23
Batman 156
Batman themes 153
Battle Creek 173
Beaches 39
Beau, Raphaël 151
Beauty and the Beast 86
Bee Gees 163
Bellis, Richard 206
Beltrami, Marco 98, 194, 201, 221, 226
Bend It like Beckham 134
Bernstein, Elmer 28, 37
Besson, Luc 46

276 Index

Better Call Saul 95, 135
Beverly Hills Cop 22, 67, 104–105
Bigelow, Kathryn 201
biopics 86, 139, 141
BioShock 133
Bird 141
Bird, Brad 53, 227
Birdman or (The Unexpected Virtue of Ignorance) 17, 30, 48, 108, 151
The Birds 11, 44
Black Swan 152
Blade Runner 2049 19, 225
Blade Runner 23, 34
The Blair Witch Project 11
Blazing Saddles 46
Blue Velvet 132
boldness 18–19
Bollywood 168–169
Bond songs 18, *see also James Bond* franchise
booth score readers 178
Bordwell, David 236
Born to be Blue 141
The Bourne Identity 225
The Bourne Ultimatum 96, 99
brass 72–73
Brave 31, 64
Breakfast at Tiffany's 41, 95, 107, 165
Breaking Bad 65, 151
Brest, Martin 104–105
Bridge of Spies 196
Bridges, Mark 50
Britell, Nicholas 17, 28
Britten, Benjamin 70
broadcaster stings 158–159
Brokeback Mountain 28, 31
Bruckheimer, Jerry 219
budgeting 14, 76, 90, 114, 118–122, 131, 149, 165, 167, 170–173, **174**, 175–182, 191, *see also* financial implications
Burrell, Carter 18
Burton, Tim 56, 156, 166
Burwell, Carter 225, 226–227

Cabaret 166
Caché 44
"Call of Duty: Black Ops" 131
Cast Away 44
Castellucci, Teddy 226
character themes **20**, 27–28, 152–153
characterization 17, **20**, 23–24, 27–28, 33, 108, 131, 138
Chazelle, Damien 46
Chicken Run 218–219
Chinatown 24
Chion, Michael 20
chords 65–66, 68
choreographers 165

Citizen Kane 154
Classical Hollywood Films 13
classical music 23, 27–28, 60–61, **125–127**, 135–140, 140
Clausen, Alf 31
clichés 31, 39, 138
click-tracks 93, 211–212
Clinton, George 29
A Clockwork Orange 138
Close Encounters of the Third Kind 37, 63
Cloverfield 11
Coen Brothers 18, 22, 226–227
collaboration 1, 8, 14, 50, 59–60, 97–98, 150, 189, 191, 196, 217, 226–228, 255
comedy **20**, 28–29
commercials 54–56, 99, 129, 194
commissioning music 149–150
communication 8, 216–217, 236, 239
compilation soundtrack albums 132–134
composer agencies 192–193
composer calls 191
composer websites 192
composers 150; availability of 195–196; collaboration with 14, 59–60, 150, 189; compensation for 9, 143–144, 171–175, 185, 193–194; coping with digital soundtracks 243–246; and dubbing 249–250; finding/hiring 190–197; long partnerships with 190, 226–228; as music consultants 11–12, 18, 44; onboarding 197–201, 202, *204*; scope of the work 183–184; and temp scores 98–99, 102; workflow 202–203, *204*, 205–215; working processes 88, 205–206, 207, 234–235
computer-generated imagery (CGI) 238–239
Condon, Bill 86
conductors 176
confidence 217
consonant music 65
Conti, Bill 134
continuity **20**, 29–30, 49
"coolness" 22
Coppola, Francis Ford 121–122
copyright 116, 118, 122, 141, 186
Corigliano, John 27, 32, 140
The Cotton Club 142
creative control 166, 217, 239, 242, 249
creative freedom 218
creative stakeholders 4, 52–53, 55, 99, 165, 189, 198, *see also* project owners
crime-comedies 29
crime thrillers 23
Crimson Tide 78
Cuarón, Alfonso 247–248, *248*
cue sheets 93, 123, 253–254
cues 25
cultural associations 16, 130, 137

Daft Punk 21, 48, 108–109, 151, 196
Dancer in the Dark 39, 168
Dangerous Liaisons 34
Dangerous Minds 131
Danna, Mychael 98–99, 197–198
Daredevil 24, 47
The Dark Knight 17, 30, 65, 86, 105, 138, 146, 155–156, 206–207, 215
The Dark Knight Rises 251–252
Das Boot 78
Davis, Garth 219
Dead Space 38, 209–210
deadlines 184
Debney, John 26
delegation 217
demos 207–211, 213, 215
Desplat, Alexandre 225
dialogue 13, 14, **20**, 30, 80, 241
Die Hard 23–24, 139–140
diegetic music 11, 41–46, 48, 108–109, 162, 164, *see also* non-diegetic music
diegetic switches 45, 46–47
digital technology 85, 88, 158, 200, 230, 232–233; CGI 238–239; coping with 243–246; phone cameras 232; software 206–208, 211, 242, 248; soundtracks 240
directors 85, 97, 250
discussions 56–59
Disney musicals 168
Disney, Walt 87
dissonant music 66
Djawadi, Ramin 56, 59–60, 108, 133, 155, 158, 205
Dogme 95 filmmakers 44
Donnie Darko 38, 133
Doom 38
doublings 177–178
Doyle, Patrick 31, 238
The Draughtsman Contract 151
dream states 32
drums/percussion 30, 73, 78–79, 108
dubbing 93, 214–215, 243, 245–246, 248–253
dubbing engineers 221, 244, 249, 251
Dunkirk 35, 152
dynamics 80–81

early arrival/departure 243–244
early arrival/late departure 245–246
East Is East 43
Easy Rider 131
Edelman, Randy 32
editing speeds 236–237
Edward Scissorhands 37
Edwards, Gareth 225
8 Femmes (8 Women) 167
8 Mile 131
Eisenstein, Sergei 24

Eisner, Michael 189
electronic music 176
Elfman, Danny 23, 56, 99
emails 216
emotional reqirements 53, *54*, 161–162
emotional responses **20**, 35, *54*
The English Patient 23
E.T.: The Extra-Terrestrial 63
Evita 166
Ex Machina 18, 87–88, 151
exclusive licenses 117
experimentation 7, 9, 47, 150–151, 213–214, 218, 237, 252
extra-diegetic music. *see* non-diegetic music
Eyre, Richard 53

Faltermeyer, Harold 104–105
Family Guy 46
Fantasia 137
Fargo 22, 135
Favreau, John 26, 56, 59–60, 168
fear 7
fee schedules 184–185
feedback 208–209
Fenton, George 34, 222–225
Ferdinand 109
Fiddler on the Roof 166
The Fifth Element 46
Fifty Shades of Grey 23
film noir 24
financial implications 145–146, 170–173; of classical music 137; and composers 191; and music supervisors 90; of musical performers 76, 214; musicals 165; popular music 128–129; recording costs 76, 90, 120, 137, 171, 181, 212, *see also* budgeting; licensing fees
Fincher, David 220, 220–221
fixing scenes via music 95
Flashdance 134
focus **20**, 26–27
focused listening 56–57
folk music **125–227**, 142–145
foreign royalties 123, 186
foreshadowing 33
Forrest Gump 36, 63, 131
The Founder 86
1492: Conquest of Paradise 35
franchises 27, 63–64, 79, 152, 156, 159–161, 163
French New Wave 47
Frozen 168
Funny Games 44

Game of Thrones 155, 158
Garland, Alex 18, 87–88, 151
Geffen, David 219, 223

278 Index

genres of music 60–61, *62*, 124
Gerrard, Lisa 35, 96, 219
Ghost 220–221
Ghostbusters 134
Giacchino, Michael 19, 32, 53, 56, 102, 160, 162, 200, 205–207, 214, 225, 227, 235–236
Gilligan, Vince 95
Giulia y los Tellarini 145
Gizicki, Steven 92
Gladiator 35, 96, 219
Glass, Phillip 45, 108, 144
Glee 157
Glow 34
Godard, Jean-Luc 47
Goldenthal, Elliot 223
Goldsmith, Jerry x, xi, 23, 28, 67
Golubić, Thomas 91–92
Good Bye Lenin! 101
The Good Wife 128–129
Good Will Hunting 39
goodie bag approach 103, 109, 244–245
Gorbman, Claudia, "Unheard Melodies: Narrative Film Music" 13
Gosling, Ryan 106
The Graduate 104, 132–133
Grand Theft Auto: Vice City 133
Granger, Farley 106
Graves, Jason 38, 192, 209–210
Gravity 247–248
The Great Gatsby 134
Greengrass, Paul 99
Greenwood, John 33, 66–67, 109
Gregson-Williams, Harry 35, 63, 113, 196, 237
Grusin, Dave 104
Guardians of the Galaxy 134

Haab, Gordy 50–51
Hale, Andrew 142
Hale, Simon 142
Halo 38
Haneke, Michael 11, 44
"Happy Birthday" 129
Happy Feet 133
harmony 65–68, *68*
harp 74
Harry Potter franchise 63
Hauschka 196, 219–220
Heil, Reinhold 108
Herrmann, Bernard 12, 18, 24, 27, 44, 139, 153–154, 201, 218
hierarchies 217, 221–222, 226
Hitchcock, Alfred 11–12, 18, 27, 37–38, 44, 95, 106, 139, 154, 201
homophony 66, 67
honesty 200–201
Hooper, Tom 166

Horner, James 53, 154
horror 37–38
horror genre 11, 66
Hotel Rwanda 144
House of Cards 65
Howard, James Newton 28, 38, 155, 196, 201, 235
The Hunt for Red October 31
The Hurt Locker 201
Hurwitz, Justin 107, 142
hymns 36

I, Daniel Blake 44, 224–225
II. Allegretto (Beethoven) 136
In the Land of Blood and Honey 213
Iñárritu, Alejandro González 48, 108
Inception 32, 82, 105
The Incredibles 53
Inouye, Charles Martin 94
instrument rental 180
instrument tuning 180
international productions 120–121
Interview with the Vampire: The Vampire Chronicles 46, 223
Iris 53
Iron Man 47, 59–60, 79
The Italian Job 35

Jablonsky, Steve 239
Jack Reacher 209
James Bond franchise 156, 160, 163
Jarre, Maurice 32, 144, 151
Jaws 104, 154
jazz music 23–24, 29, 46, 61, 66, **125–127**, 140–142
Jennings, Will 162
Jerry Maguire 142
Jewison, Norman 166
Jóhannsson, Jóhann 12, 18, 67, 102, 151, 225
Jolie, Angelina 213
Jones, Brian Jay 121–122
Jones, Trevor 32
Jordan, Neil 46, 223
The Jungle Book 26, 234
Jurassic Park 69
Justice League 130

Kamen, Michael 23–24, 37, 139–140, 153–154, 162
Katzenberg, Jeffrey 219
King Kong 103–104
Klimek, Johnny 108
Komeda, Krzysztof 38
Korngold, Eric W. 218
Korzeniowski, Abel 63
Kosinki, Joseph 21, 108
Koyaanisqatsi: Life out of Balance 78, 108

Kraemer, Joe 209
Kroc, Ray 86
Kubrick, Stanley 10, 11, 34
Kundun 144
Kurtz, Gary 121–122

La La Land 46, 106, 168
L.A. Noir 142
La tourneuse de pages [The Page Turner] 139
Lake, Peter 50
Langer, Susanne 15–16
language 15–16, 52, 226
large budgets 172, 212, 248
Larson, Nathan 36
The Last of the Mohicans 32
Lawrence of Arabia 28
Lebo M 31
legal considerations 5–6, 129; 2001: A Space
    Odyssey 100; commissioning contracts
    55, 183–187, 197; music licensing 89,
    90, 99, 101, *see also* master use licenses;
    synchronization licenses
Leigh, Mike 34, 199
Leone, Sergio 12
Les Misérables 166
Levinson, Barry 105
Lewis, C. S. 222
licensed music 89–90, 99, 101, 112–115,
    126; blanket licenses 120–121; costs /
    budgeting 118–122; exclusive licenses 117;
    jazz **126**, 141; license terms 117; master
    use licenses 114, 129, 137; non-exclusive
    licenses 117; popular **126**, 128–129,
    135; synchronization licenses 114–116,
    129, 132, 136, 143–144, 146, 183, 197;
    traditional / folk **126**, 143; vs. original
    music 162
licensing fees 115–120, 123, 128–129, 146, 167
licensing managers 118
Lievsay, Skip 247, 248
The Life Aquatic with Steve Zissou 42
Ligeti, György 34, 99–100, 137
Liman, Doug 98, 225
linear media 3, 49, 215
Lion 65, 154, 196, 219–220
The Lion King 31, 168
listening equipment 57, 59
Loach, Ken 44, 224–225
locations 10–11, **20**, 31–32, 86–87, 143
Lola Rennt (Run Lola Run) 48, 78, 108, 131,
    151, 234
The Long Walk Home 222–223
Lord, Peter 218
Love Actually 19
Love in the Time of Cholera 144
love themes 23
Luke Cage 107, 135

McTiernan, John 233
Mad Men 157
magic, reliance on music 37
Magnolia 48, 164
main titles 21–22, 155–158
major key music 66
Mamma Mia! 167
The Man Who Knew Too Much 139, 164
Mancini, Henry 95, 107, 218, 249
Mann, Hummie 29
Mansell, Clint 19, 151–152
Marianelli, Dario 140
Marvel's *Defenders* 138–139
master sound recordings 116
mechanical royalties 123, 186
media production, and digital technology 85
medium budgets 172
meetings 216
melody 62–65, 68
Mendes, Sam 232
metronomes 77
"mickey-mousing" 28
Micmacs 151
Midler, Bette 39
Miles Ahead 141
minor key music 66
Minority Report 34
misappropriation 144
Mission Impossible—Rogue Nation 139, 234
Mission Impossible franchise 139, 156, 160, 234
mixing 93, *204*, 214–215
mixing engineers 178
Modern Family 132
modes 64
modular approaches 235
monetization 90
monothematic scores 153–154, 161
montage sequences 24–25, 133–134, 163
Monty, Norman 160, 163
Moonlight 17, 28, 131
Morricone, Ennio 12
Mostow, Jonathan 98
Mother! 18
Mothersbaugh, Mark 21, 130
motifs 63
Moulin Rouge 167
Mousehunt 219
Mr. & Mrs. Smith 98
Mr. Turner 34, 67, 151, 199
music briefs 54–55
music contractors 176–177, 213
music copying 176, 211–213
music editors 92–94, 178, 211–212, 214–215
music planning 87, 233
music producers 178
music production companies 192–193
music researchers 113–115, 136

280 Index

music royalties 122–123, 186
music/sound effects overlaps *241*
music sources 113, 145–147
music supervisors 89–92, 102, 108, 113–114, 130–131, 136, 138, 147, 201, 213
music videos 134
musical directors 165
musical instruments 68–76, 82, 83
musical notation *16*
musical themes viii, x, 21–23, 33, 38, 62–64, 68–69, 105, 107, 152–164, 267
musical unity 97
musicals 107, 164–169
musicians/singers 177
My Fair Lady 165, 166

narrative film music 13, 19, **20**, 21–25, 27–39, *see also* diegetic music; non-diegetic music
narrative structure **20**, 24–25
Navarrette, Javier 224–25, 235
Network 11
networking 89–91, 94, 191
New German Cinema 47
Newman, Thomas 32, 196, 250
Nichols, Mike 132–133
No Country for Old Men 18
Nocturnal Animals 24, 63
Nolan, Christopher 86, 88, 206, 235, 252
non-diegetic music 41–42, 45, 48, 108–109, 162–163, *see also* diegetic music
non-disclosure agreements 200
non-exclusive licenses 117, 146–147
non-linear media 3, *see also* video games
non-linear workflows 230–231
non-narrative films 44–45
non-use of music 10–12, 18, 224–225
North, Alex 100
North by Northwest 12

O'Halloran, Dustin 196, 219–220
on-screen performances 106–107, 109
onboarding 4, 197–202, *204*
Once Upon a Time in the West 12
opening title themes. *see* main titles
orchestral film scores 13, 21, 23, 26, 29, 32, 34–35, 42, 45, 51, 69, 104, 155, 156, 158, 162, 172, 174, 214
orchestral leaders 178
orchestration 175, *204*, 211–214
original music 140, 161–64, 181–182
original musicals 167–168
originality 103–106
other costs 178–181
Ottman, John 160
overdubs 177–178
overtime pay 177–178

pacing, establishing **20**, 25, 35
Paesano, John 24
Park, Nick 218
past practices, observing 14
Patsavas, Alex 92
Pearce, Richard 222–223
performing rights organizations (PROs) 123, 253
permissions 116
Philadelphia 138, 163
phone calls/video conferencing 216
piano 74, 82
The Pink Panther 29, 107
Pirates of the Caribbean franchise 63–64
pitches 193–194
Planet Earth 2 194
Planet of the Apes 28, 67
planning 10–11, 53, 86–88, 95, 165–166, 241–244
Poledouris, Basil 31
Poltergeist xi
polyphony 67
polythematic scores 154–155, 161
pop music 22, 29, 35, 66, 104–105, 124, **125–127**, 128–132, 156–157
Porter, Chris 151
Porter, Dave 95
Portman, Rachel 205
post-production 85–86, 199–200, 213, 215, 231–233
potpourri musicals 167
Powell, John 22, 35, 96, 98, 99, 109, 195–196, 196, 218, 225
pre-production 86, 165, 199
pre-recording 106–107, 109, **127**, 141, 165–166, 169
Pretty Woman 134
Price, Steven 247, 248
Pride & Prejudice 140
production music 113, 132, 145–147
project owners 4–5, 9, 86, *204*, 207, 213, 221–222; control 219–220; fears of 65; firings by 223–226; and music editors 93–94; and music supervisors 91; pressure from 222–223; and trust 8, 220, 227; vague input 222, *see also* creative stakeholders
project planning 10–12, 53
project plans 198
Prometheus 32, 63
Psycho 18, 38, 201
publishing rights to compositions 116

Quantum of Solace 137
questions: about musical instruments 76; at the end of a project 254–255; for media creators on music 57, 58; when planning 53

Index **281**

Rabjohns, Paul 109
Raiders of the Lost Ark, The Truck Chase x–xi
Rain Man 105
Rami, Sam 99
Ratatouille 32, 45, 162
recording engineers 178
recording studios 179
The Red Violin 140
Reggio, Geoffrey 44–45, 108
rehearsals 165
relative volume 79–81
Requiem for a Dream 18–19, 151
Resident Evil 38
Reznor, Trent 63, 196, 220–221
rhythm 78–79
Ride of the Valkyries (Wagner) 36, 101
ritarando 77
A River Runs Through It 31
Robin Hood: Prince of Thieves 37, 154, 162
Robin Hood—Men in Tights 29
Robin Hood themes 153
Rocky 134
Rocky IV 163
Rodford, Maggie 99
Rolling Stones 46–47, 108, 131, 133
romance 23
romantic comedies 29
Rope 11, 106
Ross, Atticus 63, 196, 220–221
Round Midnight 142
Rouse, Christopher 96
The Royal Tenenbaums 130
royalties 123, 186, 253
Russ, Patrick 233
Russo, Jeff 158

sadness 38–39
Sakamoto, Ryuichi 145
Salisbury, Ben 18, 87–88, 151
Sanchez, Antonio 17, 48
Santaolalla, Gustavo 28, 144–145
Saturday Night Fever 163
scales 64
Schumacher, Joel 36
"Scope of the Work" clauses 55
score preparation 93
score producers 213
scoring sessions 93, 172, 175–179, 181–182, 200, 203, *204*, 210–214, *212–214*, 231
Scorsese, Martin 113
Scott, Tony 35
screen credits 185
Scrubs 157
Seamster, Jeff 50
self-voice 50–51
Semanick, Michael 109
Sembello, Michael 134

set design 86–87
Shadowlands 222
Shag 117–118
Shaiman, Marc 249–250
Shayamalan, M. Night 201
sheet music royalties 123, 186
Shephard, Vonda 45, 107, 133
Shine 139
showreels 192
Shrek 196
Sicario 67, 102, 151
The Silence of the Lambs 67, 138
Silvestri, Alan 98
Simon & Garfunkel 104, 132–133
The Simpsons 31, 64
Singin' in the Rain 168
The Sixth Sense 201
small budgets 171, 211
Snow Falling on Cedars 28
The Social Network 22, 63, 220–221
Soderbergh, Stephen 232
software 206–208, 211, 242, 248
The Soloist 140
sonic branding 158–159
sonic competition 240
The Sopranos 22, 79
sound design teams 198–199, 241
sound effects/music overlaps *241*
sound quality. *see* timbre
soundalikes 99, 101, 130
soundtracks 132–134, 161–163, 215, 240
source music 131–132
sourcing music 89–90
Spielberg, Steven 196, 219, 232
spotting sessions 92–93, 199–200, 202, 231
Springsteen, Bruce 163
Stalling, Carl W. 28
Star Trek: The Motion Picture x
Star Trek 19, 207
Star Trek Beyond 47
Star Trek Discovery 158
Star Trek franchise 160
Star Wars: Episode IV—A New Hope 26
Star Wars: Episode VIII—The Last Jedi 250
Star Wars: Return of the Jedi 23
Star Wars: Rogue One 160, 225
Star Wars—Episode I: The Phantom Menace 33
Star Wars—Episode VII: The Force Awakens 33, 64
Star Wars Battlefront Rogue One: X-wing VR Mission 50–51
Star Wars franchise 160
Starnes, Tim 94
Steiner, Max 103–104
stems 214–215, 250
Stoller, Ethan 94
storytelling tools 16

282 Index

Stranger Things 38
streaming shows 135, 157–158
strings 74–75
structure **20**, 24, 26
studio composers 85
studio logos 158–159
subtlety 17–18, 19
Suicide Squad 128
suites 206–208, 215
Superman franchise 160
Svensson, James 50
Sweeney Todd—The Demon Barber of Fleet Street 166
Swing Kids 142
symphonies 25
synchronization royalties 123, 186
Syriana 32

The Talented Mr. Ripley 142
Tarantino, Quentin 113
Tarzan 45
Taxi Driver 24
Team America 134
television shows 156–158
temp tracks 93, 96–103, 130
tempo 77–79
Terminator 2: Judgment Day 67
Terminator 3: Rise of the Machines 98
Terminator franchise 27, 79, 152, 160
Thalberg, Irving 66
The Darjeeling Limited 144
The Motorcycle Diaries 144
The Throne (Sado) 145
theme music viii, x, 21–23, 26–27, 33, 38, 62–64, 68–69, 105, 107, 152–164
There Will Be Blood 33, 67, 109
The Thin Red Line 101–102
Thor: Ragnarok 21
Tiersen, Yann 101
Tigerland 36
Timberlake, Justin 163
timbre 81–83
time-periods **20**, 30, 33–35, 53, 121, 130–131
timelines/deadlines 184
timing 39
tiny budgets 170–171
Titanic 39, 154, 162
To Kill a Mockingbird 26, 28
Tomorrowland 37
Toni Erdmann 44
Top Gun 36, 42, 78–79, 132
total soundtrack composition 246–248
traditional/folk music **125–127**, 142–145
tragedy 38–39
Trainspotting 131
Transformers: Dark of the Moon 239
transportation 178–179

TRON: Legacy 21–22, 48, 64, 108–109, 151
Troy 224
tutti playing 214
2001: A Space Odyssey 34, 99–100, 136, 137
Tykwer, Tom 108, 151

Ugly Betty 157
Unbreakable Kimmy Schmidt 164
"Unheard Melodies: Narrative Film Music" (Gorbman) 13
Unsane 232
Unstoppable 35, 237

Vangelis 23, 34
Veca, Don 209, 210
Verbinski, Gore 219
Veronica Guerin 113
versatility 192
Vertigo 27, 37, 95, 154
Vicky Cristina Barcelona 145
video games 3–4, 25, 30, 49–51, 144, 158, 161, 215, 244; creative workflow 87, 198, 230; horror music in 38; jazz music 142; musical guidance 27; musical responsiveness 49; pop music 131, 133
Villeneuve, Denis 19, 102, 151, 225
violins 74, 82
virtual instruments 170–171, 206, 208, 211, 247
visual-effects team 238–239
voice doubles 107
VR games 50–51

Wallfisch, Benjamin 19, 38, 152, 225
war epics 36
Warren, Diane 163
Water Drops on Burning Rocks [Gouttes d'eau ur pierres brûlantes] 131
Wayne's World 128
Weir, Peter 32
Wesson, Mel 17, 251–252
West Side Story 165–166
Westworld 64, 86, 108, 133, 135, 155, 158
Where the Wild Things Are 32
Whiplash 107, 142
Williams, John x, 34, 37, 46, 50–51, 63, 69, 104, 154, 160, 196, 214
The Wire 44
Witness 32, 151
wonder 37
woodwinds 70–72
workflows 202–203, 204, 205–215, 230, 231
Working Together: Why Great Partnerships Succeed (Eisner) 189
world music 142–143
World War Z 221
Wrath of the Titans 224–225, 235

X-Men franchise 160

Yared, Gabriel 67, 224, 237–238
The Year of Living Dangerously 144
Yershon, Gary 34, 67, 151, 199, 205

Zemickis, Robert 44
Zimmer, Hans 19, 32, 35, 88, 96, 101,
 105–106, 152, 155, 194–196, 205–207, 219,
 225, 235
Zoolander 29